European Connections

edited by
Peter Collier

Volume 28

PETER LANG

Oxford· Bern · Berlin · Bruxelles · Frankfurt am Main · New York · Wien

Gerri Kimber

For Janine

Katherine Mansfield
The View from France

To a beautiful spirit
and someone I am proud to
call my friend.

Gerri
xx
3 April 2009

PETER LANG

Oxford · Bern · Berlin · Bruxelles · Frankfurt am Main · New York · Wien

Bibliographic information published by Die Deutsche Bibliothek
Die Deutsche Bibliothek lists this publication in the Deutsche
Nationalbibliografie; detailed bibliographic data is available on the
Internet at ‹http://dnb.ddb.de›.

British Library and Library of Congress Cataloguing-in-Publication Data:
A catalogue record for this book is available from The British Library,
Great Britain, and from The Library of Congress, USA

ISSN 1424-3792
ISBN 978-3-03911-392-7

© Peter Lang AG, International Academic Publishers, Bern 2008
Hochfeldstrasse 32, Postfach 746, CH-3000 Bern 9, Switzerland
info@peterlang.com, www.peterlang.com, www.peterlang.net

Printed in Germany

This book is dedicated to Professor Malcolm Bowie (1943–2007)

Contents

Acknowledgements

I should like to acknowledge the enormous debt of gratitude I owe to Professor Malcolm Bowie, the supervisor of my original PhD thesis for two years, until ill health forced him to relinquish his role. In 2003, he encouraged me to resurrect a long-neglected M. Phil thesis, once more offering to become my supervisor. The working title of the thesis was his idea and I have kept it, in tribute to him, for the monograph. I looked forward to being able to present him with a copy of the final thesis, but, sadly, he passed away three months before its submission. Nevertheless, Malcolm's supervisory guidance permeates every chapter of the revised book and I hope he would have approved of the end result.

Professor Lisa Downing, also a former student of Malcolm's, kindly took over the supervision of the thesis after his illness was diagnosed, and I am immensely grateful to her. Her sound advice and encourage-ment at every stage have been invaluable, and any meritorious sections of the present book are undoubtedly a product of her erudition and ana-lytical skills. It has been a rare privilege to have had two such brilliant scholars as supervisors.

The internationally renowned New Zealand critic, poet and novelist, Professor C. K. Stead, CBE, ONZ, became a mentor and friend during the latter stages of writing the thesis and several sections bear witness to my discussions with him on the subject of Katherine Mansfield. I am im-mensely grateful to him for agreeing to write the foreword to the present volume. Professor Vincent O'Sullivan, the world's foremost Mansfield scholar, has also been exceedingly generous with his time and talking 'Mansfield' with him is one of life's great pleasures.

Finally, I should like to thank Ralph Kimber and Annabel Kimber for their constant support and encouragement during the research for this book, when their needs frequently took second place to those of Kather-ine Mansfield.

Abbreviations

All page references to Mansfield's stories in English are taken from the *Collected Stories* (London: Constable, 1945), and follow directly after any quotation. Unless stated otherwise, all page references to the stories in French are taken from *L'Œuvre romanesque de Katherine Mansfield* (Paris: Stock, 1955).

The following reference abbreviations are used as standard throughout the book:

Primary Texts

IGP	*In a German Pension* (London: Stephen Swift, 1911)
Bliss	*Bliss and Other Stories* (London: Constable, 1920)
GP	*The Garden Party and Other Stories* (London: Constable, 1922)
Poems 1	*Poems* (London: Constable, 1923)
Dove's Nest	*The Doves' Nest and Other Stories* (London: Constable, 1923)
SC	*Something Childish and Other Stories* (London: Constable, 1924)
J1	*Journal*, ed. by John Middleton Murry (London: Constable, 1927)
L1, i, ii	*The Letters*, 2 Vols, ed. by John Middleton Murry (London: Constable, 1928)
NN	*Novels and Novelists*, ed. by J. Middleton Murry (London: Constable, 1930)
SB	*The Scrapbook*, ed. by J. Middleton Murry (London: Constable, 1939)
L2	*Letters to John Middleton Murry 1913–1922*, ed. by J. Middleton Murry (London: Constable, 1951)

J2	*Journal, Definitive Edition*, ed. by J. Middleton Murry (London: Constable, 1954)
CL1	*The Collected Letters, Volume One, 1903–1917*, ed. by V. O'Sullivan and M. Scott (Oxford: Clarendon Press, 1984)
CL2	*The Collected Letters, Volume Two, 1918–1919*, ed. by V. O'Sullivan and M. Scott (Oxford: Clarendon Press, 1987)
CL3	*The Collected Letters, Volume Three, 1919–1920*, ed. by V. O'Sullivan and M. Scott (Oxford: Clarendon Press, 1993)
CL4	*The Collected Letters, Volume Four, 1920–1921*, ed. by V. O'Sullivan and M. Scott (Oxford: Clarendon Press, 1996)
CS Alpers	*The Stories of Katherine Mansfield – Definitive Edition*, ed. by Antony Alpers (Auckland: Oxford University Press, 1984)
Poems 2	*Poems*, ed. by V. O'Sullivan (Oxford: Oxford University Press, 1988)
NB1, NB2	*Notebooks, Vols. 1 and 2, Complete Edition* ed. by M. Scott (Minnesota: University of Minnesota Press, 2002)

Principal French Translations

Félicité	*Félicité*, trans. by J.-G. Delamain, pref. by Louis Gillet (Paris: Stock, 1928)
FGP 1	*La Garden Party et autres histoires*, trans. by Marthe Duproix, pref. by Edmond Jaloux (Paris: Stock, 1929)
FJ1	*Lettres*, trans. by Madeleine T. Guéritte, pref. by Gabriel Marcel (Paris: Stock, 1931)
La Mouche	*La Mouche*, trans. by Madeleine T. Guéritte and Marguerite Faguer, pref. by Madeleine T. Guéritte (Paris: Stock, 1933)
PA	*Pension allemande et nouvelles diverses*, trans. by Charles Mauron and Marguerite Faguer (Paris: Stock, 1939)
CN	*Cahier de notes*, trans. by Germaine Delamain, intro. by J. M. Murry (Paris: Stock, 1944)
Poèmes	*Poèmes*, trans. by Jean Pierre Le Mée (Paris: Éditions de la Nouvelle Revue Critique, 1946)
VI	*Le Voyage indiscret*, trans. by Didier Merlin (Paris: Éditions du Seuil, 1950)

FL2, I, ii, iii   *Lettres, Vol. 1: 1913–1918, Vol. 2: 1918–1919, Vol.3: 1920–1922*, trans. by Anne Marcel, intro. by André Bay (Paris: Stock, 1954)

OR   *L'Œuvre romanesque*, trans. by J.-G. Delamain, Marthe Duproix, André Bay, Marguerite Faguer, Didier Merlin and Charles Mauron, pref. by André Maurois (Paris: Stock, 1955)

FJ2   *Journal: Édition définitive*, trans. by Marthe Duproix, Anne Marcel and André Bay, pref. by Marcel Arland, intro. by J. M. Murry (Paris: Stock/ Les Librairies Associés, 1956)

FGP2   *La Garden-Party et autres nouvelles*, trans. and pref. by Françoise Pellan (Paris: Gallimard, 2002)

Nouvelles   *Les Nouvelles de Katherine Mansfield*, pref. by Marie Desplechin (Paris: Stock, 2006)

Principal Biographies

Alpers   Alpers, Antony, *The Life of Katherine Mansfield* (London: Jonathan Cape, 1980)

Meyers   Meyers, Jeffrey, *Katherine Mansfield: A Biography* (London: Hamish Hamilton, 1978)

Tomalin   Tomalin, Claire, *Katherine Mansfield: A Secret Life* (London: Viking, 1987)

Foreword

To look into the question of Katherine Mansfield and France requires a clear head and a steady hand. A brilliant mind and a volatile temperament, self-dramatising and sometimes self-mocking, living life constantly close to the edge, and sometimes on the brink of disaster, Mansfield was drawn to France and its literature, at once fascinated, charmed, challenged and repelled by what she encountered there. Returning to Paris early in January 1918 she is at first happy, excited to be back:

> It is snowing hard. The streets are all ice and water – and so slippery qu'on marche comme un poulet malade. All the same I am unreasonably deeply happy. I thought I would be disenchanted with France this time, but for the first time I seem to recognize my love for it and to understand *why*. It is because, whatever happens, I never feel *indifferent*. [...] There is [...] a wonderful spirit here – so much humour, life, gaiety, sorrow, one cannot see it all & not think with amazement of the strange cement like state of England (CL2, p. 5, 9 January 1918).

One reads this, as Jack Murry must have read it, thinking, 'Yes, of course. But how long will it last?' By the end of the month she is writing from the Cote d'Azur:

> This country [...] is really ideally beautiful. It is the most exquisite enchanting place –Yet I am very sincere when I say I *hate* the French [...] they have no heart – no heart at all (CL2, p. 44, 27 January 1918).

A few days later this is repeated: 'I simply loathe and abominate the french bourgeoisie' (CL2, p. 52, 1 February 1918). A week further on it has turned to comedy, focussing on their 'absorbed interest in evacuation':

> What is constipating and what not? That is a real *criterion* . . At the end of this passage there is a W.C. Great Guns! They troop and flock there . . and not only that. They are all victims of the most amazing Flatulence imaginable. Air Raids overs London don't hold a candle to 'em. This I suppose is caused by their violent purges and remedies, but it seems to me very 'unnecessary'. – Also the people of the village have a habit of responding to their serious needs (I suppose by night) down on the shore around the palm trees. Perhaps its the sailors but my english

15

gorge rises & my english lip curls in contempt. The other day one palm tree had a placard nailed on it *Chiens Seulement* (CL2, p. 59, 6 February 1918).[*]

The same contradictions are present in her fiction. There are stories which express her feeling that there is something 'special' about France and the French, a refined, sophisticated, aesthetic quality, a style to be valued especially by those whose essentially British culture lacks it. Others show her dislike, her feeling of being shut out, equally by French courtesy and discourtesy, from what is perceived to be valuable but can be viewed only from the outside. One story at least, 'Je ne parle pas français', begins in the negative about the French temperament and becomes something like a celebration of it. After writing the first few pages she tells Murry, in a letter, that the story will be 'a cry against corruption' – the corruption, that's to say, of its French narrator, Raoul Duquette. But by the end of the story she has written herself so far into the character that the feeling has changed. She is enjoying herself, enjoying *being* Duquette, untrustworthy, equivocal, sophisticated, a comedian, above all *French*. To moralise the story, ironing out its ambiguities, seeing it (as Murry did) simply as that 'cry against corruption,' is to lose its final richness, its animation, the quality of 'real life' that characterises the best of her work.

In her brief adult life Mansfield seems to have been constantly escaping to France, and then escaping from it. The War made it more than ever real and important to her – and, indeed, to everyone. It was the centre of the world's attention. Her dearly loved brother died and was buried there. It was there she went, to Gray in the war zone, to act out her brief affair with Francis Carco; to Paris, and later Bandol, to live with Jack Murry the idyll of being 'writers together'; to Menton for a climate that would be kinder to her diseased lungs; to the Gurdjieff Institute at Fontainebleau, in the hope of an escape, or a reprieve, from death. France gave her new ways of looking at herself and the world. From France she saw the New Zealand of her childhood, and her New Zealand family, more truthfully than she saw them from England. That 'Gallic lens', as Dr Kimber calls it, was very important in her development as a writer; but it was also often uncomfortable, and at times intolerable. So it was

---

[*]   Dr Kimber tells us that offending passages such as these were omitted from the first French edition of her letters.

from France she escaped, back to England and to Murry, to the English language and the English lens, when loneliness, linguistic deprivation, fear, and simply the *Frenchness* of it all, grew too much for her.

Her wish to write a 'new kind of fiction', the seriousness of her search for the means of achieving this, her indifference to conventions of length ('the novel', 'the short story') and willingness to let the internal dynamic of the story determine its shape – all of these stylistic matters pushed her in the direction of France for models, theory, examples and inspiration. In the literary climate of England the 'short story' was not paid proper attention; it was a form that suited the 'yarn', or a child's attention span. For French writers and critics, on the other hand, the *conte* was a proper literary mode, to be taken as seriously as any other. Fragmentation, mysteriousness, indirection and allusion, these were aspects of Modernism deriving largely from French Symbolism. Mansfield, pursuing goals of originality and modernity, could not avoid French literary influences; and Dr Kimber traces where these were found and how, in particular, the work of Baudelaire, and later of Colette, played important roles in the development of her style.

All these elements, together with early death, and revelations of a life that could be said to have been lived in pursuit of '*l'idéal*', combined to make the posthumous Mansfield of intense interest to the French, who for a long time took her more seriously than she was taken in England. But they would have her only on their own terms – the delicate, francophile stylist, in search of spiritual truth and enduring love. Sick, sad and saintly – it is not that there was no truth at all in the image. Those elements were there in her work; but as long as others which contradicted or complemented them were overlooked, the picture was so partial as to be false. So the 'Katherine Mansfield' created in England after her death by Jack Murry, her (at first) grieving husband, and (later) prospering editor and copyright holder, was further enhanced in France, air-brushed towards perfection.

Dr Kimber traces the development of this unlikely figure, 'La Perle de l'Océanie' – part genius, part Virgin Mary – in the literary consciousness of France; shows too how the few who saw that it was a misrepresentation tried and failed to dislodge it. The facts of her biography, as they emerged, were too upsetting, too shameful, and those who wished to reveal them were ignored or deplored. A saint could fall victim to tuberculosis; only a sinner could have contracted gonorrhoea. Perhaps the problem was that the challengers of the Mansfield myth in France failed, themselves, to see, or anyway to persuade others, that there was marvellous middle ground between these extremes. None had the critical authority to make clear, and make known, how much richer, more rewarding in both human and literary terms – how much *better* indeed – the real writer was than either the saint or the sinner. France was to have one or the other, or none at all. At present it seems it is the sad last of these three possibilities France has settled for.

Nothing could be better for Mansfield's reputation in France, and in general, than to have the complex and contradictory truth told – about her real relations with French literature and society, about their actual influence and importance in her life, and about exactly how they are represented in her fiction, her thought, her letters and journals. Though Dr Kimber's focus might seem at first glance narrow – Mansfield and France, France and Mansfield – it proves, in her comprehensive, corrective account, a topic so broad in its implications that it becomes in effect a review of the whole subject of the writer Mansfield.

C. K. Stead

Introduction

The New Zealand short story writer Katherine Mansfield (1888–1923), spent all her adult life in Europe, of which approximately three years in total were spent in France, where she eventually died. Following her death, Mansfield became a celebrated author in France, with interest initially focused on her personal writing (her *Journal* and *Letters*), and to a lesser extent on the stories themselves. Critical texts on Mansfield may be numbered in the hundreds, and although there have been occasional articles devoted to a discussion of Mansfield's reputation in France, the focus has always remained a narrow one, centred around a superficial exposé of the French critics' creation of a legend surrounding her life.[1]

This book takes a different and original viewpoint in its assessment of why Mansfield's reputation in France has always been greater than in England. In addition to examining the ways in which the French reception of Mansfield has idealised her persona to the extent of crafting a hagiography, I ask: What were the motives behind the French critics' desire to put Mansfield on a pedestal? How did the three years she spent on French soil influence her writing? How do the translations of her work collude in the hagiography of her personality? This book covers new ground in Mansfieldian studies in its endeavour to establish interconnections between Mansfield's own French influences (literary and otherwise), and the myth-making of the French critics and translators.

I have divided my book into five chapters. Chapter One places Mansfield in the general literary context of her era, exploring French literary tendencies at the time and juxtaposing them with the main literary trends in England. Few Mansfield scholars have researched her literary influences and even fewer critics have turned their attention to a discussion of the historical, literary background which would go on to shape

---

1   See in particular: Pierre Citron, 'Katherine Mansfield et La France', *Revue de littérature comparée* (April–June 1940), 173–93. Christiane Mortelier, 'The Genesis and Development of the Katherine Mansfield Legend in France', *AUMLA* (November 1970), 252–63. Jeffrey Meyers, 'Murry's Cult of Mansfield', *Journal of Modern Literature* (February 1979), 15–38.

Mansfield's own writing. Mansfield studies today centre for the most part on feminist critiques of her work and a re-reading of her narrative art from a feminist/Modernist viewpoint, without undertaking a detailed analysis of its historical roots, which is what I propose here. In addition, in focusing this chapter from an Anglo/French perspective, I am entering new ground in Mansfield studies. The analysis proposed here contributes to the field of reception studies in general, and specifically to the study of the cultural exchange between Britain and France in the late-nineteenth and early-twentieth-centuries.

The second chapter concentrates on the writer's trips to France, demonstrating the influence of the French experience on her life and works. Mansfield was a nomadic figure, constantly on the move both in England and abroad, but finally choosing to spend more and more time in France. Through a detailed examination of her notebooks and correspondence, I shall demonstrate how this body of work reveals an idiosyncratic yet evocative account of early-twentieth-century France. It was inevitable that these prolonged exposures to French culture, literature and people would influence her writing and thinking. An examination of her personal writing shows her reacting in a subjective way to the sights and sounds around her, often in a good mood, humorous and content; sometimes depressed, suffering and acerbic. Her occasional negative responses to France in the light of these ever changing moods were not the impression of Mansfield that Murry sought to portray after her death; this would lead him down the path of editorial subterfuge in order to 're-create' certain aspects of his dead wife's personality, which is the subject of Chapter Four.

Chapter Three concentrates on Mansfield's knowledge of specific French writers and the influence they bring to bear on her own creative output. This focus incorporates specific new readings of Mansfield's writing, reflecting its deep-rooted French literary influences from the earliest stages of her career, thereby corroborating the debt she owed to France, which went beyond the merely superficial one of 'health tourist'. Mansfield's own unique form of Modernism was, therefore, not derivative of other contemporary English language writers. I shall demonstrate how her Modernism was, in fact, partly a product of her early symbiosis of specifically French late-nineteenth-century techniques and themes. From her late teens onwards, when her tastes and preferences started to take shape, she began, with the Symbolists and the Decadents as her dominant influences, to write the sort of fiction which was committed to the possibilities of narrative experimentation. I also examine Colette's *L'Envers du music-hall*, arguing how this early work remained a constant reference point for Mansfield throughout her writing career, drawing parallels in the texts of both writers which, to my knowledge, have not been alluded to by other Mansfield scholars. Both thematically and stylistically, Mansfield's use of this early Colettean work is considerable. These first three chapters will enable the reader to understand more fully the French influence – in whatever form it took – in Mansfield's life.

In Chapter Four, new critical ground is covered when I demonstrate how the translations of her personal writing, together with her fiction, collude in the misrepresentation of her personality, and how the beliefs and principles expressed in the original texts have been diluted and even censored during the translation process. I shall highlight fundamental problems of translating writing such as Mansfield's and determine, via the use of in-depth analysis of the translated texts, whether her narrative and personal ideologies, literary nuances, themes and artistic abilities survive translation from English to French. I shall provide examples of how her writing was edited, manipulated and mistranslated in order to aid the creation of the 'French' Katherine Mansfield. An examination will also be made of more than one translation of the same text, where such translations exist, to determine whether these newer translations help to demystify or promote the legend. Finally, I ask whether any of the translations or the inadequacies of the translation process itself contribute to the process of hagiography.

The last chapter will consider Mansfield's critical reception in France, both during her lifetime and after her death, via the evolution of a conceptual pattern, relating the perception of Mansfield to the varying French critical responses, together with a brief analysis of the more contemporary approach. Though in England Mansfield is not perceived as a literary giant, nevertheless she commands respect; her short stories have never once been out of print since her death. The contrast to how she is viewed in France could not be more marked. There, her saint-like persona has been set in stone since it was invented in a few short years after her death and the critics who have attempted to oust this popular perception have seen their viewpoints submerged by the huge tidal wave of French critical opinion, determined to uphold this falsely created persona at whatever cost to historical accuracy. Murry's influence over, and manipulation of, the French critics will be emphasised, disclosing how he decided to promote her work and her life by printing as much of the material she left behind as possible and by promulgating a personality cult of his dead wife, which was enthusiastically taken up by the French. The chapter will concentrate primarily on the development and entrenchment of the legend up to the 1940s, followed by a briefer overview of the situation since the 1950s and will argue that the critical opinion was almost exclusively a Catholic and reactionary one. I shall be incorporating new documentary evidence to support my argument, making this chapter the most comprehensive discussion of the phenomenon of the Mansfield legend in France yet undertaken.

The division of the book in this way allows me to highlight how these various strands combine to create a legend which has little basis in fact, thereby demonstrating how reception and translation determine the importance of an author's reputation in the literary world. This research also contributes to the field of reception studies, as well as gender studies, since the hagiography of Mansfield in France is a specifically gendered one.

Chapter One
Influences and Innovations

'England built London for its own use, but France built Paris for the world'.

Ralph Waldo Emerson, *Complete Works, Volume 7 – Society and Solitude* (Boston: Houghton, Mifflin, 1894), p. 487, Journal, July 1848.

This chapter will serve to contextualise my argument within a general analysis of English and French literary activity, from the close of the nineteenth century, through the first two decades of the twentieth century, up until Katherine Mansfield's death in 1923. It will focus on the principal writers who were contemporaries and interlocutors of Mansfield, such as T. S. Eliot and Virginia Woolf. In addition, general literary transactions and connections between England and France during these years will also be examined.

Mansfield was inevitably a product of her own generation; as a writer she was influenced by people, places, trends in literature, and the books she read. In this chapter I aim to elucidate what exactly these influences were, their origins, and how they helped to shape the fiction she produced. (Specific French authorial influences will be discussed in Chapter Three.) Mansfield studies today centre, for the most part, on feminist critiques of her work and a re-reading of her narrative art from a feminist/Modernist viewpoint, with little analysis of its historical roots. The Anglo-French focus of this chapter should engage those with an interest in reception studies in general and especially those with an interest in the cultural exchange between Britain and France in the late-nineteenth and early-twentieth-centuries.

Beginnings

The end of the nineteenth century saw the rise of a great number of literary genres and movements in both England and France, which frequently overlapped each other in ideas and adherents.[1] Both Henry James and George Moore have been credited with a specific transformation of English fiction, according it an esteem and value similar to that in France. Both men spent time in Paris during the 1870s, which culminated for James in the publication in 1878 of *French Poets and Novelists*,[2] where he discusses authors such as Balzac, Gautier and Baudelaire. Bernard Bergonzi suggests that:

> Towards the end of the nineteenth century many writers felt that literature and art had moved into a new phase, and that even though Queen Victoria continued to be very much alive, the Victorian era was already passing away [...] The 'nineties', whether qualified as 'naughty' or 'mauve' or 'yellow', can still exert a striking appeal [...] And yet to refer to a single decade in this way can be misleading, since many of the essential attitudes of the nineties had their roots in the eighties or even in the seventies; specifically the Aesthetic Movement [...] [which] was essentially a manifestation of the previous decade [...] The word 'Decadence' has a broader application, but suffers from its ambiguity; some of the time it suggests a combination of physical lassitude and psychological and moral perversity – as exemplified for instance in J.-K. Huysman's novel *A Rebours*, which was much admired in the nineties – although more properly it should refer only to language.[3]

Gradually during the 1880s, as a direct result of French influence and the spread of theories such as Art for Art's Sake and Naturalism, a new conception of fiction arose in England to challenge the adherents of Realism, such as Dickens and Thackeray. The naturalist school itself would undergo modification as the new century arrived, with authors such as John Galsworthy, Arnold Bennett and H.G. Wells creating their own form of indigenous Realism.

1   The interplay of literary influences between France and Britain has a long and well-documented history. See for example: Enid Starkie, *From Gautier to Eliot* (London: Hutchinson, 1960).
2   Henry James, *French Poets and Novelists* (London: Macmillan, 1878). This was the first of James' books to be published in England; there was no concurrent American edition.
3   Bernard Bergonzi, *The Turn of a Century* (London: Macmillan, 1973), p.17.

In the decades straddling the end of the nineteenth and the beginning of the twentieth centuries, Paris was considered a literary and artistic Mecca. It would be so for Mansfield and her husband, the critic John Middleton Murry, as it had been for hundreds of writers before them. (There was the old adage that it was cheaper to enjoy oneself in Paris than be bored in England.) By the end of the nineteenth century, Paris had become the literary, artistic and musical world's most important city, with her indigenous artists, writers and musicians ranked second to none, spreading their movements and influence elsewhere.[4] It was considered essential for those of a literary or artistic persuasion to spend time there, perfecting their craft; both British and Americans writers and artists sought refuge and artistic inspiration in France, Americans in particular fleeing the limitations and social restraints of their native country. This state of affairs would continue into the twentieth century up to the outbreak of the Second World War.

From a historical point of view, this was an unsettled and disturbing period for Europe and especially for France; the years 1898 and 1899 according to Alan Schom, 'stand out as among the most unpleasant and divisive since the Hundred Years' War'.[5] He continues:

Zola, Dreyfus, dishonourable army personnel, corrupt and opportunistic politicians, the assassination of President Carnot, the public beating of President Loubet [...], the amazing blunder of Fashoda, the renewed threat of war, this time with England, and the ever-present threat from Germany – everything served to undermine the established order (p. 200).

4   English writers, such as Algernon Swinburne and Walter Pater, were responsible for the Art for Art's Sake movement crossing the Channel from France to England whilst writers such as Henry James continued to advocate the principles of Realism and Naturalism.
5   Alan Schom, *Émile Zola: A Bourgeois Rebel* (London: Queen Anne Press, 1987), p. 200.

The *Fin de Siècle*

Thus, literary turmoil and innovation were intertwined with political and social upheaval. The term *'fin de siècle'* appears; Bernard Bergonzi claims for it a looser time scale than one would imagine, showing how it, 'clearly points to the preoccupations of the last years of the nineteenth century, without being limited to a single decade, and which can cover such particular manifestations as "aestheticism" and "decadence"' (p. 18). He goes on to state:

> The phrase *fin de siècle* was applied to a wide range of trivial behaviour, provided it was sufficiently perverse or paradoxical or shocking. Yet in so far as *fin de siècle* refers to a serious and consistent cultural attitude, it has two essential characteristics: the conviction that all established forms of intellectual and moral and social certainty were vanishing, and that the new situation required new attitudes in life and art; and the related belief that art and morality were separate realms, and that the former must be regarded as wholly autonomous; hence the aesthetic doctrine of 'art for art's sake' (p. 18).

With the advent of the new century everything seemed suddenly to be different. As W. B. Yeats expressed: 'Everybody got down off his stilts; henceforth nobody drank absinthe with his black coffee; nobody went mad; nobody committed suicide; nobody joined the Catholic Church; or if they did I have forgotten'.[6] Many English authors, however, resisted change, whatever its nomenclature. George Gissing and H. G. Wells, for instance, opposed the influences of the continental Naturalists and continued to retain a prejudice against the French, preferring Dickens as a role model to Zola, unlike Arnold Bennett who remained a great Francophile, influenced by Flaubert, Zola and Maupassant.

Émile Zola (1840–1902), had first hand experience of the English *fin-de-siècle* literary scene. In 1893, he had been invited by the Institute of British Journalists to give a speech in London; accepting the invitation was an act of bravery in itself, since his work had received poor reviews in England – indeed, some of his novels had been banned by parliament. However, it was in England that he sought refuge following the Dreyfus

6   W. B. Yeats, ed., *The Oxford Book of Modern Verse: 1892–1935* (Oxford: Clarendon Press, 1936), p. xi.

affair, though he was obliged to go into hiding, his infamy being such that his face was nearly as well known in England as it was in France. His novel *Fécondité*,[7] written in 1899, contains a harsh sociological survey of France and the French.

George Moore (1852–1933), was an Anglo-Irish novelist, dramatist and short story writer. He lived and worked in Paris for many years and when he eventually returned to England he was determined to imbue the English novel with more naturalistic and realistic techniques, as exemplified by the French authors he had come to admire, such as Zola, Flaubert, the Goncourts and Balzac. Richard Ellmann calls him 'the main middle man between English and French culture at that time'.[8] In the late 1870s Moore met Villiers de L'Isle-Adam, who introduced him to the Decadent and Symbolist movements. He also made the acquaintance of Mallarmé and Verlaine, both of whom are mentioned alongside many others in his *Confessions of a Young Man*.[9] Richard Ellmann states that:

> It was Moore who introduced Huysmans' *A Rebours* (1884) before Wilde described the book in *The Picture of Dorian Gray* (1890). As he was inclined to boast, Moore also wrote the first articles in English on Rimbaud, Laforgue, and Verlaine, collecting them in 1891 in his *Impressions and Opinions*. Edmund Gosse was to follow him by writing the first English critical essay on Mallarmé in his *Questions at Issue*, published in 1893. This was the year, too, when Verlaine came to England in November to lecture at Oxford; a little later, in March, 1894, Mallarmé also lectured at Oxford and at Cambridge. The same month Villiers' *Axel* was produced in Paris for the first time, and in the audience was W. B. Yeats, who was so moved that he entered it thereafter among his 'sacred books'. Translations of the symbolist writers began to appear in the middle 'nineties' (p. ix).

This was a fecund time for French influence on English literature, as exemplified by the the French Decadent and Symbolist movements, both of which would go on to have a lasting influence on the fiction of Katherine Mansfield, as I shall demonstrate in Chapter Three.

7   Émile Zola, *Fécondité* (Paris: Fasquelle, 1899).
8   Arthur Symons, *The Symbolist Movement in Literature*, intro. by Richard Ellmann (New York: Dutton, 1958), p. ix.
9   George Moore, *Confessions of a Young Man* (London: Swan Sonnenschein, 1888).

Decadence and Symbolism

All these developments in French literature were described for the English reader in 1899, by Arthur Symons (1865–1945), in his seminal work, *The Symbolist Movement in Literature*,[10] dedicated to W. B. Yeats, which was to profoundly influence the next generation of writers and poets, including the Imagists and poets such as T. S. Eliot. It would introduce many English readers to French literature – including Mansfield; indeed no one was more influential than Symons in importing French literary ideas to England and fostering a new spirit of internationalism. (Yeats, Eliot and Pound all stressed their debt to Symons for having introduced them to Symbolism.[11]) In 1893, Symons had arranged for Verlaine to visit England and in the same year his essay 'The Decadent Movement in Literature' was published,[12] leading him to be acclaimed the foremost English interpreter of foreign literary trends. *The Symbolist Movement in Literature* was an attempt, after the death of Verlaine in 1896 and Mallarmé in 1898, to collate and elucidate what George Moore and other English writers had merely touched upon. Symons described Symbolism thus:

> [It is] an attempt to spiritualize literature, to evade the old bondage of rhetoric, the old bondage of exteriority. Description is banished that beautiful things may be

10   Arthur Symons, *The Symbolist Movement in Literature* (London: Heinemann, 1899).

11   Michael Levenson explains further, 'Yeats, like Symons, positioned himself against the hegemony of scientific explanation and continued to insist on the possibility of transcendence (via symbols) to a unified spiritual realm. Symbolist literature represented an attempted overcoming of the materialist spectre, and against the tendency of scientific literature (by which he referred to literary Naturalism) "to lose itself in externalities of all kinds," Yeats urged a return to "suggestion" and "evocation". A symbol, he writes, "is indeed the only possible expression of some invisible essence, a transparent lamp about a spiritual flame," and the symbolist work of art points past itself and past the physical world to "something that moves beyond the senses"'. Michael Levenson, *A Genealogy of Modernism: A Study of English Literary Doctrine 1908–1922* (Cambridge: Cambridge University Press, 1984), pp. 109–10.

12   Arthur Symons, 'The Decadent Movement in Literature', *Harper's New Monthly Magazine*, November 1893. This essay would later be expanded to become *The Symbolist Movement in Literature*.

evoked, magically; the regular beat of verse is broken in order that words may fly, upon subtler wings. [...] Here then in this revolt against exteriority, against rhetoric, against a materialistic tradition; in this endeavour to disengage the ultimate essence, the soul, of whatever exists and can be realised by the consciousness; in this dutiful waiting upon every symbol by which the soul of things can be made visible; literature, bowed down by so many burdens, may at last attain liberty, and its authentic speech (Symons, *Symbolist Movement*, p. 5).

I shall show how this literary ideal is evoked in Mansfield's style in Chapter Three. Of his own attempts at poetry, Symons explains that, 'I tried to do in verse something of what Degas had done in painting. I was conscious of transgressing no law of art in taking that scarcely touched material for new uses'.[13] Of course, writing at the time the movements are still in vogue means that he is able to take up the position of guide and mentor in his writing:

The latest movement in European literature has been called by many names, none of them quite exact or comprehensive – Decadence, Symbolism, Impressionism, for instance. It is easy to dispute over words, and we shall find that Verlaine objects to being called a Decadent, Maeterlinck to being called a Symbolist, Huysmans to being called an Impressionist. These terms as it happens, have been adopted as the badge of little separate cliques, noisy, brainsick young people who haunt the brasseries of the Boulevard Saint-Michel, and exhaust their ingenuities in theorizing over the works they cannot write (Symons, *Selected Writings*, p. 72).

From an early stance of viewing both Decadence and Symbolism somewhat disparagingly, Symons eventually came to view Symbolism as one of the most important movements in European Literature, especially in poetry, with 'Le Symbolisme' implying the search for the highest and noblest reality, via spiritual experience (which Baudelaire had already expounded before him), suggested through analogies or *symbols* within the written word, which thus was always to remain an imperfect image or reflection. Mallarmé was accorded the title of chief high-priest of 'Le Symbolisme', all aspects of the movement leading to his door, both figuratively and literally: '[Mallarmé used] to gather round him on Tuesday evenings in his house on the rue de Rome a wide cross section of the writers, artists, and musicians of fin-de-siècle France, Belgium and

13   Arthur Symons, *Selected Writings*, intro. by Roger Holdsworth (Manchester: Carcanet Press, 1974), p. 93.

England'.[14] The movement struggled on into the early part of the twentieth century, but its lofty ideals and inspirations could not be sustained in a modern world; its followers found themselves unable to uphold tenets which were so artificial and divorced from reality, and so moved on.

Modernism and its Roots

In literary terms, the nineteenth century ends with the beginning of the Great War in 1914, in the same way that the eighteenth century closes in 1815 with the ending of the Napoleonic Wars. Not only did the Great War mark the end of a century, it also heralded the beginning of many new literary genres and ideas. The war itself would profoundly influence the literature of the era in England and particularly in France, where there would develop a post-war pressure on French writers to engage politically and to write with patriotic sentiment. A Modernist view of the world would eventually be born out of this new order with a new set of formal innovations, both experimental and language-focused. Men and women were affected differently – the men at the front experiencing injury and death, the women working in factories and hospitals, enjoying a freedom they had not known before; Melanie Hawthorne notes how:

> World War 1 also changed the climate of gender politics. [...] Feminism and calls for women's rights suddenly seemed selfish coming from a segment of society that had not been called on to make any personal sacrifice in the war (or so it was perceived). The symbols of female emancipation – childlessness, short hair – were viewed with mixed feelings.[15]

Notwithstanding the perception of the emancipated woman's selfishness, this cultural moment allowed female writers to innovate intellectually, becoming a time of liberation and eventually recognition. Certainly, by the 1920s, Sylvia Beach's Parisian bookshop and the rooms of Gertrude

---

14   Rosemary Lloyd, *Mallarmé: The Poet and His Circle* (Ithica: Cornell University Press, 2005), p. 6.
15   Melanie C. Hawthorne, *Rachilde and French Women's Authorship: From Decadence to Modernism* (Lincoln: University of Nebraska Press, 2001), pp. 205–06.

Stein thronged with women writers in a way that would have been un-thinkable before the war. Clare Hanson goes so far as to suggest that:

> The initial impetus for modernism came in fact from women writers, so that to talk of a female version of modernism – implying a secondary position for women – is misleading. One might suggest rather that modernism as we have been taught it is a male parasite on a body of experience and a way of seeing pioneered by women.[16]

Early literary historians of Modernism concentrated on a select band of male authors, such as Eliot, Pound and Joyce in England, and Gide and Proust in France, ignoring the work of the female writers of the time, believing them to be of little or no interest. Bonnie Kime Scott relates how:

> In 1965, [...] Richard Ellmann and Charles Feidelson assembled *The Modern Tradition*. Of its 948 pages, fewer than nine were allotted to women writers (George Eliot and Virginia Woolf) [...] While modernist studies are rolling off the presses at an unprecedented rate, a surprising number still find interest only in canonised males (Scott in *GOM*, p. 7).

According to Virginia Woolf, 'In or about December 1910, human character changed'.[17] She was referring to the end of the Edwardian era, together with the Post-Impressionist exhibition, mounted by Roger Fry in London at the end of 1910, with the implication that all forms of trad-

---

16 *The Gender of Modernism: A Critical Anthology*, ed. by Bonnie Kime Scott (Indianapolis: Indiana University Press, 1990), Chapter 14, 'Katherine Mansfield', ed. Clare Hanson, p. 303. (Volume hereafter referred to as *GOM*.) This point is made frequently by other women critics and especially Mansfield scholars like Sydney Kaplan: '[In] the story of the development of modernism – that combination of revolt against Victorian fathers, recognition of the artist's alienation, pursuit of the contemporary in language, psychology and behaviour, creation of dynamic original forms in which to contain a newly awakened sense of present reality – it is still necessary to restate the fact that until recently the academic critical tradition generally ignored the presence, let alone the overwhelming significance, of women writers in the creation of the movement'. Sydney Janet Kaplan, *Katherine Mansfield and the Origins of Modernist Fiction* (Ithaca: Cornell University Press, 1991), p. 6.

17 Virginia Woolf, 'Mr Bennett and Mrs Brown', in *Collected Essays*, vol. 1, ed. by Leonard Woolf (London: Hogarth Press, 1966), pp. 319–37 (p. 320).

tional mimetic representation, both in literature as well as art, would never be the same again. Suzette Henke explains how:

> The Georgian writer will try to capture a new style of psychological verisimilitude contingent on fluid, evanescent impressions of a subjective life-world. Deconstructing the props of traditional fiction, Woolf calls for a reconstruction of art to reflect the semiotic dimensions of ordinary life. She tacitly evokes the chorus of Greek drama and urges that the common man or woman be foregrounded in modern fiction – that heroic activity be redefined, that the range of literary topoi be expanded to include the whole panoply of quotidian existence.[18]

Women writers of the era, when they *are* mentioned by their almost exclusively male contemporaries, are praised for their literary technique, but never for their ideological or political views. Beatrice Hastings, one time friend of Mansfield and the mistress of A. R. Orage when he was editor of the influential literary paper the *New Age*, is one such woman whose importance escaped the almost exclusively male literary critics. She moved to Paris during the Great War, became Modigliani's lover and as stated by Kaplan, 'played a crucial role in initiating, encouraging, criticising and eventually countervailing the dominant thrusts of the modernist movement' (p. 141).

Every book on Modernism seems to have a different take on its definition as a literary movement. For Michael Levenson it encompasses:

> The use of heterogeneous styles, discourses, and semantic positions; the refusal of continuities, such as narrative, and the substitution of a quality of 'undecidability':

---

18   Suzette Henke, 'Virginia Woolf', in *GOM*, p. 625. In Roger Shattuck's story, 'The Poverty of Modernism', one of the characters states: 'Modernism is not a period, like the Victorian era. It's not a proper school or movement like Surrealism. It has no geographical character or associations, like *Der Blaue Reiter*. It serves no heuristic purpose, like the Enlightenment or Romanticism. It suggests no stylistic practice, like Baroque or Imagism. It's the weakest term we've had since Symbolism, which even Verlaine mocked by spelling it with a c and an a. But best of all [...] modernism embodies a disabling contradiction. It has cancer. The only general characteristic of the modern era is the celebration of individual experience, of particular feelings in particular circumstances, not repeatable. Every epiphany is *sui generis*. The term "modernism" tries to make a category of items that will not fit into a category'. Roger Shattuck, 'The Poverty of Modernism', in *The Innocent Eye: On Modern Literature and the Arts* (New York: Farrar, Strauss & Giroux, 1984), pp. 329–41 (p. 338, p. 340).

the foregrounding of textuality; the use of text and graphics at variance with each other. So much of the artistic passion of the period was stirred by questions of technique, where 'technique' should not suggest attention to 'form' as opposed to 'content,' but should imply rather the recognition that every element of the work is an instrument of its effect and therefore open to technical revision.[19]

For John Harwood, the mood is rather one of resignation to a literary label that has little or no significance:

> The problem is straightforward: any 'modernism' broad enough to embrace the variety of literary experiment in the first quarter of this century turns out to be nothing more than a portmanteau label, a synonym for 'innovative or experimental writing'. Once reified, it inevitably becomes a straitjacket: the diverse history of the period has to be flattened and denatured in order to justify the existence of the concept.[20]

Significantly, both men concentrate on the male tradition of Modernism, moving from Conrad and Ford to Pound and Eliot, expounding the tenets of experimental, innovative avant-garde writing in the early part of the twentieth century. Whatever the principles of Modernism may have

---

19   Michael Levenson, ed., *The Cambridge Companion to Modernism* (Cambridge: Cambridge University Press, 1999), p. 3.

20   John Harwood, *Eliot to Derrida: The Poverty of Interpretation* (Basingstoke: Macmillan, 1995), p. 13. Marysa Demoor discusses the dating of the Modernist movement. 'Sullivan explains the start of modernism in the preface to his book as "a reaction to the social and economic realities brought about by the First World War". [...] According to him this led to the marriage of politics, literature and economics. The definition is exact if, like him, one chooses 1914 as the starting point of modernism. Still, some periodicals and some writers had flaunted a modernist spirit well before the First World War. An analysis of pre-war cultural Europe caused critics like Michael Levenson [...] to make a distinction between an early and a late modernism, with the early phase being almost diametrically opposed to its later form: "modernism was individualist before it was anti-individualist, anti-traditional before it was traditional, inclined to anarchism before it was inclined to authoritarianism". [...] Clarke suggests "1923" as the crucial date in the change from "early" to "late" with Eliot's launching of the *Criterion* as its most manifest sign. He also seems to agree with Marjorie Perloff in considering the period between 1910 and 1914 as the zenith of early modernism. It seems perfectly warranted then cautiously to consider an overlap period between the modernist period and the Victorian era'. Marysa Demoor, *Their Fair Share: Women, Power and Criticism in 'The Athenaeum', from Millicent Garrett Fawcett to Katherine Mansfield, 1870–1920* (Aldershot: Ashgate Publishing Ltd, 2000), p. 140.

been, they nevertheless dominated poetry, fiction and criticism up to the Second World War, with Eliot, Pound and the Bloomsbury group as the 'lawgivers'. Thus in the simple term 'Modernist', we find encompassed a complex value-judgement which does not require overtly evaluative terminology. The institutionalisation of the movement came in 1922 with the founding of *The Criterion*, with Eliot as editor, providing both him and others with a legitimate forum for their work – *The Waste Land* appeared in its first issue.

In France, the critic Louis Gillet (1876–1943), played a crucial role in ensuring that new experimental English writers were being read and discussed in France, notably in the periodical *La Revue des deux mondes*. (In Chapter Five I shall analyse his major contribution to both the development and dissemination of the Mansfield legend in France.) Fluent in six languages, he was able to take on the important role of an exponent of the up and coming foreign writers who were as yet unknown in France. He was to present, analyse and often translate the works of authors such as Conrad, Woolf, Mansfield and especially James Joyce, with whom he was to strike up a lasting friendship.

Early Modernism also had to compete for acolytes with Imagism. In the autumn of 1912, Ezra Pound (1885–1972), an American poet who came to Europe in 1908, started publishing articles on French poetry in the English literary journal, *The New Age*. These were swiftly followed by his collection of poems entitled *Ripostes*, whose preface included the term 'Imagiste' for the first time.[21] In the spring of 1913, Pound published an article in the periodical *Poetry* in which he outlined the aims and principles of the Imagist movement, advocating the use of free rhythms, together with solidity and concision of language and imagery.[22]

21 'As for the future, *Les Imagistes*, the descendents of the forgotten school of 1909, have that in their keeping'. Ezra Pound, *Ripostes of Ezra Pound* (London: Stephen Swift, 1912), p. 59.

22 Ezra Pound, 'A Few Don'ts by an Imagiste' in *Poetry: A Magazine of Verse* (March 1913). F. S. Flint's essay, 'Imagisme' appeared in the same issue, opening with a definition of an image as 'that which presents an intellectual and emotional complex in an instant of time'; he continues with the following succinct statement of the group's position:
'1. Direct treatment of the 'thing', whether subjective or objective.
2. To use absolutely no word that does not contribute to the presentation.

He suggested that his English readers should set their sights on French rather than English writers and that, 'English poets should study Rémy de Gourmont for rhythm, Tailhade for form, Régnier for simplicity of expression, Francis Jammes for human interest, and Corbière for intensity'.[23] At the same time they should turn their back on the sentimentality associated with Victorian poetry. He praised Yeats for following these lines of development, whilst at the same time distinguishing Imagism from the Symbolism to which Yeats still adhered. Although the Symbolists had moved away from the material towards the spiritual, the Imagist saw the image as sufficient in itself. In 1914, the group of poets associated with Pound produced their first anthology entitled *Des Imagistes*,[24] having been heavily influenced by T. E. Hulme's famous essay 'Romanticism and Classicism', published in 1912, which had called for a return from the 'spilt religion' of Romanticism to 'dry and hard' Classicism.[25] The rules of Imagism were set out in the preface to the anthology and included employing the language of common speech and using *exact* words to convey meaning, creating new rhythms, and advising concentration as the essence of poetry.

Also in 1914, Pound met Eliot and first read 'Prufrock', and Joyce began serialising *A Portrait of the Artist as a Young Man* in *The Egoist* (which would also eventually go on to publish the early chapters of *Ulysses*).[26] Vorticism, a literary and artistic movement founded by

3. As regarding rhythm: to compose in sequence of the musical phrase, not in sequence of the metronome'.

Pound's own essay and list of 'don'ts' is in broad agreement with Flint's position, stating, 'It is better to present one Image in a lifetime than to produce voluminous works'. Quoted in L. Rainey, ed., *Modernism: An Anthology* (Oxford: Blackwell, 2005), pp. 94–95.

23   Quoted in Starkie, pp. 157–58.

24   Ezra Pound, ed., *Des Imagistes* (London: Poetry Bookshop, 1914).

25   T. E. Hulme, 'Romanticism and Classicism' in Hulme, *Speculations: Essays on Humanism and the Philosophy of Art,* ed. by Herbert Read. (London: Kegan Paul, Trench, Trubner, 1936), pp. 113–40. 'This is the point I aim at, then, in my argument. I prophesy that a period of dry, hard, classical verse is coming. I have met the preliminary objection founded on the bad romantic aesthetic that in such verse, from which the infinite is excluded, you cannot have the essence of poetry at all' (pp. 132–33).

26   It was serialised in *The Egoist* in twenty-five instalments from 2 February 1914– 1 September 1915 (vol. 1, no. 3 – vol. 2, no.9).

Wyndham Lewis and based on Cubism – which also had its roots in France – came into being during this year of the new and the experimental. It had its own, short lived journal entitled *Blast*, which ran for two issues in 1914 and 1915.[27] Wyndham Lewis would go on to describe Pound, Eliot, Joyce and himself as 'the Men of 1914' which would provide literary historians with a useful label. Bergonzi emphasises another French connection:

> In his early, pre-1914 phase, Lewis was more purely an artist; *Blast*, for all its stridency of manner, was the vehicle of a dynamic formalism [...] Apollinaire's manifesto *L'Antitradition futuriste*, published in Milan in 1913 [...] anticipates both the tone and the typographical peculiarities of *Blast* (p. 185).

In 1915, Ford Madox Ford, founder in 1908 of *The English Review* (which published the first stories of D. H. Lawrence), wrote what was to become his most famous novel, *The Good Soldier*, in which he summarised his personal reaction to the English fictional tradition.[28] Anthea Trodd tells us that, 'he later quoted an admirer who described it as "the finest French novel in the English language", praise which confirmed Ford's hope that his novel could be seen as existing in the European tradition of commitment to formal perfection exemplified by such writers as Flaubert and Maupassant'.[29]

However, it was *The New Age*, under the editorship of A. R. Orage, which first published Pound's views on French poetry and which would go on to play a major role in the literary life of Mansfield. Its importance to the development of Modernism is not always appreciated. From its

---

27   Michael Levenson explains the philosophy of both movements further: 'Both Imagists and Vorticists shared the hostility to an established and constraining tradition and its entrenched dogmas, in particular the notion that certain forms have a validity sanctioned by long use. In Rémy de Gourmont's phrase: "What we need is less models and more of the free light of life which you hide from us". When an angry letter writer took Pound to task for inattention to classical norms, he rejoined: "The modern renaissance, or awakening, is very largely due to the fact that we have ceased to regard a work of art as good or bad in accordance with whether it approaches or recedes from the 'Antique', the 'classical' models"' (Levenson, *Genealogy of Modernism,* p. 77).

28   Ford Madox Ford, *The Good Soldier: A Tale of Passion* (London: Bodley Head, 1915).

29   Anthea Trodd, *A Reader's Guide to Edwardian Literature* (London: Harvester Wheatsheaf, 1991), p. 109.

conception in 1907, under the sponsorship of George Bernard Shaw, most of the important literary figures of the ensuing decade left their mark on its pages. Through Arnold Bennett, its readers were introduced to Chekhov and Dostoevsky who were just starting to be translated into English; it also made fashionable the works of Claudel, Valéry, Stendhal, Romain Rolland and Gide to an English speaking audience, encouraging its reading public to turn against the old giants of Victorian literature and to make a literary voyage of discovery across the Channel.[30]

Another periodical which could claim a long connection with Modernist authors and artists was the *Athenaeum*, which from the turn of the century had started publishing articles by Clive Bell, artist, founder member of the Bloomsbury group and Virginia Woolf's brother-in-law, as well as Roger Fry, another Bloomsbury artist and art critic. From 1919 onwards, under the editorship of Mansfield's husband, John Middleton Murry, its list of reviewers would include Virginia Woolf, Katherine Mansfield, T. S. Eliot, Aldous Huxley and Ezra Pound.

---

30   John Carswell discusses the reasons for the success of *The New Age*: 'There was
        nothing eye-catching about the *New Age* – that was part of its success. In format it
        resembled one of the established weeklies such as the *Spectator* (the organ of con-
        servative clubmen and clergy) and the *Athenaeum* (the organ of dons and estab-
        lished literary men). From the first it assumed a confident, even jaunty air of com-
        plete authority, whether the subject was politics (the first half of the paper) or lit-
        erature (the second half). As a result the magazine extended, for the price of a
        penny a week, the stimulus of an apparently classic weekly to a new, literate, but
        relatively unprivileged public; while at the same time filling a void in journalism.
        The earlier radical press, though it had a genealogy stretching back to Leigh Hunt
        and Wilkes, had been strident, scandalous, seditious, and above all sectarian. *The
        New Age* was as much a journal of ideas as of comment, and it chimed with the as-
        pirations of thousands of individuals and small groups throughout the country who
        were uncommitted, progressive and for the most part, young'. John Carswell, *Lives
        and Letters: A. R. Orage, Beatrice Hastings, Katherine Mansfield, John Middleton
        Murry, S. S. Koteliansky, 1906–1957* (London: Faber, 1978), p. 35.

Eliot and Laforgue

T. S. Eliot's utilisation of the French literary tradition is well documented.[31] Only a few weeks older than Mansfield, their paths were to cross several times.[32] American by birth, he settled in England in 1915, having lived in Paris since 1910.[33] His literary awakening came in 1908 at Harvard when he also read Symons' *The Symbolist Movement in Literature*, and was deeply struck by Symons' call for a spiritual vision to eclipse the realist tradition. In Eliot's own words, 'I myself owe Mr. Symons a great debt. But for having read his book, I should not, in the year 1908, have heard of Laforgue and Rimbaud, I should probably not have begun to read Verlaine, I should not have heard of Corbière. So the Symons book is one of those which affected the course of my life'.[34] As Lyndall Gordon confirms:

> Arthur Symons's quotations from late-nineteenth-century French poets had the effect of a mirror that flashed back to Eliot an image clearer, larger, and more dramatic than anything he had imagined. Particularly in the account of Jules Laforgue,

31   For example: 'Eliot was [...] very much formed as a poet by le romantisme français as it existed around the turn of the century'. Louis Menand, 'T. S. Eliot', in *Modernism and the New Criticism, The Cambridge History of Literary Criticism,* vol. 7, ed. A. Walton Litz, Louis Menand and Lawrence Rainey (Cambridge: Cambridge University Press, 2000), p. 46.

32   As Alpers relates: '[Mansfield] also met the new young poet T. S. Eliot more than once, and in fact was at a dinner party with him only a few days after her reading of "Prufrock" at Garsington' (Alpers, p. 243). In a letter to Ottoline Morrell, Mansfield recounts a meeting with Eliot: 'Jack tied a white apron round himself and cut up, trimmed and smacked into shape the whole of America and the Americans. So nice for poor Eliot who grew paler and paler and more and more silent. [...] I came away with Eliot and we walked past rows of little ugly houses hiding behind bitter-smelling privet hedges; [...] I liked him very much and did not feel he was an enemy' (CL1, p. 312, 24 June 1917).

33   Lyndall Gordon writes: '[In 1910] Eliot crossed the Atlantic to an imaginary Paris filled with the spiritual malaise and morbidity of the decadent late-nineteenth-century poets he admired. ("La France représentait surtout, à mes yeux, la poésie", he declared many years later.) He planned to "scrape along" in Paris, and gradually give up English and write in French'. Lyndall Gordon, *Eliot's Early Years* (Oxford: Oxford University Press, 1977) p. 37.

34   T. S. Eliot, *Essays Ancient and Modern* (London: Faber and Faber, 1936).

he saw possibilities for himself. A poet, Symons revealed, could be 'eternally grown-up'; he did not have to be a Byronic *enfant terrible* to be a hero. There were others, Eliot discovered, who spoke with mature irony, others whose dreams dissolved in the grim business of the grown-up world. The crucial difference between the poems Eliot wrote before and after he read Symons is that the latter contain at their centre a wilfully defeatist identity (p. 29).

The French poet Jules Laforgue (1860–1887), a Decadent and forerunner of Modernism, was to be a major influence on Eliot. In many of Laforgue's provocative poems the author is perceived as 'pierrot', a sad and pitiable clown. It was Laforgue's 'pierrot' which inspired Eliot's 'marionette' and 'clown' poems as well as his 'Conversation Galante',[35] also published by The Egoist Press. Eliot shared a type of pessimism with Laforgue (and Baudelaire), together with a certain antagonism towards society, resulting in a self-destructive introspection which remained with him for the rest of his life. He even took to imitating the physical image of Laforgue which would eventually become a useful literary tool.[36] When Eliot created the character of J. Alfred Prufrock in 1911, Gordon states, 'the Laforgian split into mocking commentator and droll sufferer is reworked as a split into prophet and groomed conformist' (p. 31). In his preface to *The Sacred Wood: Essays on Poetry and Criticism*,[37] Eliot also acknowledges his debt to Rémy de Gourmont and his critical writings. It was through Gourmont that Eliot came into contact with Flaubert's thoughts on art and literature, which he would incorporate into his own thinking; he would also absorb into his writing the then almost unknown spiritual aspect of Baudelaire's work.

---

35   T. S. Eliot, 'Conversation Galante' in *Prufrock and Other Observations* (London: The Egoist Press, 1917).

36   Gordon elucidates further: 'He proceeded to cultivate the *dandysme* of his hero, the polished image described in Symons's book: "des cravats sobres, des vestons anglais, des pardessus clergyman, et de par les nécessités, un parapapluie immuablement placé sous le bras". Eliot no doubt elaborated his polish in imitation of Laforgue but, as one critic noted, he probably did not have to alter himself that much: "There was an element of Laforgue already in him: it was easy to progress to the pose from the urbane dandyism, the perfection of dress, manners, and accomplishments, which was the Harvard style of his time and in which he excelled"' (Gordon, pp. 30–31).

37   T. S. Eliot, *The Sacred Wood: Essays on Poetry and Criticism* (London: Methuen, 1920).

In 1916, whilst living in England, Eliot was introduced to the Bloomsbury group, and through them was befriended by Lady Ottoline Morrell's circle where he was to meet both Mansfield and John Middleton Murry. Gordon relates how, 'when [Aldous] Huxley met [Eliot], in December 1916, he wrote him off as "just a Europeanised American, overwhelmingly cultured, talking about French literature in the most uninspired fashion imaginable"' (p. 83). Returning to Paris in 1917, Eliot took to writing poetry in French, using Corbière as a model.[38] Throughout 1919 and 1920 he read the instalments of *Ulysses* as they were being published, and was full of admiration for Joyce's literary experiment. When interviewed many years later, referring to Joyce, Eliot acknowledged that, 'what he was tentatively attempting to do, with the usual false starts and despairs, had already been done, done superbly and it seemed to him finally, in prose which without being poetic in the older sense, had the intensity and texture of poetry' (quoted in Harwood, p. 63). Of course, he was talking about *The Waste Land*, his work in hand, which appeared for the first time in *The Criterion*,[39] which Eliot founded and became editor of in 1922, the same year that saw the publication of *Ulysses* and Katherine Mansfield's *The Garden Party and Other Stories*.[40] Louis Menand makes the following point:

[If *The Waste Land*] was indeed intended as a kind of deliberate dead end, an explosion of the nineteenth-century metaphysics of style leaving nothing in its place, this ambition was perhaps one of the things Eliot learnt from Joyce. *Ulysses*, Eliot told Virginia Woolf in a famous conversation, 'destroyed the whole of the nineteenth century'. It left Joyce with nothing to write another book on. It showed up

---

38   According to John Harwood, Richard Aldington claimed that the association of Eliot with Laforgue was 'verging on cliché; an "affinity of mind" had been misconstrued as imitation. Eliot had as much in common with Rimbaud and Corbière; he was a direct descendent, not an imitator, of the younger Symbolists' (Harwood, p. 91).

39   *The Waste Land* appeared in *The Criterion* in October 1922 followed by publication initially in New York and then England. *The Waste Land* (New York: Boni and Liveright, 1922). *The Waste Land* (Richmond: Hogarth Press, 1923). *The Criterion* was modelled on *La Nouvelle revue française*, founded in France by Gide and his associates in 1909, and it meant that Eliot now had a permanent place in which to propagate his own views of literature. *The Criterion* ceased publication in 1939.

40   James Joyce, *Ulysses* (Paris: Shakespeare and Company, 1922).

the futility of all the English styles [...] [T]here was no 'great conception': that was not Joyce's intention [...] Joyce did completely what he meant to do (p. 56).

Proust, Bloomsbury and France

The most important French novelist writing at this time, who would come to exert a powerful influence over James Joyce and many other English writers, was Marcel Proust (1871–1922). Pervading the entire cycle that comprises *A la recherche du temps perdu*,[41] is a concern with solitude; the artistic satisfaction it affords and the human strains it imposes, together with the importance of momentary impressions in recapturing the sense of the whole. Its power lies precisely in the triviality of the events, the characters' lives dominated by receding shadows, in a chiaroscuro world of memory, secrets and repressions. Every character, every relationship, is made up of the accretions of a palpable past.[42] His work would go on to influence generations of novelists and thinkers and both his vision and technique are now perceived as vital to the development of European Modernist literature. For the Bloomsbury group he became an icon:

> Even for members of the group brought up on Racine, Marcel Proust became the most revered French writer. The Bloomsbury circle plunged into the Proustian text 'with extreme emotion.' The original members of the group had embraced G. E. Moore's emphasis on states of mind [...] It was almost a given, therefore, that Proust would have an enduring impact on the work, reading, and lives of many

---

41   It was published in seven volumes – three of them posthumously. *Du côté de chez Swann* (Paris: Nouvelle Revue Française, 1913), *A l'ombre des jeunes filles en fleurs* (Paris: Nouvelle Revue Française, 1919), *Le Côté de Guermantes* (Paris: Nouvelle Revue Française, 1920/1921), *Sodome et Gomorrhe* (Paris: Nouvelle Revue Française, 1921/1922), *La Prisonnière* (Paris: Nouvelle Revue Française, 1923), *Albertine disparue* (Paris: Nouvelle Revue Française, 1925), *Le Temps retrouvé* (Paris: Nouvelle Revue Française, 1927).

42   Proust's own earlier influences included John Ruskin, whose works *Bible of Amiens* and *Sesame and Lilies* he had translated into French. John Ruskin, trans. Marcel Proust, *La Bible d'Amiens* (Paris: Mercure de France, 1914). John Ruskin, trans. Marcel Proust, *Sésame et les lys* (Paris: Mercure de France, 1906).

members of Bloomsbury. Never was there a group of painters, writers, and thinkers for whom the sense of the moment counted more: it had a lasting power.[43]

Indeed, the work of Virginia Woolf can be seen to capture some of
Proust's innovatory techniques and ideas. A similar sort of movement to
Bloomsbury in France both before and after the Great War, centred on
the journal *La Nouvelle revue française*, known as the *NRF*, mentioned
in the previous paragraph, which had been founded by André Gide,
Jacques Copeau and Jacques Rivière, amongst others, in 1909. (It would
eventually evolve into the Gallimard publishing house.) Gide had wanted
to create a mouthpiece for the new literature that was replacing Symbolism. He and his co-founders now sought to encourage a more classical
form of writing, more sober, restrained and without ideological con-
straints; they launched the careers of many writers including Duhamel,
Giraudoux and Romains.[44] For many critics, Gide became the nearest
French equivalent to the Bloomsbury intellectual.

Mary Ann Caws and Sarah Bird Wright contend that the connection
between Bloomsbury and France should not be understated:

> The interchange between French artists and writers and those of Bloomsbury was
> immensely fruitful and of long duration. The Bloomsbury figures counted among
> their close friends some of the artists and writers who shaped European culture
> during the Belle Époque: Henri Matisse, André Dérain, Jacques Copeau, Sergei
> Diaghilev, Marcel Proust, Pablo Picasso, Gertrude Stein, Jacques Cocteau. […]
> The aesthetic dialogue between Bloomsbury and France was at its height during
> the decade immediately before and after World War I. During these years the art-
> ists were invigorated by their months on the coast of the Midi and in Paris; the
> writers, similarly, were stimulated not only by their travels but also by the new
> theories and techniques developed by French novelists, poets and critics (p. 19).

England also attracted her share of French artists, Monet being perhaps
the most famous. André Derain, who was painting in London during his
Fauve period, came to be associated with the Bloomsbury group because

43 Mary Ann Caws and Sarah Bird Wright, *Bloomsbury and France: Art and Friends*
    (Oxford: Oxford University Press, 2000), p. 11.
44 Ethel Tolansky writes: 'The *NRF* soon became a fundamental reference point in
    the cultural scene, leading Otto Abetz, German ambassador in Paris, to state that:
    "Il y a trois forces en France: le communisme, la grande banque, et la *NRF*"'. Peter
    France, ed., *The New Oxford Companion to Literature in French* (Oxford: Claren-
    don Press, 1995), p. 573.

of his friendship with Clive Bell and Roger Fry, and it was Fry and Bell who organised the two Post-Impressionist Exhibitions of 1910 and 1912 in London which were to have an unprecedented impact on both English artists and writers alike (including Mansfield), by introducing new modes of French aesthetic perception. Fry, in his constant quest of bridge-building between the continental and British worlds of art, also mounted an exhibition in Paris in July 1912, entitled, 'Exposition de Quelques Artistes Indépendants Anglais' at the Galerie Barbazanges.[45]

Other French writers associated with Bloomsbury included Charles and Marie Mauron, who became close friends of Roger Fry and E. M. Forster. It was Fry who put Mauron, critic and translator, in contact with Gide, via the *NRF*.[46] The relationships become a spider's web of contacts and resources; Roger Martin du Gard and Gide became close friends of the Strachey family and it was Lytton Strachey's sister, Dorothy Bussy, who became Gide's translator in England.[47]

The critical reception of English writers in France, as of French writers in England at this time depended on the work of a number of

---

45   Bloomsbury could, however be selective in its French gleanings, as Caws and Wright note: '[They] seem not to have taken notice of the excitement in Paris from 1911 to 1914 about the "simultanist" or "nowist" movements associated with Blaise Cendrars and Guillaume Apollinaire, nor did they pay much attention to the abstract experimentation of Robert and Sonia Delaunay' (p. 10).

46   Fry had first made contact with Gide in Cambridge in 1918; they instantly hit it off and Gide was complimentary about Fry's first translations of Mallarmé's poems. From 1892, when he first started studying painting in Paris, until his death in 1934, having just translated Charles Mauron's *Aesthetics and Psychology,* Fry continually demonstrated a deep attachment to all things French.

47   The founders of the *NRF* also came to be associated with the meetings at Pontigny, as described by Caws and Wright: 'One of the more celebrated meeting places of French intellectuals from about 1910 through the 1930's was the medieval Cistercian Abbaye de Pontigny, in the Yonne. Here many of the Bloomsbury group had an occasion to mingle with writers, critics, and other noted figures. Paul Desjardins had initiated the conferences on an estate he had inherited; Pontigny was to be a place for international meetings on topics of aesthetics, politics, and institutions such as the law. [...] In order to be invited to Pontigny, it was necessary for foreign participants to be known to the French for their general erudition... From the outset a heavily Roman Catholic preserve, it was dominated by Paul Desjardins, the founder, [...] by Charles du Bos, the vice-president, [...] and by André Gide, Jacques Rivière, Jean Schlumberger, Jacques Copeau, and Roger Martin du Gard' (Caws and Wright, pp. 291–92).

translators. (A discussion of the translations of Mansfield's work in French will form another chapter in this book.) There was keen excitement about these linguistic exchanges, and Roger Fry often acted as an intermediary. For example, it is no accident that Virginia Woolf and Henry James both had the same translator at this time – Charles Mauron; Fry, who revered both novelists, thought that only Mauron would cope with the linguistic and conceptual difficulties inherent in their work. (Mauron would go on to translate Mansfield's *In a German Pension*, in 1939, discussed in Chapter Four.) It was through the translations of Fry, with commentaries by Mauron, that Mallarmé was introduced to the English reading public, laying the groundwork for a burgeoning appreciation of French Symbolist poetry.[48] Fry's ongoing collaborations with Mauron would have an invaluable impact on future Mallarmé studies. As Caws and Wright point out:

> For Fry, only the poet Mallarmé could equal the great modernist novelists, breaking the theme to pieces, as Fry said, then reconstructing it in a cubist fashion. Since art and poetry were always indissolubly linked in Fry's imagination, he compared Mallarmé's unequivocal intensity with that of Cézanne (p. 364).

The most famous member of the Bloomsbury group, Virginia Woolf (1882–1941), would develop an uneasy friendship with Mansfield; when the latter died, she claimed that Mansfield's work was, 'the only writing I have ever been jealous of'.[49] Early in her writing career she had already found herself at odds with the state of the novel in England as exemplified by the likes of Wells and Galsworthy. For her they were too materialistic and not capable of understanding the new and the radical; like Proust, Joyce and Flaubert she too was questioning the relevance of a plot, favouring instead philosophical introspection. Her general dissatisfaction with English novelists expressed itself in an essay she wrote in 1919, declaring that in their 'realistic' representation of life they were succeeding merely in obscuring or even falsifying it.[50] Woolf's work has always been of interest to writers, critics and translators in France. *To the*

---

48   Stéphane Mallarmé, trans. Roger Fry, *Les Poèmes de Mallarmé* (Oxford: Oxford University Press, 1937).

49   *The Diary of Virginia Woolf, vol. 2, 1920–1924*, ed. by Anne Olivier Bell; assisted by Andrew McNeillie (London: Hogarth Press, 1978), p. 227.

50   Virginia Woolf, *The Common Reader* (London: Hogarth Press, 1925), p. 22.

Lighthouse, published in England in 1927, was serialised first in France and won the *Femina Vie Heureuse* Prize in 1928.[51]

Joyce and Gillet

James Joyce (1882–1941), was exactly the same age as Virginia Woolf and died in the same year. Between them they contributed to the development of what was to become known as the psychological novel, which had its origins in France, its greatest exponent being Proust, as outlined above. From his childhood in Dublin, Joyce had been immersed in French literature and in 1903, at the age of twenty-one, he took himself off to Paris, as so many others had done before him, to find inspiration as a writer, staying in a hotel on the Left Bank where, 'he rented a top room with a patched length of carpet [...], the hard roll for a pillow and families of mice behind the cracked skirtings. There, on a spirit stove, he cooked in one saucepan which was rarely washed out'.[52] He would live, on and off, in Paris, for most of his life. According to Symons, it was after reading *En route* by Huysmans (the sequel to *Là-bas*),[53] that Joyce came to an understanding of how the novel could compete with both poetry and philosophy. It was from Flaubert's correspondence that he drew much of his aesthetic doctrine at this time. Cordell Yee makes the point that, 'Joyce claimed to have read "every line" Flaubert wrote and is said to have memorised whole pages of his works [...] Flaubert shares Joyce's interest in justifying the claim that verbal art can match the appeal of visual art [...] Like the young Joyce, Flaubert calls for precision in language'.[54] In addition, John Houston underlines this argument when he states that, 'Joyce, like Flaubert himself, tended, in putting together

---

51   Virginia Woolf, *To the Lighthouse* (London: The Hogarth Press, 1927). '[Roger Fry] made many suggestions during the period in which Mauron was translating the middle part of *To the Lighthouse,* published in the French literary journal *Commerce*' (Caws and Wright, p. 352).
52   Patricia Hutchins, *James Joyce's World* (London: Methuen, 1957), p. 56.
53   Joris-Karl Huysmans, *En route* (Paris: Tresse et Stock, 1895).
54   Cordell D. K. Yee, *The World According to James Joyce: Reconstructing Representation* (Lewisburg: Bucknell University Press, 1997), p. 139, n. 69.

literary sentences of a parodic intent, to make sure that, in many technical ways, they were polished and elegant'.[55]

In these early years, most of Joyce's success was based on scandal and shock value, particularly after the publication, by Shakespeare and Company, of *Ulysses* in Paris in 1922. Until this point he was completely unknown to the French reading public. *Ulysses* was followed by *A Portrait of the Artist as a Young Man*, translated into French in 1924.[56] For Starkie, *Ulysses'* roots are firmly in the French tradition:

> There is very little in *Ulysses* which derives from the English tradition in fiction, but it has many affinities with France. In form it is classical in its integrated structure and its strict unity of time – twenty-four hours. But, in the same way as Racine, Joyce has succeeded in making use of the whole life of the characters depicted. In its plan it has the almost architectural inevitability of *Madame Bovary*, and it is as strictly composed. Like all great psychologists – whether in drama or fiction – like Flaubert when writing *Madame Bovary*, or Racine when composing *Bérénice*, Joyce wished to liberate himself from the tyranny of plot, from the artificial convention of a story – he succeeds in this aim. [...] The *monologue intérieur* which he uses in this work is an extension of the method employed by Flaubert, Edouard Dujardin, and Proust, but it has been taken to its most extreme limits (pp. 191–92).

The French critic, Louis Gillet, read *Ulysses* in 1925 and went on to meet Joyce in 1931; the essays he published on Joyce in France contributed significantly to the author's fame in that country. He wrote of these essays:

> Toutes ces études ont paru à la *Revue des deux mondes* [...] Et si je songe qu'il était défendu par les lois d'y nommer Gide ou Proust, je m'étonne encore d'avoir eu le droit d'y hasarder ce que j'osais dire de Joyce: c'était une bombe dans le Saint des Saints. Le directeur savait peu de chose des auteurs étrangers. C'est à cette circonstance que je dois d'avoir eu carte blanche.[57]

For him, Joyce's work was the inevitable outcome of the literary movements of the preceding generation:

---

55   John Porter Houston, *Joyce and Prose: An Exploration of the Language of Ulysses* (Lewisburg: Bucknell University Press, 1989), p. 40.
56   James Joyce, *Dedalus: Portrait de l'artiste jeune par lui-même,* trans. by Ludmila Savitsky (Paris: Éditions de la Sirène, 1924).
57   Louis Gillet, *Stèle pour James Joyce* (Marseille: Sagittaire, 1941), p. 30.

C'était écrit: le roman devait en arriver là. Après Browning, Meredith, Henry James, Huysmans, Proust, il ne restait qu'un pas à faire; le voilà fait. Nous avions déjà les aventures de M. Folantin à la recherche d'un bifteack passable. Il n'est pas jusqu'à l'idée du roman d'une journée qui ne se rencontre en France vers 1880; il y avait la Belle Journée d'Henry Céard, et qui relirait ce petit conte de M Edouard Dujardin, *Les Lauriers sont Coupés*, serait surpris d'y découvrir l'indication de beaucoup d'effets qu'on croit propres à l'auteur d'*Ulysse*. Il est curieux que cette espèce de roman intégral, la tentative la plus soutenue qu'on ait faite pour épuiser la somme du réel, soit issue en même temps du naturalisme et de la boîte de Pandore du symbolisme. Et cependant, cela s'explique, puisque tout le réel consiste dans la connaissance claire ou confuse qu'on en a: 'L'âme', déclare M. Joyce, 'l'âme, en un sens, est tout ce qui est' (Gillet, pp. 40–41).

It was Gillet who had the most influence in shaping the French reaction to Joyce and especially to *Ulysses*, when the French translation appeared in 1929. The two men were to become close friends and Gillet was able to gain valuable insights for his criticism through lengthy discussion with the author himself. He never wrote for Joyce scholars, but rather for the French general public, who at that time were prejudiced against the Irish writer. Georges Markow-Totevy claims that:

There is still a more valuable contribution of Gillet's criticism. At a time when Joyce was recognised only by the vanguard of English letters in Europe, England and America, the French critic raised his voice from the solemn circle of literary tradition and respectability to defend what seemed then the most extravagant and lascivious of literary charlatans. It is almost a paradox that Gillet, given his background and his responsibilities of official critic and future Academician, should be the man to place, as he says, 'this bomb in the holy of Holies'. Because of his renown and influence over public opinion he did more than the other excellent French friends and critics of Joyce to establish and strengthen his fame in France.[58]

58   Louis Gillet, *Claybook for James Joyce*, trans. and intro. by Georges Markow-Totevy (London: Abelard-Schuman, 1958), p. 22.

The Modernist Short Story

Both Virginia Woolf's *Mrs Dalloway* and James Joyce's *Ulysses* were originally conceived as short stories.[59] As Dominic Head argues, 'In the stories of Joyce, Woolf and Mansfield, there is a substantial common ground in terms of method and effect; and, for each writer, formal dissonance is both a yardstick of generic innovation and a vital key to interpretation'.[60] He goes on to explain how all three writers incorporate a complex view of the interaction between individual experience and social organisation. Clare Hanson claims that for the most part:

> Much of the criticism levelled against Mansfield upholds the assumption that the short story is a minor art form; in other words her choice of form determines the status of her art, which is thus marginalised. The short story may be seen as having a form of exclusion and implication 'its tendency towards the expression of that which is marginal or excentric to society'. [...] This bias remains the reason why the short story has been such an important literary form for female writers, many of whom have made their entire reputation on the short story form (Hanson in *GOM*, p. 300).

Elsewhere, she makes an important distinction between the 'short story' and 'short fiction':

> The modernist short story grew out of the psychological sketch of the 1890s. Like the psychological sketch, it is more properly called a type of short fiction for one of its leading characteristics is a rejection of the 'story' in the accepted sense. Modernist short fiction writers distrusted the well-wrought tale for a variety of reasons. Most importantly they argued that the pleasing shape and coherence of the traditional short story represented a falsification of the discrete and heterogeneous nature of experience.[61]

There was no real tradition of short story writing in England, and few worthy examples until the twentieth century, whereas the opposite was true in France, with a well-established high quality tradition, dating back

---

59   Virginia Woolf, *Mrs Dalloway* (London: Hogarth Press, 1925).
60   Dominic Head, *The Modernist Short Story* (Cambridge: Cambridge University Press, 1992), p. 139.
61   Clare Hanson, *Short Stories and Short Fictions, 1880–1980* (London: Macmillan, 1985), p. 55.

at least two centuries. The ascendancy of the modern short story in England was concurrent with the emergence of Modernism. The 'old-fashioned' story with a plot, is now set against 'a slice-of-life', unstructured, psychological story, as exemplified by Woolf and Joyce, and especially Mansfield.[62]

Katherine Mansfield

In one sense or another, Mansfield is associated with many of the complex literary movements and influences outlined above; in addition to her personal acquaintance of several of the writers mentioned in this chapter, echoes of the French symbolists, Walter Pater, Oscar Wilde and the Decadents are to be found in much of her prose writing, as I shall demonstrate in this book. For Kaplan:

> Pater and Symons provided techniques that Mansfield would use later to uncover, at its deepest level, the culturally determined condition of women. By importing symbolist devices into realistic fiction, Mansfield exemplifies how the male-bonded nineteenth-century aesthetes became absorbed into the twentieth-century feminist consciousness. Some of her brilliance lies in her realisation that the symbolism of the aesthetes could be joined, as well, to a twentieth-century epistemology – partially Freudian, partially feminist. Her use of the '90s influence veers away from the occult, abstract direction it took with Yeats, for example, and it never goes to the extremes of Joyce with his preoccupation with symbolic language, myth, and metafiction (p. 64).

---

62   Dominic Head takes this discussion one stage further: 'Suzanne Ferguson defines these two types as simple (the anecdote or tale) and complex (the episode). Simple stories concern "a single character in a single, simple action", while in the complex episode "the forming elements are thus marshalled towards the ordered revelation of character or, in some cases, the development of symbol, rather than towards plot". Eileen Baldeshwiler has supplied alternative terms for this binary opposition: she distinguishes between the conventional, plot-based story ("epical") and the "lyrical" story, often open-ended, which focuses upon "internal changes, moods, and feelings"' (p.16).

Conversely, for Starkie:

> Katherine Mansfield had less knowledge of France and French literature than Somerset Maugham, and probably knew little of either before she arrived in Europe, but thereafter she stayed for long periods in France – she even died there – and felt affinity with the French people. She was obviously influenced by Maupassant, but there is no doubt that she was also greatly affected by Chekov, and that his spiritual qualities, his qualities of soul, were more sympathetic to her than the materialism of Maupassant. [...] There is something of Gallic irony in 'At the Bay', and its visual descriptions are more French than Russian – she has managed here to transpose Maupassant's method to the New Zealand scene. Also, the ending of 'The Doll's House' possesses the kind of pathos which he understood, and she can frequently be as merciless and as cruel as he. Her writing, however, shows a delicate tenderness at times – a kind of virginity even – a feeling for poetry, which is found nowhere in his work, which brings her nearer to Chekov, and which also places her achievement, in spite of its limitations, on a nobler and more moving plane than Somerset Maugham could ever reach (p. 201).

The difference in viewpoint is marked. Starkie's summary of Mansfield's method, influences and writing style displays all the commonplace misunderstandings that characterise early Mansfield criticism. Even more noticeable are the references to a saintly, ethereal Mansfield, a persona invented by the French critics (as I shall demonstrate in a later chapter); this is amply demonstrated by Starkie's vocabulary and the use of words and phrases such as 'pathos', 'delicate tenderness', 'virginity', 'nobler and more moving plane'. This was for many years, the common view, that of Mansfield as minor Modernist writer, dealing in a delicate, feminine way with the domestic aspects of life – the literary equivalent of painters such as Berthe Morisot and Mary Cassatt with whom her work is often compared. By contrast, the points Kaplan raises mark Mansfield out as an innovator, a Modernist and a feminist, and a 'great' writer.[63] This dichotomy of viewpoints has always been a marked presence in Mansfield criticism, and has only diminished in the last twenty or

---

63   In addition, Kaplan remarks: 'What Mansfield might have discovered in the prose poem was the possibility of deconstructing the phallocentric structures of conventional narrative and producing instead a kind of writing from the body, such as that advocated by contemporary postmodernists like Hélène Cixous. (Accordingly, many of the examples used by the French feminists come from the same symbolist writers about whom Mansfield was learning through reading Arthur Symons.)' (Kaplan, p. 48).

so years, with the advent of detailed biographies and myriad numbers of critical works. For some of the current revisionary critics of Modernism, Mansfield remains a marginalised writer of short stories, virtually eliminated from the history of the movement. For critics writing in the twenties and thirties, however, she was viewed as highly significant to the development of Modernist fiction and was widely imitated and discussed. In Michael Levenson's *The Cambridge Companion to Modernism*, published as recently as 1999, she is not mentioned once, though her novelist friend, Virginia Woolf, merits detailed discussion. This is an inexplicable oversight which demonstrates how short story writers are frequently marginalised. Clare Hanson makes the point that Mansfield is, 'a marginal not a minor writer – marginalised in particular ways during her lifetime and in rather different ways after her death' (Hanson in *GOM*, p. 299). For both Hanson and Kaplan, Mansfield belongs, together with Virginia Woolf, at the heart of British Modernism. One of Mansfield's biographers, Ian Gordon, writes, 'She had the same kind of direct influence on the art of the short story as Joyce had on the novel. After Joyce and Katherine Mansfield neither the novel nor the short story can ever be quite the same again'.[64]

Most modern critics agree that Mansfield's own unique form of Modernism was not derivative of other contemporary writers but was rather a product of her symbiosis of late-nineteenth-century techniques and themes, for the most part introduced through her reading of Symons, from her late teens onwards, when her tastes and preferences started to take shape and she began, with the Symbolists and the Decadents as her dominant influences, to write the sort of fiction which was committed to the possibilities of narrative experimentation.

This then, is the literary ether into which Mansfield was immersed. She was either associated with, or drew inspiration from, most of the schools of thought outlined in this chapter. Her first 'adult' stories were published in the *New Age* and Orage remained a life-long friend. She knew all the Bloomsbury set, was friends with Virginia Woolf and is said to have had an affair with Bertrand Russell. She and her partner, John Middleton Murry, set up their own short lived magazine entitled *Rhythm*, an

---

64   Ian Gordon, *Katherine Mansfield*, Writers and Their Work, no. 49 (London: Longmans, Green & Co., 1954), p. 17.

avant-garde publication with Francis Carco sending articles from France, with a bias towards Symbolism, the arts and Post-Impressionism, the music of Debussy and Mahler and the philosophy of Bergson. The list of contributors, unknown at the time beyond the confines of the Left Bank, reads impressively today and included Derain, Picasso and Tristan Derème. Like Joyce, Eliot and countless others, Mansfield and Murry lived for a while in Paris; their attempt proved short-lived as Murry was declared a bankrupt whilst they were there, forcing them to return to England. For a while he was the French literary critic on *The Times*, thereby influencing and directing Mansfield's reading and understanding of French texts; her reading of French novels was prodigious, her influences numerous. When Murry became editor of *The Athenaeum*, Mansfield became its main book reviewer. She met both Eliot and Joyce and read their works, and before her death came to know and appreciate the writing of Proust.[65]

In short, she was aware of – when not actually participating in – most of the literary activity taking place during the years before and after the Great War; she also spent months at a time living and writing in France. Though never particularly integrated into the principal intellectual and political currents of French life, nevertheless she would assimilate into her own thought patterns and creativity, a strong infusion of something outside the familiar – a reorientation of vision perhaps, a view of life, literature and art through a Gallic lens, which was to be of infinite and lasting value, and which is the subject of my next chapter.

---

65   On the subject of *Ulysses*, Virginia Woolf relates how: 'One day Katherine Mansfield came, and I had it out. She began to read, ridiculing: then suddenly said, but there's something in this: a scene that should figure I suppose in the history of literature' (*Diary of Virginia Woolf*, vol 2, p. 240). So far as Eliot and Mansfield are concerned, Kaplan makes the following points: 'They had, in fact, some important things in common: they were exactly the same age [...] and they were both outsiders in London – he an American, she a New Zealander. Yet most of the similarities between these two writers appear to be the result of parallel development rather than influence. Critics of modernism make much of the fact that Eliot read Symons's book on symbolism in December 1908 and that it catapulted him into his first efforts at modernist verse. Mansfield's knowledge of Symons came even earlier than Eliot's and her awareness of symbolism independently shaped her first creative attempts' (p. 76).

Chapter Two
Falling for France

'I love this place more and more. One is conscious
of it as I used to be conscious of New Zealand. I
mean if I went for a walk there & lay down under a
pine tree & looked up at the wispy clouds through
the branches I came home plus the pine tree – don't
you know? Here it's just the same. […] Why I
don't feel like this in England heaven knows. But
my light goes out, in England, or it's a very small
& miserable shiner'.

Katherine Mansfield, CL4, p. 89, 28 October 1920.

As shown in the previous chapter, it was the complexity of cultural reson-
ances collectively known as the *fin de siècle* which made France – and
especially Paris – such a magnet for writers and artists at the turn of the
last century, underlining Ralph Waldo Emerson's opinion that, 'England
built London for its own use, but France built Paris for the world'.[1] However, Britain was also a nation in upheaval during this period, teeming
with the excitement of innovation and change. Suffragettes were de-
manding votes for women; Ireland was preparing for a confrontation
between nationalists and unionists; inventions such as the motor car and
the movies were beginning to transform society.

This literary climate of innovation allowed experimental writers
like Katherine Mansfield to flourish. She was most definitely a writer of
her time and of the moment, reading all the 'right' French books –
Baudelaire, Rachilde, Colette – producing the 'right' sort of work – innovative, modern and experimental – and even dying in the 'right'
(suitably occult) place – with Gurdjieff at Fontainebleau. The smartly
cynical metropolitan satirist of her youth would metamorphose into an
innovative, creative writer with an overtly Modernist style and a covertly

---

1   Ralph Waldo Emerson, *Complete Works, Volume 7: Society and Solitude* (Boston:
     Houghton, Mifflin, 1894), p. 487, in journal for July 1848.

hidden social and spiritual agenda. In the last months of her life she was so receptive to the new and the challenging that she was even prepared to stay at Gurdjieff's 'Institute for the Harmonious Development of Man'. It is therefore essential to bear in mind this multi-faceted portrait of Mansfield, with an emphasis on her radical open-mindedness, when examining the French influence which informed almost her entire adult life.

This chapter focuses on Mansfield's response to France and the French and how this manifested itself in her writing. In Chapter Five I shall reveal how the French critics – as well as Murry – would distort these views in order to aid the creation of the legend surrounding Mansfield's personality in France. Using all available material – notebooks, letters and journals – I have collated Mansfield's opinions, remarks and responses to all things French and presented them here, in their most comprehensive form, for the first time. Thus, any falsification of this response by the French critics and Murry after her death will be easily exposed.

Mansfield was a nomadic figure, constantly on the move both in England and abroad, but finally choosing to spend more and more time in France. Through my detailed examination of her notebooks and correspondence I shall demonstrate how this body of work reveals an idiosyncratic yet evocative account of early-twentieth-century France. Up until her death in 1923 at the age of thirty four, if all her many separate visits are added together, then approximately three years of her life were spent on French soil. [See Appendix A for a brief chronology of these trips.] It was inevitable that these prolonged exposures to French culture, literature and people would influence her writing and thinking, in some form or another. It is the remit of this chapter to elucidate the extent to which this influence would colour her writing.

An examination of her personal writing shows her reacting in a subjective way to the sights and sounds around her, often humorous and content; sometimes depressed, suffering and acerbic. Her occasional negative responses to France in the light of these ever changing moods were not the impression of Mansfield that Murry sought to portray after her death; this would lead him down the path of editorial subterfuge in order to 'recreate' certain aspects of his dead wife's personality. This chapter concentrates on Mansfield's perceptions of France and the French and the influence they brought to bear on her own creative output.

Specific French literary influences will be discussed in the next chapter. I hope thus, to understand more fully the French influence – in whatever form it took – in Mansfield's life.

Why France?

Mansfield spent several months in Bavaria early on in adulthood, taken there by an exasperated and weary mother in 1909, when it was discovered that she was pregnant. Her parents also feared she might be 'suffering' from possible lesbian tendencies, for which, at that time, a water cure – a German speciality – was deemed particularly helpful.[2] After 1914, for obvious reasons, it was neither appropriate nor desirable to holiday in Germany. France was nearer, she had a good working knowledge of French language and literature, but most importantly, and as outlined above, France, and Paris in particular, was a magnet for all the creative forces of the day; it was, quite simply, *the* place to be.[3] Notwithstanding the influence of Murry, who had spent months living in Paris as a young student prior to meeting Mansfield (and who introduced her to his Parisian acquaintances, one of whom – Francis Carco – was to become a major player, both in her life, her art and the legend after her

---

2   Late-nineteenth and early-twentieth-century sexologists and doctors saw homosexuality as a degenerative disease to be treated and cured; a perception which only partially changed with the publication of Sigmund Freud's *Three Essays on the Theory of Sexuality* in 1915 (trans. by James Strachey (London: Imago, 1949)). Mansfield's parents were in fact right to 'fear' that her daughter might have lesbian tendencies, though ironically she had conducted at least two lesbian relationships whilst living at home in New Zealand – with an old school friend, Maata Mahupuku (a Maori princess), and Edie Bendall, an art school student. There are several references to her sexual feelings for Maata and Edie in her notebooks of 1907, including the following: 'Last night I spent in her arms, and tonight I hate her – which being interpreteth meaneth that I adore her, that I cannot lie in my bed and not feel the magic of her body [...] I feel more powerfully all those so termed sexual impulses with her [Edie Bendall] than I have with any men' (NB1, p. 99).
3   See previous chapter for my brief overview of the French/English literary scene during Mansfield's life-time.

death), Mansfield's response to France was to become a wholly personal one.

Early French Influences

During 1903–1906, from the age of fifteen to eighteen, Mansfield was in England being educated, together with her two older sisters, at Queens' College in Harley Street. At this time, France for her was no more than a tourist destination. Reading books in French was more of a duty than a pleasure: 'I have read Amiel, & I am going to be frank. I like him in bits, but I do not think he is always logical – I hope I have not offended you dear' (CL1 p. 17, 15 February 1905). Mansfield's command of the French language was to develop over her life time, from school girl hesitancy to fluent conversationalist. Even as early as February 1908, back in New Zealand after her schooling in London, and resolute in her determination to return to Europe, she was writing in her journal in French, no doubt because it made her feel sophisticated, and probably in the hopes that prying eyes at home would not be able to understand what she was writing. 'Night. J'attends pour la première fois dans ma vie la crise de ma vie' (J2, p. 35, February 1908). There are many instances of this use of French peppered throughout the early diaries and notebooks.[4] As a special concession, obtained through contacts of her father, Harold Beauchamp (Governor of the Bank of New Zealand and friend of the New Zealand Prime Minister of the day, R. J. Seddon), she was allowed to borrow books from the library attached to Parliament House in Wellington; records at this time show that she was reading Maupassant, Balzac, Mérimée and Flaubert – all in French.

---

4   Other examples include: 'C'est de la misère. Non, pas ça exactement. Il y a quelque chose – une profonde malaise me suive comme un ombre [sic]. Oh, why write bad French? Why write at all? J2, p. 138, 20 June 1918. 'SATURDAY a horrible morning and afternoon. Je me sens incapable de tout [...] J'ai l'envie de prieur [sic] au bon Dieu comme le vieux père Tolstoi. Oh Lord make me a better creature tomorrow. Le cœur me monte aux lèvres d'un gout de sang. Je me déteste aujourd'hui' (NB2, p. 3).

In October 1908, within a few months of returning to England (having finally obtained permission from her family allowing a permanent move), she visited Paris once more, with a friend. Her response to this trip is fortunately well documented in her notebooks and letters, where we see, for the first time, Mansfield's intoxication with the pleasures of travel – which remained with her all her life – together with her enthusiastic response to the attractions of Paris itself:

> Yesterday we spent the day at Versailles [...] Looking back upon it all I feel I must have dreamed so much beauty – the pictures – the rooms which Louis XV gilded with the very blood of the people – the chapel built by Madame de Maintenon to 'purify the Palace'! [...] We left the garden in the evening – outside there was a great Fair. Long, brilliantly lighted booths which made me feel like a child – especially the toys and gingerbread frogs – and kites and cakes and books and sweets [...] and the queer little old Frenchman seemed to be so pleased with my delight that he made me a present tied with ribbon of confiserie fearful and wonderful [...] Today I have been to the Arc de Triomphe and the very top of Notre Dame – and the Tomb of Napoleon and the Luxembourg – I feel very tired with so much beauty and fascinating new thoughts and conceptions [...] I am more than sorry to leave Paris [...] The picturesque aspect of it all – the people – and at night from the top of a tram – the lighted interiors of the houses – you know the effect – people gathered round a lamp lighted table – a little, homely café – a laundry – a china shop – or at the corners the old chestnut sellers – the Italians selling statuettes of the Venus de Milo – and Napoléon encore Napoléon (CL1, p. 77–78, 24 October 1908).

This vivid description evokes all the delight and sense of intoxication of a young girl revelling in the sights and sounds of a foreign city. Mansfield's descriptive skills capture the imagination of the reader; the juvenile, breathless quality of the prose – here is the origin of Kezia in 'Prelude' and 'The Doll's House' – reinforced by images and sounds perceived as if through the eyes of a child. Mansfield, aged twenty, reverts to the pleasure-seeking of someone half her age; even 'the queer little old French man' is drawn into the game, as is the reader. Everything she highlights at the fair are items that would particularly delight a child – 'a ribbon of confiserie fearful and wonderful'– the childish delight taken in the wrapping of an article as much as for the contents inside. The adjective 'fearful' is exactly right – for a child, so much excitement can seem almost overwhelming. The inclusion of the gingerbread frog – such an exotic and unforgettable species – foreshadows the nascent attention to detail that was to be the hallmark of all her greatest work. Towards the end of the passage she delineates a view of night time Paris from the top of a tram; again we perceive the echoes of stories not yet dreamed of – 'a lamp lighted table' transformed many years later into – 'I seen the little lamp' (p. 401), in 'The Doll's House'. Mansfield's ability to look on a scene, and, with a few deft strokes of her pen, tell us everything we need to know, is already present in this early letter. Paris, in this instance, is thus used as a catalyst, enabling her to develop her descriptive technique as well as storing up memories of sights and sounds that would return, to be used, in years to come.

At this time Mansfield was reading voraciously, especially in French. It appears that she alone was directing this reading, all the while making school-girl type entries in her notebooks with critical comments and quotations to refer back to:

> Mallarmé
> 'La chair est triste, hélas! Et j'ai lu tous les livres'. […]
> Mérimée has les idées très arrêtées. […]
> *Maupassant* – his abundant vitality. Great artists are those who can make men see their particular illusion. (That is true with limitations.)
> *Balzac*. He makes his characters so demean themselves that their slightest gesture shall be the expression of their souls. So there is more colour. It is a portrait, but the flesh covers the bones. He was trained under the severe eye of Flaubert
> (NB1, pp. 165–66, April 1909).

This process of reading and analysing foreshadows her literary reviews, an additional source of income in later years.[5]

The seeds of the relationship between Mansfield and France were being sown in these youthful years in Europe. With her base in London, she was now travelling through France, Belgium and Germany, armed with an eclectic library of books, loose purse strings provided by a wealthy father, and a desire to experience 'life'.[6] Some of the experiences during these itinerant years would return to haunt her in many different ways; the symptoms of the gonorrhoea she contracted around

---

5   Murry collected her many reviews and published them after her death in *Novels and Novelists*.

6   Claire Tomalin recounts one incident in Mansfield's early troubled youth where, in the autumn of 1908, aged 20, 'she told two friends at Beauchamp Lodge that she had been taken ashore from the Papanui at Montevideo and drugged, and now feared she might be pregnant' (Tomalin, p. 57).

1911 would slowly reduce her to a semi-invalid – the infection was not formally diagnosed by a doctor until 1920.[7] Biographers are in agreement that it was most probably at this time that she contracted the tuberculosis that was eventually to kill her.[8] Letters written by her during this period would cast a shadow, many years later, by way of blackmail; in 1920, she paid her entire £40 advance on *Bliss* to have them returned.[9]

France and Murry

In May 1912, having only commenced her relationship with Murry a few weeks before, the couple took off for Paris on a sort of 'honeymoon', being unable to marry until 1918, since Mansfield was already married to someone else.[10] On this particular occasion she was travelling not so much as a tourist but as a published author, having had her first collection of stories *In a German Pension* published in 1911; she was also now

---

7   See Tomalin, pp. 75–78, for a detailed discussion of Mansfield's infection with gonorrhoea. Tomalin concludes: 'From 1910 she was a chronic invalid; as such, her vulnerability to the tuberculosis bacillus must have been considerably increased. The picture of Katherine as a classic case of tuberculosis is true enough, but over it we have to superimpose another picture, that of the classic female victim of gonorrhoea' (pp. 77–78).

8   Antony Alpers suggests that the little 'East End' boy sent to Bavaria by Ida Baker, in order to help Mansfield come to terms with the loss of her still-born child, may have transmitted tuberculosis to her: 'Yet Katherine did not learn that she had tuberculosis until the end of 1917. Her only known recent contact was A. E. Randall; but little Charlie Walter, who went to Wörishofen, was almost certainly another, and a closer one' (Alpers, p. 127).

9   Vincent O'Sullivan notes how a former lover, Floryan Sobienowski, whom she had met in Wörishofen, 'had got in touch with Murry, [in 1920], asking £40 payment for the return of letters KM had written him ten years before [...] KM regarded him as a considerable nuisance, and wanted her letters back' (CL4, p.40, n.1).

10   Her first husband was George Bowden, whom she married on a whim, panic-stricken in her knowledge that she was pregnant by another man, on 2 March 1909, after two-three weeks acquaintance, leaving him on her wedding night.

joint magazine editor of *Rhythm* with Murry.[11] The pair thus found themselves with a certain literary cachet – Murry took his new partner to the
Latin Quarter and introduced her to his many literary acquaintances
there.[12] The Paris correspondent of *Rhythm* at that time was Francis
Carco, an impoverished young 'fantaisiste' poet and journalist whom
Murry had made friends with on a previous visit and hailed as another
Rimbaud.[13] He offered to give the pretty, young Antipodean French les-
sons. Years later, in 1918, Mansfield would write one of her most famous and cynical stories, loosely based on this meeting, titled 'Je ne
parle pas français'.[14]

In December 1912, the young couple were again in Paris, this time
with friends the Campbells and the Cannans. Beatrice Campbell subsequently remembered in her memoirs, a vibrant, bold and confident
Mansfield during this visit:

> I remember her gaiety, the way she would flounce into a restaurant and sweep her
> wide black hat from her bobbed head and hang it among the men's hats on the rack. I
> remember a group of men at a table running their tongues round their lips saying 'Oh
> la la' [sic] and her little muted laugh, delighted with herself [...] At night we went

11   *Rhythm* was first published in the summer of 1911, by Murry and his Oxford friend
      Michael Sadleir (who would eventually become Mansfield's publisher at Con-
      stable's), at the time still an undergraduate at Oxford. Murry claims that by the
      autumn of 1912, '*Rhythm* had become at last a *succès d'estime*. Gradually, most of
      the prominent writers of the younger generation had gathered round it: Gilbert
      Cannan, Hugh Walpole, Frank Swinnerton [...] Walter de la Mare, Rupert Brooke
      [...] and finally D. H. Lawrence'. John Middleton Murry, *Between Two Worlds,
      An Autobiography* (London: Jonathan Cape, 1935), p. 238.
12   In *Between Two Worlds*, Murry states, 'I think of those few days in Paris in the full
      spring of 1912 as of a brief interlude when we: "thought there was no more behind/
      But such a day to-morrow as to-day/ and to be child eternal." That was our honey-
      moon' (p. 216).
13   Francis Carco will be discussed in more detail in a later part of this chapter. Also
      listed as a 'foreign correspondent' for *Rhythm* was another 'fantaisiste' poet, Tris-
      tan Derème, who wrote several 'Lettres de France' for the journal, commenting on
      the Parisian literary and artistic scene at the time.
14   This story first appeared in 1919, in a privately printed edition from Murry's own
      'Heron Press'. It was subsequently edited and re-published in *Bliss*.

from café to café; there always seemed to be some terrific psychological drama going on, and we had to keep avoiding someone or other.[15]

This description, written by a close friend at the time, demonstrates the freedom of expression – both in appearance, emotions and situations – that Paris was able to effect on Mansfield.[16]

Exactly a year later, in December 1913, their finances in an unhealthy state, Mansfield and Murry decided on a permanent move to Paris, naïve in their belief they would be able to live more cheaply there, that Murry would be able to review French books for the *Times Literary Supplement* and write a novel. In fact it was Mansfield who settled easily into Parisian life and Murry who floundered, unable to find work, harassed by Carco and other French associates who believed he could find *them* work writing for English papers.[17] Initially she wrote to her sister:

> The weather is icy but Paris looks beautiful [...] I am going to enjoy life in Paris I know. It is so human and there is something noble in the city – Then the river is so much more a part of it than the Thames. It is a real city, old and fine and life plays in it for every one to see. Jack and I are dropping into speaking French together and leaving English alone until we have really mastered the other (CL1, p.133, 22 Dec 1913).

These remarks demonstrate how, even allowing for difficulties arising from a practical viewpoint, the charm of Paris was influencing her thoughts and hence her reactions. During this month she wrote the story 'Something Childish but Very Natural',[18] the first of her stories to be

---

15   Lady Beatrice Glenavy, *Today We Will Only Gossip* (London: Constable, 1964), p. 58.

16   Claire Tomalin also comments on another friend of Mansfield's description of a 'self-conscious and self-dramatizing Katherine who appeared at the Closerie des Lilas on different nights in clothes so different they seemed almost disguises, now a hat covered in cherries, another time a cloak and a white fez, or a turban, with bright, red-lipsticked mouth: a bold and confident Katherine; a Katherine who reminds one of her own heroine in 'The Swing of the Pendulum', telling herself, "I wasn't born for poverty – I only flower among really jolly people, and people who are never worried"' (Tomalin, pp. 113–14).

17   Murry made the following comment on Carco, using the initials R.D. – Raoul Duquette from Mansfield's story 'Je ne parle pas français': 'My French friend, R. D., eager to consolidate his own precarious position, introduced me everywhere as *le correspondent littéraire du Times*' (Murry, *Between Two Worlds*, pp. 272–73).

18   This story was only published after Mansfield's death, in *Something Childish*.

written in France. [See Appendix B for a complete list of all Mansfield's stories written in France.] It was much longer than any story she had written up to that point and was her first attempt at writing in 'episodes'. Her new situation had helped to turn her creative processes in a different direction and made her experimental both in scope and vision.

Within a few short weeks however, financial complications lead to a more cynical tone in Mansfield's personal writing:

> January. Paris.
>
> Tea, the chemist and marmalade –
> Far indeed today I've strayed,
> Through paths untrodden, shops unbeaten,
> And now the bloody stuff is eaten.
> The chemist, the marmalade and tea,
> Lord, how nice and cheap they be!
>
> Tips and fares and silly femmes
> Have skipped about my day like lambs,
> And great their happiness increased
> Since I am the one who has been fleeced!
> (NB1, p. 266, January 1914).[19]

This is the first reference in her notebooks to a more judgmental view of France and the French, the eulogising being replaced by a more critical, though humorous, response.

It was now becoming obvious that Murry could not make a living in Paris, bankruptcy proceedings were threatening in England; he returned briefly to London in an attempt to sort out his affairs but to no avail. With their hopes for a new life in Paris dashed, after only three months away, they were forced to return to England, having disposed of all their

---

19   Murry omitted from both editions of the *Journal*, the following third 'verse': 'Blast you for a mingy churl / You stop a baiting of a girl! / Just you try and pick my pocket / I'll put you into <Hell> & lock it!' (NB1, p. 266, January 1914). This is a classic example of Murry editing out passages from Mansfield's personal writing which he felt might not correlate with her burgeoning reputation. See Chapter Four for many more examples.

worldly goods for a pittance to brothel owners helpfully provided by Carco.[20] Murry himself commented on the episode:

> What remains to me of that strange interlude in Paris [...]? A glimpse [...] of a tall slim man in black with a sickly yellow face: that was Marcel Proust. A glimpse [...] through the windows of his little shop [...] of a man with a pince-nez set awry on his nose, tying up a parcel: that was Charles Péguy.[21]

However, the most important outcome of this stay in Paris was the relationship that developed between Mansfield and Francis Carco, which led to a further – and now famous – clandestine meeting between them a year later, and all of which culminated in the production of two of her most famous stories, 'An Indiscreet Journey' and 'Je ne parle pas français'.

Relationship with Carco

Francis Carco (1886–1958), who was born in Noumea in the South Pacific, always liked to claim his 'South Sea' connection with Mansfield. Together with his Corsican parents, he moved back to France at the age of ten. During the First World War he became Corporal Carco (holding the same rank as 'le petit caporal' in 'An Indiscreet Journey'). Bohemianism, as a life-style choice for Carco and a horde of similar writers, artists, performers and hangers-on, seems largely to have been a matter of surviving on boiled eggs and devising increasingly ingenious ways to shock the bourgeoisie.[22] But they also had serious ambitions to liberate and educate society at large, by rejecting the intellectual, emotional and

---

20   In a letter written on the day of their departure, Mansfield describes their predicament: 'Everything is packed of ours – the book packer is here now & we are waiting for the man to come and take away the furniture. Grimy and draughty and smelling of dust, tea leaves and senna leaves and match ends in the sink – cigarette ash on the floor – you never saw an uglier place – now, or more desolate [...] Jack in a moment of desperation yesterday sold even the bedding' (CL1 p. 138, 24 February 1914).

21   Murry, *Between Two Worlds*, p. 278.

22   See Chapter One for a general overview *of fin-de-siècle* Paris.

sexual strictures inherited from the previous generation. Carco's connections at that time included Picasso, Modigliani, Apollinaire, and significantly, Colette. He became one of the founders and guiding lights of the 'poètes fantaisistes', as well as an art critic, novelist, essayist, memoirist, biographer, cabaret performer, song writer and movie script writer. As a poet he was especially influenced by Verlaine, Baudelaire and Villon. He would become particularly famous for his novels depicting Montmartre and the Paris underworld; indeed it was Carco specifically, who helped to shape our popular image of Montmartre as a place of drug addicts and opium dens, homosexuality, pimps, prostitutes, brothels and criminals. His first sensational novel, *Jésus-la-Caille*,[23] was written almost entirely in Parisian street-slang; it is now considered an early master-text in Parisian homosexuality and a precursor of Genet.[24] Henri Clouard brings Mansfield herself into a discussion of Carco's fiction, writing in 1949, with the knowledge that that they had been close friends:

> Les romans qui le firent connaître, *Jésus la Caille* (1914) [...] peignent les gens du 'milieu', les mauvais garçons, les filles, la crapule. Romancier des bas-fonds de la capitale, il l'est, selon la remarque de Katherine Mansfield, avec 'une sorte d'humour tendre, aperçu du dedans comme si c'était tout simple, tout naturel'.[25]

Mansfield would have read some of Carco's early poetry, which had been published in *Rhythm*, and Murry would have described the 'Paris Correspondent' to his new lover. *Rhythm* had a strong French literary bias; both Tristan Derème and Carco were regular correspondents and contributors, as previously mentioned, though Claire Tomalin is critical of their contribution: 'Carco contributed *Lettres de Paris* alternately with another poet, Tristan Derème; The plan looked good, but the articles

---

23   Francis Carco, *Jésus-la-Caille* (Paris: Mercure de France, 1914).
24   As Melanie Hawthorne notes: 'The post-World War 1 period saw a relaxation of attitudes in France and a flourishing of gay male culture, especially in Paris [...] This tolerance resulted in part from the homosociality of wartime experiences, which had thrown men and women together (men in the trenches, women in the land army or auxiliary services), experiences that were not simply forgotten about after the war' (Hawthorne, pp. 218–19).
25   Henri Clouard, *Histoire de la littérature française du symbolisme à nos jours: de 1914–1940* (Paris: Albin Michel, 1949), p. 225.

provided were not, Carco and Derème both being better poets than journalists' (Tomalin, p. 99).

Hence, on their few days 'honeymoon' in Paris in May 1912, Murry was eager to introduce Mansfield to his friend, whom he himself had met a couple of years before when, as a young Oxford undergraduate, he had spent time in Paris. Mansfield and Carco instantly hit it off, and as Christiane Mortelier wryly observes: 'For an itinerant young woman in conscious pursuit of life in the raw, he was the perfect tourist guide'.[26] Carco noted Mansfield's apologetic 'je ne parle pas français' to him when they were introduced; the threesome spent many evenings in each other's company roaming the streets of Montmartre, as depicted by Carco in his autobiography of 1938, *Montmartre à vingt ans*: 'Nous avions beau sortir, le soir, en camarades, hanter les bal-musettes de la Montagne-Sainte-Geneviève ou les petits cafés-concerts de la place d'Italie et rentrer quelquefois à l'aube'.[27]

During their disastrous attempt at living in Paris, Carco was constantly on hand and the relationship intensified as a consequence. He recorded the following impression of Mansfield, 'La jeune femme, parmi ses malles, dans la grande pièce de la rue de Tournon, me souriait et me faisait jurer de m'installer à Londres, dès que tout irait bien' (Carco, *Montmartre*, p. 188). These memoirs were written in 1938, almost twenty five years after the events described and with an eye for upholding the myth that had become the personality of Mansfield.[28] In Murry's first novel, *Still Life*, published in 1916, but started during this trip to France, the character Dupont, who is Carco's fictional equivalent, tells the character named 'Morry' that he must never love a woman more than three or four days, but that during those three or four days he must: 'Never think of anything else, never leave her for a moment, and thus, knowing her to the last hiding-places of her mind, break with her once and for all, leaving no thread of the unknown or the unexplored to bind

26   Christiane Mortelier, 'The French Connection: Francis Carco', in Roger Robinson, ed., *Katherine Mansfield: In from the Margin* (Baton Rouge: Louisiana State University Press, 1994), pp. 137–57 (p. 146).

27   Francis Carco, *Montmartre à vingt ans* (Paris: Albin Michel, 1938), p. 183.

28   In 1949, Henri Clouard noted the following: 'Carco a l'expérience d'un tragique assez superficiel, mais immédiat et pressant, intensément réel, envers lequel il montre cette gravité attentive [...] même quand il y guidait la muette curiosité de Katherine Mansfield' (Clouard, p. 224).

you to her'.[29] From what we know of Carco historically, this cynical advice would have fallen easily from his own lips and therefore tallies with how Mansfield was eventually to present him in her own fiction, though we have almost nothing on record to denote her attitude towards Carco at this time, as she prepared to leave Paris with Murry in February 1914. In a letter to a friend, she merely noted: 'I have given Carco a few souvenirs – the egg timer which *charmed* him and some odd little pieces like that' (CL1, p. 138, 24 February 1914).[30]

On returning to England, Mansfield began to find herself more and more disillusioned with her life and more specifically with her relationship with Murry, which began to go sour as he disappeared into his work and his own circle of male friends, leaving her feeling isolated and alone. In this disaffected state, when a letter arrived from Carco addressed to Murry, Mansfield, receptive and emotionally in need, wrote in her journal:

> A letter from Francis Carco. I had not expected it and yet when it came it seemed quite inevitable – the writing – the way the letters were made, his confidence and his warm sensational life. I wish he were my friend – he's very near me. His personality comes right through his letters to Jack – and I want to laugh and run right into the road (J2, p. 62, 16 November 1914).

According to Carco's memoirs, her feelings were more than reciprocated. We know now how his 'souvenirs' of Mansfield were very much developed to fit an image, an icon, in whose life he had fortuitously found himself playing a minor – if significant – role:

> Cette séparation, si gaiement acceptée, devait exercer sur moi l'influence la plus imprévue […] J'ignorais tout de l'amitié qu'un homme peut éprouver à l'égard d'une femme, et ce sentiment si complexe, auquel, sans que je m'en fusse douté, Katherine Mansfield m'avait initié, se développa brusquement de telle sorte que d'abord je ne compris rien à ce qui m'arrivait. Je n'osai m'en ouvrir à personne (Carco, *Montmartre*, p. 189).

29   John Middleton Murry, *Still Life* (London: Constable, 1916), p.10.
30   Murry's relationship with Carco pre-dates this trip, as already mentioned. In *Between Two Worlds*, he describes how, 'I had been taken by him [Carco] before to desolate brothel-bars in forlorn suburbs, with that queer tired atmosphere of dingily commercial vice, which he was himself to render so impressively in his novels, and which sorted so well with his own queer faded ivory face' (pp. 276–77).

In Chapter Five, I discuss in detail Carco's duplicity concerning the 'recollections' of his relationship with Mansfield, which would play a significant part in the entrenchment and solidification of the hagiography of her personality in France.

Her journal entries now show a marked disaffection for Murry as her interest in Carco grows, the tone ever more urgent:

> F. may be leaving Besançon soon for the front, he told me, and he said 'Je vous aime chaque jour d'avantage'; and he told me that all the while we had been in Paris he had loved me. Well, he thinks so, now. And that he would like to love in a little hut on the edge of the world where no one would ever come, and that at times now he has merely an awful sensation of emptiness. He would like to lie in the road and let the world pass over him 'et quand je m'endors, je vous prends dans mes bras – et j'éprouve une tristesse affreuse' – and – ever so much more. The day after this letter he sent me another, very short – 'Chère Katherine, je ne veux que vous. Vous êtes et vous serez toute ma vie' (J2, p. 62, December 1914).

The journal continues in this vein for several entries, spread over a number of weeks.

At the beginning of 1915, Mansfield's younger brother Leslie Beauchamp, over in England for a visit, met with his sister in London. With money she obtained from him Mansfield was at last able to visit Carco, now stationed in the war zone, working as a military postman in Gray (Haute-Saône), in north-east France. Arriving in Paris, her courage failing her for the difficult journey ahead, she wrote a letter to Carco:

> Je suis venue ici à cause de vous. Je me suis promenée jusqu'à la nuit. Voici les étoiles déjà et le petit vent qui vient toujours avec elles. Dans la salle prochaine, on joue du billard. J'entends le clic! clac! des balles. La femme qui vend les cigarettes ici porte un chapeau. Pourquoi? Chéri, j'ai commencé à pleurer et pleurer … Dans l'après-midi j'ai trouvé un petit banc dans un jardin et je restais là, disant: Courage […] Courage! Mais tout était inutile (CL1, p. 149, mid-February 1915).[31]

Even in her simple French, Mansfield's distinct prose style is evident: in the 'clic! clac!' of the balls and descriptions of seemingly insignificant details, such as the cigarette girl wearing a hat and the breeze that she claims always accompanies a starry night.

---

31   In *Montmartre à vingt ans*, Carco quotes from other letters written by Mansfield in French to him – see p. 187 in particular.

Nevertheless, her courage did not fail her and on 19 February 1915, Mansfield undertook a difficult journey to the battlefront (forbidden to women), hoodwinking the French Army Officials by falling back on the old tale of a sick relative. The pair – each emotionally ravenous, though for different reasons – fell upon one another, Carco having taken a room in a village house. She describes their encounter quite dispassionately in her journal:

> It was like an elopement [...] Laughing and trembling we pressed against each other a long, long kiss [...] the whole affair seemed somehow so ridiculous and at the same time so utterly natural [...] In the most natural manner we slowly undressed by the stove. F swung into the bed. 'Is it cold?' I said. 'No, not at all cold. Viens, ma bébé, don't be frightened. The waves are quite small.' His laughing face and his pretty hair, one hand with a bangle over the sheets, he looked like a girl [...] The sword, the big ugly sword, but not between us, lying in a chair.
>
> The act of love seemed somehow quite incidental, we talked so much. It was so warm and delicious, lying curled in each other's arms, by the light of the tiny lamp [...] only the clock and the fire to be heard. A whole life passed in the night: other people, other things, but we lay like two old people coughing faintly under the eiderdown, and laughing at each other (NB2, pp. 11–12).

After four nights with her new lover, she suddenly returned to London and Murry on 25 February, disillusioned, but with plenty of copy. (Carco appeared to be following his own rules to the letter regarding the way to treat women, as set down by him for Murry.) Though Mansfield may have been disillusioned with Carco as a lover, nevertheless she clung onto the relationship for a few more months – long enough to make use of his apartment in Paris, on the Quai aux Fleurs, overlooking the Seine and the Ile de la Cité.

The story 'An Indiscreet Journey',[32] which Mansfield wrote in Paris in May 1915 (whilst borrowing Carco's apartment), is an account of her visit to Gray. Its importance lies in the fact that it is one of the earliest fictional accounts of World War One written in English, and what is more, written by a woman, with first hand experience of the scenes she was describing. Though lightly handled on the surface, as with so much of Mansfield's work, this 'simple' story is made the vehicle for a rich

---

32   The story was never published in Mansfield's lifetime, appearing in the posthumous collection *Something Childish*, in 1924.

freight of ideas and impressions. She summons up the peculiar atmosphere of village life caught up in the middle of war and by so doing, her story eventually ends up speaking for an entire generation, shocked and intimidated by a war that was still in its infancy at the time she is writing.

Here we find, in fiction, and possibly for the first time, a description of the after effects of gas poisoning on a soldier and added to the story of her escapade.[33] It is most probable that she witnessed the effect of this gassing (chlorine gas having only been introduced by the Germans for the first time on 22 April 1915 at Ypres), whilst residing in Paris in May of that year at Carco's flat – for it was to Paris that the dying and injured from the trenches were brought in their thousands – and thus that she was able to incorporate what she saw directly into a story which perhaps might be more correctly termed 'literary journalism'.

The fake letter from a relative, used by the unnamed female protagonist to enable her to reach her lover at the front, was based on the original sent by Carco to Mansfield for the exact same purpose. An analysis of this story serves to highlight how any critical interpretation of her written response provides many clues to her internal, hidden response. The connection has now been made, with France as an agent at work in her thoughts and, as we can see, now firmly transferred to the written page.

At this point in her life, as Jeffrey Meyers observes,[34] she was both disillusioned by the selfishness of Carco and wounded by the indifference of Murry:

> I don't miss Jack at all now. I don't want to go home. I feel quite content to live here in a furnished room & watch […] Life with other people becomes a blur; it does with Jack, but its enormously valuable & marvellous when I'm alone – the detail of life – the life of life. Carco feels that too – but nobody else. Perhaps in a negative way, Lesley does. Yes, she does (NB2, pp. 56–57).

---

33 Alpers states that, 'her horrific portrayal of a gassed French soldier in a café […] must have been based on something seen very recently, in Paris' (CS Alpers, p. 554).
34 See Meyers, p. 85.

In the *Definitive Journal*, the last three sentences of the above quotation were edited out, diminishing the importance Mansfield accorded Carco in her life at this time. The trip to Gray having somehow not come up to her expectations, she had returned to Murry, only to leave him *again* a few days later to return to Paris and Carco's flat. Two weeks later she is back in England, a month later she is back at Carco's flat again. And all the while she is writing cheery, loving letters to Murry and breezy, vaguely flirtatious ones to Carco (having told Murry she was no longer in contact with him), perhaps, cynically, because she wanted the use of his flat, perhaps because she still held a candle for their relationship. On 8 May she sent Carco this from his own flat:

> L'homme qui éclaire les lampes est venu avec sa petite étoile au bout d'une grande canne. Quand je vois ça, mon cœur tremble toujours, pour tous les soirs, dans toutes les grandes cités. [...] Deux jeunes gens sont arrêtés sur le quai et, malgré le froid , en face du vent, un long oh! un très long baiser... Et puis, ils sont disparu ...oui...aussi vite que possible, comme si la maison brule chez eux [sic] (CL1, p. 182, 8 May 1915).

Yet on the very next day she writes to Murry:

> I went out on the landing just now to get some water. The concierge was sweeping the stairs and the woman below me came out to talk to her. 'The little lady upstairs came in very late last night,' said she. 'Who.' 'La maîtresse de Francis Carco,' bawled the voice [...] I am still trembling with fury (CL1, p. 183, 9–10 May 1915).

To add to an already duplicitous picture, Carco too was writing back, perhaps hoping for another visit from his new lover, since I have discovered the following unpublished letter from him, sent under a pseudonym, with an invitation to stay, which would certainly have facilitated another journey to the front:

> Ma chère amie
>
> Je vous remercie bien vivement de votre dernière lettre. Vous voilà donc à Paris j'en suis fort heureuse. Cela me permettra ainsi d'aller vous voir après la guerre comme nous nous le sommes promis et de passer avec vous d'excellentes journées. Mais en attendant mon voyage, je vous rappelle que maman met ici une chambre à votre disposition pour le temps que vous voudrez. Je sais bien que chez Gray n'est pas très intéressant, surtout en temps de guerre. Mais il fait beau et peut-être ne serez vous [sic] pas fâchée de trouver ici plus de tranquillité qu'à Paris où les zeppelins font des

peurs. Venez donc nous voir. Maman en serait enchantée [...] En ce cas obtenez un laisser passer valable pour un certain temps. Je ne pense pas qu'on fasse au consulat des difficultés pour l'obtenir [...].

Marguerite Bompard [35]

There would appear to be all sorts of promises and expectations hidden in this letter and in the game of cat and mouse which is being played. It is certainly unclear as to who exactly was playing the predatory role in the relationship. Mansfield did not go back to her French soldier, but nevertheless made full use of the flat on offer. According to Tomalin however, Carco had given her more than just 'copy' for her stories:

> According to Karen Usborne's study of 'Elizabeth', her companion A.S. Frere heard Murry telling her that Katherine had contracted syphilis after her visit to Carco at the front in 1915, when she is alleged to have had her hair cropped like a soldier's and visited the trenches in uniform. Apart from the fact that she did come back with her hair cropped very short, this seems an unreliable bit of reporting by someone known to be hostile to Katherine, as Frere was; but it may be a garbled version of Katherine's gonorrhoea, which very possibly flared up again as a result of the Carco episode. It does suggest that Murry spoke of his wife in less exalted terms during her lifetime than later (Tomalin, p. 226n).

As Tomalin intimates above, Murry glossed over Mansfield's misdemeanours after her death in order to 'sanctify' her personality, but he was not above criticising her whilst she was alive.

The ramifications of the Mansfield/Carco relationship are to be felt in the annals of French as well as English literature, for in Carco's novel of 1916 entitled *Les Innocents*, he portrays Mansfield unsympathetically as Winnie Campbell:

> Winnie s'assit devant son bureau. Elle alluma une cigarette et elle jouait d'un coupe-papier avec son épais bloc-notes dont les pages étaient couvertes d'une écriture nette et détachée.
> 'Ce n'est rien, voler', dit-elle en se décidant enfin à rompre le silence. 'J'ai volé autrefois, et vous aussi, vous savez ouvrir, doucement, une porte et prendre l'argent'.
> 'Oui', fit-il à voix basse.

---

35   This unpublished letter, handwritten by Carco, dated 26 March 1915, is held in the archives at the Alexander Turnbull Library, Wellington [MS – Papers – 4003 – 05].

'Il y a beaucoup plus difficile. Il y a, par exemple, tuer pour voler... et puis, tuer pour tuer'.[36]

Many years later, backtracking on his original characterisation, Carco says of this portrayal:

> Pourtant, c'est à Katherine Mansfield que je dois d'avoir écrit mon meilleur livre, car elle m'en a, en partie, procuré les éléments. Si c'est elle qu'à maints détails on reconnaît dans la Winnie des *Innocents*, elle n'a posé du personnage que ce qu'il présente de pur, d'intact (Carco, *Montmartre*, p. 196).

There is, however, very little 'de pur, d'intact' about the character of Winnie, who comes across as predatory and exploitative.[37] Carco could not alter his novel, but he certainly could and did change his attitude towards Mansfield and in particular his written portrayal of her. With the passage of time, Mansfield's reputation in its ascendancy, and not wishing to rock any critical boats, his biographical portrait of Mansfield was considerably softened and romanticised in order to accommodate the sentimental French legend which had developed after her death. It is important to stress, however, that whilst she was alive, this not-too flattering portrait of herself as Winnie, which she undoubtedly read, had already entered the domain of French literature via Carco's novel, published seven years before her death.

In 'An Indiscreet Journey', the personality of Carco is drawn with a very light pen; but in the story 'Je ne parle pas français', the character of Duquette is much more easily recognisable as having been drawn from Mansfield's memories of him. Mansfield went so far as to mention his name in connection with the story, in a letter she wrote to Murry: 'The subject I mean lui qui parle is of course taken from – Carco & Gertler & god knows who. It has been more or less in my mind ever since I first felt strongly about the French' (CL2, p. 56, 3 and 4 February 1918). Carco is depicted as a writer, a gigolo and possibly bisexual. This may well have been a measured and deliberate response by Mansfield to Carco's portrayal of Winnie (Mansfield) as bisexual in *Les Innocents*. She also satirises Carco's literary endeavours at this time through the

---

36 Carco, *Les Innocents* (Paris: Albin Michel, 1916). p. 96.
37 Alpers, for example, describes the character of Winnie as, 'a predatory huntress out for "copy"' (Alpers, p. 173).

titles she invents for Duquette's novels: 'False Coins' (71), 'Wrong Doors' (75), and 'Left Umbrellas' (75). Carco comments on the story in his autobiography:

> Je me reconnais avec elle et son futur mari, John Middleton-Murry [...] Pour moi, c'est un peu comme un conte que j'aurais pu écrire et que je n'écrirai jamais. Les trois portraits y ont un air étrange, si frappant qu'il semble presque halluciné. Dans cette nouvelle, *Souris* est Katherine Mansfield (Carco, *Montmartre*, pp. 177–78).

Mansfield termed this story her 'cry against corruption',[38] and it serves as a powerful reminder of how France and the Gallic lens were influencing her language, viewpoint and creative endeavours.

The story concerns a Frenchman, Raoul Duquette, an Englishman, Dick Harman and his naïve English woman friend Mouse, abandoned by Dick in Paris and then by Duquette who does not want to be burdened with her.[39] For Alpers:

> There were three main impulses behind its writing. One was the irrational loathing that she had developed for the French since coming away this time; another was her profound despair about the war and what it was doing to everything she loved ('it's never out of my mind, and everything is poisoned by it'); but the strongest impulse she acknowledged was her love for Jack (Alpers, p. 270).

Mansfield wrote to Murry about this story, remarking on the development of her art: 'I don't want to exaggerate the importance of this story or to harp on it; but it's a tribute to Love you understand and the very best I can do just now' (CL2, p 66, 10 and 11 February 1918). Her experiences with Carco were certainly uppermost in her mind when she began the story, but also her love of France as a country did not necessarily always endear her to the French people. In the middle of writing this story, she scribbled a note, part way through the manuscript:

---

38 'Not a protest – *a cry*, and I mean corruption in the widest sense of the word, of course' (CL2, p. 54, 3 February 1918).

39 Mansfield resurrects Carco in Duquette's description of himself in the first part of 'Je ne parle pas français': 'I confess without my clothes I am rather charming. Plump, almost like a girl, with smooth shoulders, and I wear a thin gold bracelet above my left elbow' (68). Mansfield had originally written in her journal after her liaison with Carco, 'With his laughing face, his pretty hair, one hand with a bangle over the sheets, he looked like a girl' (J2, p. 78, February 1920).

> But Lord! Lord! how I do hate the French. With them it is always rutting time. See them come dancing and sniffing round a woman's skirt.
>
> Mademoiselle complains that she has the *pieds glacés.*
>
> 'Then why do you wear such pretty stockings and shoes, Mademoiselle?' leers Monsieur.
>
> 'Eh – oh la – c'est la mode!' [sic]
>
> And the fool grins well content with the idiot answer.
>
> Note: A muff like a hard nut. (Mouse in *Je ne parle pas.*)
>
> (J2, p.128, February 1918).

This personal interjection suggests strongly for Alpers that, 'On the subject of love [...] the author and the French (perhaps including Maupassant, whose stories Mansfield did not admire), don't speak the same language at all' (CS Alpers, p. 561).

During her two stays in Paris at Carco's flat during the spring of 1915, two other stories were completed and one commenced. On the first trip in March, and less than a month after her trip to Gray, she wrote 'The Little Governess', a story which explores the fears and vulnerability of a young woman travelling alone (a recurring theme in Mansfield's writing, discussed in greater detail in the next chapter), who inadvertently becomes the prey of a lecherous old man. The simplicity of the narrative belies a clever and beautifully executed story, fairy-tale-like in its themes of innocence and wickedness, using the settings of foreign trains and hotels, territory well known to her, together with all the difficulties of her recent trip to the battlefront so fresh in her mind.

Her letters home on this visit were full of the colour, sounds and smells of Paris, with an eye for a certain sort of detail that others would not think to mention and which would always characterise her best work:

> Having a besoin to faire mon service I went into one of those little 10c places. In the passage stood an immense fat and rosy old market woman, her skirts breast high, tucking her chemise into her flannel drawers and talking to an equally fat old ouvrier – who began to help her arrange her affairs, saying as he tugged and buttoned 'mais tu sais, ma petite tu ne peux pas sortir comme ça' (CL1, p. 171, 28 March 1915).

There were to be two more meetings between Carco and Mansfield, both brief in nature and painful in different ways for her. The first involved a certain amount of humiliation, for having been caught in the bombardment of Paris in the spring of 1918, ill, and with finances desperately low her friend Ida Baker (LM), relates how: 'Katherine summoned up her courage to go out and see someone she would have given anything *not* to see – or was it feared to see? I suspected it was Carco, but I did not dare to ask her. She came back with enough money for our tickets home'.[40] On the second and last occasion before her death, Carco himself recounts a brief meeting with Mansfield and Murry in Paris in 1922, where, sick and with only a few months to live, she had gone for irradiation treatment as a possible cure for her tuberculosis:

> C'était un soir, à l'Univers, près du Théâtre-Français. Elle se trouvait assise à gauche, dans la première salle du café, en compagnie de John Middleton-Murry. J'allai la saluer, puis je m'assis à sa table. Il y avait huit ans que nous ne nous étions vus. Ses beaux yeux sombres brillaient de la même ardeur, de la même fièvre. Une sorte de magnétisme s'en dégageait, mais elle avait mauvaise mine et ses pauvres petites mains si pâles, si amaigries, m'emplirent d'une peine affreuse. Je m'efforçais en vain de me raisonner. Elle cacha ses mains sous la table et, tandis qu'avec son mari j'essayais de parler d'autre chose, je ne pouvais détacher mon regard de cette table. Au bout d'un court moment, ne sachant plus que dire, je pris congé. Ce fut notre dernière rencontre (Carco, *Montmartre*, pp. 204–05).

No mention is made in this account of the furtive meeting described by Ida Baker in 1918, but, in view of all that had passed between the pair, the meeting may well have taken place and remained a secret. Meyers sums up Mansfield's relationship with Carco as follows:

> Though Carco was ugly and had a sinister character, Katherine was nevertheless attracted to his confidence, vitality and sensuality: 'he is so rich and so careless – that I love.' Frieda Lawrence felt Katherine was attracted to peculiar men and had odd attachments; Anne Rice thought Carco was repulsive and could never understand why Katherine wanted to sleep with him. But Carco reminded her of Gaudier, Gertler and Lawrence, and provided a powerful contrast to the handsome but priggish Murry. [. . .] She wanted to have an adventure, find sexual satisfaction, achieve artistic inspiration, assert her independence [and] provoke Murry (Meyers, pp. 112–13).

All of the above serves to demonstrate the importance of Carco in the life and art of Mansfield, especially when considering her relationship with France and the French. Carco was there at the beginning of this re-

40   Ida Baker, pseud. 'Lesley Moore', *Katherine Mansfield: The Memories of LM* (London: Michael Joseph, 1971), p. 110.

lationship, as well as the end. He is the sole French voice writing 'authentic' descriptions of Mansfield. He is also the only French author using Mansfield as a personality in his literary output, both during her lifetime and after her death.

Descriptions of France

Mansfield's most poignant personal association with France concerned the death of her younger brother Leslie, at Ploegsteert Wood, near Armentières, on the Franco-Belgian border, blown to pieces by his own hand grenade during a military training exercise on 7 October 1915. Haunted by his death for years to come, she would later write to Ottoline Morrell in November 1918: 'I keep seeing all these horrors, bathing in them again and again (God knows I don't want to) and then my mind fills with the wretched little picture I have of my brother's grave. What is the meaning of it all?' (CL2, p. 290, 17 November 1918). This bereavement now rekindled myriad memories of her childhood turning her focus once more towards her homeland, New Zealand, in search of creative inspiration. In mid-November 1915, unable to cope with the memories of living in a house in London where her brother had been such a recent visitor, Mansfield set off for France once more, this time heading for the Mediterranean and accompanied by Murry. After a brief stop over in Marseilles, she wrote to a friend, 'All my observation is so *detailed* as it always is when I get to France' (CL1, p. 199–200, 19 November 1915). Now, for the first time since leaving New Zealand, Mansfield was able to enjoy prolonged proximity to the sea, which, as well as helping her through the grief she was experiencing, must have aided her memories of her homeland, which now came flooding back. She wrote again: 'For one thing, and it's awfully important, the sea is here – very clear and very blue. The sound of it after such a long silence is almost unbearable – a sweet agony, you know – – – like moonlight is sometimes' (CL1, p.

200, 28 November 1915). As Jacqueline Bardolph states, 'the power of the elements connected her directly with her New Zealand self'.[41]

Murry left for England on 7 December, leaving Mansfield at the Hotel Beau Rivage in Bandol. Her letters to him at this time are vivacious and colourful, more so than the ones from Paris the previous spring, even allowing for the fact that she was not well and confined to bed some of the time; nothing could penetrate and cloud this mood of joy. She says of her maid:

> Not counting the number of times she put her fat face round the door & said, nodding & smiling as only a Frenchwoman can, with an air of delighted gaiety (!) 'Vous souffrez toujours.' You see little Wig giving her smile for smile & nod for nod & saying 'Ah, oui, un peu' (CL1, p. 211, 13 December 1915).

Her infamous love/hate relationship with France had its origins on this trip, where, initially, all seemed perfect: 'When I woke this morning & opened the shutters & saw the dimpling sea I knew I was beginning to love this place – this South of France' (CL1, p. 220, 19 December 1915).

Murry returned on 31 December to a house Mansfield had found for them, the Villa Pauline, forever associated with one of the happiest and most creative periods of her life. As she was to write two years later:

> I've two 'kick offs' in the writing game. One is joy – real joy – the thing that made me write when we lived at Pauline, and that sort of writing I could only do in just that state of being in some perfectly blissful way at peace. Then something delicate and lovely seems to open before my eyes, like a flower without thought of a frost or a cold breath – knowing that all about it is warm and tender and 'steady'. And that I try, ever so humbly to express. (CL2, p. 54, 3 February 1918).

Her happiness and contentment during this stay in France was reiterated many years after her death by Murry, for as he said, in Bandol, 'she had been happier than she had ever been before or was ever to be again'.[42] Here it was that she now picked up the unfinished manuscript of 'The Aloe', started in Paris in Carco's flat, transforming it into her most celebrated story, 'Prelude'.

41   Jacqueline Bardolph, 'The French Connection: Bandol,' in Robinson, pp. 158–72 (p. 161).
42   John Middleton Murry, *Katherine Mansfield and Other Literary Portraits* (London: Peter Nevill, 1949), p. 21.

Although, as stated above, this visit to France was a particularly happy one, nevertheless the witty, acerbic Mansfield was still sharp enough to mock the place she had come to love, in a marvellously tongue-in-cheek letter to her close friend, Frederick Goodyear (killed in action in France a year after this letter was written):

I feel sentimental about England now – English food, decent English waste! How much better than these thrifty French whose flower gardens are nothing but potential salad bowls. There's not a leaf in France that you can't 'faire une infusion avec', not a blade that isn't bon pour la cuisine. By god, I'd like to buy a pound of the best butter, put it on the window sill and watch it melt to spite em. They are a stingy uncomfortable crew for all their lively scrapings […] For instance, in their houses – what appalling furniture – and never one comfortable chair. If you want to talk the only possible thing to do is go to bed. It's a case of either standing on your feet or lying in comfort under a puffed up eiderdown. I quite understand the reason for what is called French moral laxity – you're simply forced into bed – no matter with whom – there's no other place for you […] Supposing a young man comes to see about the electric light & will go on talking and pointing to the ceiling, or a friend drops in to tea and asks you if you believe in Absolute Evil. How can you give your mind to these things when you're sitting on four knobs and a square inch of cane. How much better to lie snug and give yourself up to it (CL1, p. 249, 4 March 1916).

Mansfield's acerbic wit and sharp observational skills come to the fore in this irreverent take on French life.

This idyllic visit came to an end on 7 April 1916, when reluctantly, with mounting pressure and a grim sense of foreboding, the couple were persuaded to attempt a form of communal living with their friends D.H. Lawrence and his wife Frieda, in Cornwall. Yet the effect of her prolonged contact with France continued to reverberate through her thoughts and her writing, even though she was now back in England, sometimes to great comic effect:

And the French – what espèce de Niblickisme will they make of it? Shall we read in the French papers next week of someone qui a manqué de Niblick. Or that 'Au milieu de ces événements si graves ce qu'il nous faut c'est du courage, de l'éspoir et du niblick le plus ferme – – ' I wondered, taking off the rhubarb (NB2, p. 94, April 1917).

In a piece written for *The New Age* in 1917, she even mocked her own habit of reverting into French for no apparent reason: 'The creature in the glass gives a short laugh and says: "C'est pour rire, ça". But you reply severely: "Don't speak French if you're English; it's a vulgar habit"'.[43] She continued to read in French and to discuss what she was reading:

> I have been reading this past week the poems of Mistral and of his young friend Aubanel. I wonder if you have read a book called La Miougrano – the Pomegranates by Aubanel [...] Toutes les branches sont en fleurs; tout chante, tout rit, car la vie est si charmante! – – – these men write with such lovely ease. But oh they make one feel what madness it is to live out of the sun (CL1, p. 306, 24 April 1917).

Also at this time, *The New Age* published a translation by Mansfield of Alphonse Daudet's 'La Chèvre de M. Seguin', taken from the *Lettres de mon moulin* of 1868. Mansfield refers to this story in her correspondence, viewing it almost as an allegory of her own life.[44]

Illness and France

The memory of her idyllic time in Bandol was still fresh in Mansfield's mind when, in December 1917, having caught a chill, she fell ill with pleurisy; discovering a 'spot' on her right lung, her doctor advised she seek a warmer climate. On 7 January 1918 therefore, she set off for Bandol once more, 'femme seule', since Murry was working for the War Office and could not get leave.[45]

Conditions were now very different from two years before. France was exhausted by three years of war that had severely weakened the country's infrastructure. The journey to the south of France proved frightening and difficult; as Murry wrote, 'She arrived at Bandol much

---

43 *New Age*, 19 April 1917, p. 595.
44 Katherine Mansfield, 'M. Séguin's Goat', in *New Age*, September 6, 1917, pp. 411–12. In a letter to Murry she parodies the story, relating it to her consumptive symptoms – the spitting of blood: 'I'm still better, so that old ugly one has gone back to his lair after a final growl' (CL2, p. 91, 24 February 1918). In Daudet's story, the little goat, 'lay down on the ground in her lovely white fur, all spotted with blood . . . And the wolf jumped on to the little goat and ate her up' (trans. Mansfield).
45 In 1920, Murry was awarded an OBE for his war work as Chief Censor.

more ill than she ever had been before' (Murry, *Literary Portraits*, p. 21). Nevertheless, for a short time, the country worked its inevitable charm, Mansfield was not yet bitter at being left alone again by Murry and there was plenty of 'copy' for her correspondents to enjoy:

> I am unreasonably deeply happy. I thought I would be disenchanted with France this time, but for the first time I seem to recognise my love for it and to understand why. It is because, whatever happens, I never feel indifferent. I feel that indifference is really foreign to my nature and that to live in a state of it is to live in the only Hell I really appreciate. There is too, dispassionately speaking, a wonderful spirit here – so much humour, life, gaiety, sorrow, one cannot see it all & not think with amazement of the strange cement like state of England. Yes, they do feel the war, but with a difference (CL2 p. 5, 9 January 1918).

This letter was written to Murry from Paris, on her way to Bandol; there is an exhilarated responsiveness to the excitement as well as the exasperations of foreign travel. Six days later, finally installed in a much altered Hotel Beau Rivage, she was writing in a different vein to her friend J.D. Fergusson, again with the customary humour in the face of adversity that her friends had come to expect of her:

> Take the word of a 'sincere well wisher' and never attempt this journey during the War. [...] There were no pillows for hire. We were hours late [...] The French do not suffer as we do on these occasions. For one thing I think they obtain great relief by the continual expression of their feelings, by moaning, groaning, lashing themselves into their rugs, quietening their stomachs with various fluids out of bottles, and charming the long hours away with recitations of various internal diseases from which they and their friends have suffered (CL2, p.13, 15 January 1918).

She was able to make a joke of her suffering, but the journey had left her weak and incapacitated. Within three weeks of arriving, she was writing of her hatred of the French and at the same time had begun writing 'Je ne parle pas français'. The attractions of being in the south of France were now not enough to prevent depression taking hold. Mansfield herself wrote, 'I have a horror of the way this war creeps into my writings' (CL2, p. 70, 12 February 1918). She felt ill, alone, isolated and, because of the war, was now unable to return to England. Her ill temper was vented on everything around her, including most of the population of Bandol:

I simply loathe and abominate the French bourgeoisie. Let me put it on record again. There are around a dozen of them descended on this hotel and all, after a day or two, in each other's pockets, arms round each other, sniggering, confiding internal complaints & 'elle m'a dit' et 'mon mari m'a dit' and the gentlemen with their 'passez – mesdames' – god how I detest them (CL2, p. 52, 1 February 1918).

And yet, a few days later she was writing to Murry, 'This place does seem to launch me – I am simply packed with ideas and ways of writing which are important ones as I see it' (CL2, p. 61, 7 February 1918). Her dissatisfaction even extends to the French language itself:

But I do find the French language, style, attack, point of view, hard to stomach at present. It's all tainted. It all seems to me to lead to dishonesty – Dishonesty Made Easy – made superbly easy! All these half words – these words which have never really been born – and seen the light – like 'me trouble' – 'tiède' – 'blottant', 'inexprimable' (these are bad examples but you know the kinds I mean & the phrases and whole paragraphs that go with them) – They won't – at the last moment – do at all. Some of them are charming – and one is loathe to do without them – but they are like certain plants – once they are in your garden they spread & spread & spread – and make a show, perhaps, but they are weeds. No, I get up hungry from the French language. I have too great an appetite for the real thing to be put off with pretty little kickshaws – and I am offended intellectually that 'les gens' think they can so take me in. It's the result of Shakespeare – I think. The English language is damned difficult but it's also damned rich and so clear and bright that you can search out the darkest places with it (CL2, p. 96, 27 February 1918).

Arriving finally in Paris, Mansfield found that she was unable to travel any further – the bombardment of Paris by the Germans with their huge new long range gun had begun and there were strict regulations regarding foreigners crossing the channel. Even finding a hotel proved a difficult and demoralising business. Mansfield had never witnessed anything like it – the true horrors of the war were all around her:

And then, this battle and this bombardment of Paris. I don't know what the English papers say about it. [....] The spring this year seems to me hateful – cruel – cruel – like pigeons are cruel – all the leaves burst into claws. But perhaps it's just me […] I feel that corruption and destruction are in the air & we may just survive. The world is hideous (CL2, p. 138, 24 March 1918).

Money was fast running out, necessitating the clandestine visit to Carco; at times the bombardment was taking place every eighteen minutes, making any semblance of normal life impossible. Mansfield vented her fear and anger on the French, 'If you knew how I hate Life at this moment and all these Parisian dogs and their b—ches. What a set! How vile they are' (CL2, p. 141, 26 March 1918). The inhuman actions associated with wartime, including a scene she witnessed where workmen were parading in clothes found in the debris of a bombed house, left her shocked.[46] Finally, on 11 April 1918, the two women were able to cross the channel.

Gradually, however, the horrors of wartime France faded in her memory to be replaced with nostalgia for the country and its people, so that in October of the same year, back in England, she was able to write: 'Oh, I have such a longing for France. Can you hear that street cry – Marchand d'habits – It sounds like "Chandabi" and is said or sung with a sort of jump in the middle' (CL2, p. 281, 15 October 1918). Confined to bed now, her memory playing tricks on her, the French way of doing things seemed infinitely preferable:

> A little clock outside strikes three in a way that raises your eyebrows – 'My dear child – I am perfectly prepared to believe you; there is no earthly need to insist on it'. I hate that clock – Now in France, a little clock like that would strike as though it were all astonishment & amusement at finding itself at three or four or five but – however it's no matter (CL2, p. 286, 1 November 1918).

This see-sawing of emotions began to form a pattern that would be visible in her personal writing for the rest of her life:

> I wish we were all in France with a real Xmas party in prospect – snow, huge fire, a feast, wine, old, old French tunes on a guitar, fancy dresses, a Tree, and everybody too happy for words. Instead we are wondering whether to give the postman 5 shillings, or, since we have only been here since August will 3 be enough? Etc.

---

46 She wrote: 'I crept back to bed and to sleep and woke to a perfect deafening roar of gunfire. […] Two workmen arrived to clear away the debris. One found, under the dust, a woman's silk petticoat. He put it on & danced a step or two for the laughing crowd – – – that filled me with such horror that I'll never get out of my mind the fling of his feet and his grin and the broken trees and the broken house' (CL2, p. 150, 2 April 1918). Three days before, Mansfield had written: 'Yesterday the lady [long-range gun] called "Long Sighted Lizzie" became so violent that I got a bit jumpy & decided at any rate it was no use simply sitting here & waiting for the 18 minutes to be up before another crash came. So LM and I went off to an underground cantine at the Gare du Nord for soldiers and refugees – & got taken on to start today – at 1.30' (CL2, p. 147, 31 March 1918).

Etc. Etc. This cursed country would take the spirit out of a Brandied Cherry (CL2, p. 297, 19 December 1918).

Influence of Murry

Murry, in addition to his war work, was also reviewing French books for the *TLS*: 'Murry is exhausted again. He comes out of Watergate House, shakes himself, only to dive into another weedy little tank, trying to catch French fish for the Times' (CL2, p. 255, 19 July 1918). He was thus able to supply Mansfield with books of interest plus occasional review work, although as Vincent O'Sullivan points out, her only identified review of any French writer during these months in England is her notice of Paul Margueritte's *Pour Toi, Patrie* which appeared in the *TLS* on 4 July 1918 (CL2, p. 189, n2, 23 and 24 May 1918). It was Murry who encouraged her to read Georges Duhamel (who now attracted her attention and who is mentioned frequently during this period), he having recommended that she read 'Les Amours de Ponceau', one of the stories in Duhamel's new collection *Civilisation 1914–17*.[47] Her attraction was immediate:

> I read the book last night. […] He (Duhamel) is the most sympathetic Frenchman I've ever read – I think he is really great – Well, that's not a very illuminating remark. It's his dignity of soul which is so strange to find in a Frenchman – You know what I mean? (CL2, p. 209, 1 June 1918).

Georges Duhamel (1884–1966), during the time that Mansfield was alive, wrote passionately against war and its atrocities, which he had experienced first hand as a major in charge of a surgical unit for the gassed and gangrened. The notes he took on his patients formed the basis of two books: *Vie des Martyrs* and *Civilisation*,[48] which went on to win the Prix Goncourt and which was the first book of his that Mansfield read. After reading *Civilisation*, Murry had been profoundly affected and wanted

---

47   Georges Duhamel, *Civilisation 1914–1917* (Paris: Mercure de France, 1918).
48   Georges Duhamel, *Vie des martyrs* (Paris: Mercure de France, 1917).

Mansfield to share his experience, sending her a copy of the *Mercure de France*, where an article by Duhamel had recently appeared: 'I want you to read the thing by Duhamel in it: 'La Recherche de la grâce'. It seems to me very remarkable indeed that there should be another man not merely feeling what we feel, but using our words to express what he feels' (CL2, p. 228, 8 June 1918). The effect of Duhamel's writing on her had been stored, to become part of her French literary experience, its influence to be felt at a later date. 'O – Love – the Beauty of the human soul – the Beauty of it – the Beauty of it. Don't let us *ever* forget – You and I know it – Duhamel knows it – There will be others – we will build an altar' (CL2, p. 244, 16 June 1918). And although there is no discernable direct influence on Mansfield's own literary endeavours, nevertheless, two years after writing the above, she was still able to use him as a term of reference, when describing a French doctor who had recently examined her to Murry: 'He is only about 33 – and I feel that his experiences at the war had changed him. In fact he seemed to be awfully like what a young Duhamel might be' (CL4, p. 72, 16 October 1920).

Meanwhile, in July 1918, she was writing the following in her notebook:

> I have read – given way to reading – two books by Octave Mirbeau – and after them I see dreadfully and finally, (1) that the French are a filthy people, (2) that their corruption is so puante I'll not go near 'em again. No, the English couldn't stoop to this. They aren't human; they are in the good old English parlance – monkeys. I must start writing again. They decide me. Something must be put up against this (J2, p. 142, 5 July 1918).

Two of the novels of Octave Mirbeau (1848–1917), *L'Abbé Jules* and *Le Jardin des supplices*, are explicit and powerful expressions of anarchist thought.[49] Though demoralised by the First World War, Mirbeau nevertheless remained firmly anti-militarist. Mansfield was an innovator, but she was no anarchist. Though profoundly affected by the war and the deaths of her brother and close friends, she always remained patriotic. Most of Mansfield's published fiction dates from 1914; she died in 1923 and towards the end of her life was too sick to write much of any consequence. Thus, the most productive phase of her short writing career coincided with the duration of the war and its immediate aftermath.

---

49   Octave Mirbeau, *L'Abbé Jules* (Paris: Ollendorff, 1888); *Le Jardin des supplices* (Paris: Charpentier, 1899).

There is evidence that in 1919 Mansfield had started translating another French story into English: 'I am idiotic from translating. I am turning into English La Jeune Fille Bien Elevée [sic] for an American publisher, and every moment one wants to say: but it's so much better in French – do let me leave this little bit in French' (CL2, p. 321, late May 1919).[50] Unfortunately, there is no record of this translation of René Boylesve's work ever being published, or any evidence of the actual translation in her papers. It remains merely a tantalising glimpse into her thoughts on the role of translator and the ensuing difficulties, which, ironically, were to be much in evidence in translations of her own work, discussed in a later chapter. For the rest of this period in England, Mansfield continued her reading of French authors, the influence of Murry much in evidence: 'M. knows nothing of the new André Gide. The other books he says are not up to much' (CL2, p. 331, 18 June 1919), and again a few weeks later:

> Has anything happened in the world while I have lain under my dark umbrella? Murry tells me nothing – except that he went to the exhibition of French pictures and liked some very much – especially Derain and Lhote. He (Lhote) is going to write for us in the Athenaeum on French Art (CL2, p. 346, 13 August 1919).

The French influence was thus all around her – both literary and artistic – even when she was not actually *in* France.

Search for a Cure

As her health continued to deteriorate, Mansfield's doctor advised that she should spend her next winter on the Riviera again. By February 1920, after an initial visit to the Italian Riviera, she was ensconced in the Villa Flora in Menton, owned by her wealthy cousin Connie Beauchamp and a friend, where she was cosseted and surrounded by luxuries such as she had not experienced in a long while. They hoped for a Catholic con-

---

50   René Boylesve, *La Jeune fille bien élevée* (Paris: H. Floury, 1909). René Boylesve (1867–1926), is now recognised as one of the precursors of Marcel Proust. He was elected to the Académie Française in 1919.

vert for their troubles, and at one point it looked as if they might get their wish but ultimately Mansfield realised she had 'no use for the "personal deity" of the Catholic Church' (Alpers, p. 312).[51]

On this trip, Mansfield was still attracted to the French countryside, if not the people. On more than one occasion she noted how the area reminded her of New Zealand and of how much she had grown to love it. But there is no love lost between her and the French themselves: 'Oh, how I have come to love this S. of France – and to dislike the French' (CL3, p. 280, 12 April 1920). After her death, and with the translations of her *Journal* and *Letters* appearing in France, Murry, as editor of both works, was keen to downplay any negative references to the French and rather to concentrate on presenting images such as:

> Oh, could I bring the flowers, the air, the whole heavenly climate as well: this darling little town, these mountains – It is simply a small jewel – Menton . . . and it's band in the jardins publiques with the ruffled pansy beds – the white donkeys, standing meek, tied to a pole, the donkey women in black pleated dresses with flat funny hats. All, all is so terribly attractive. I'd live here years with you (CL3, p. 287, 20 April 1920).

In England from April to September 1920, she was now reading Flaubert: 'I shall try and read Madame Bovary again before you come back' (CL4, p.9, 10 May 1920). Three stories were written, one, 'The Escape', being set in France, again with the characters of an English married couple abroad with the themes of travelling, trains and frustration embedded within it. [See Appendix C for complete list of stories set in France or containing a French influence.]

Knowing she could not risk another winter in England because of her deteriorating health, Mansfield set off for Menton again in September 1920, this time staying at another of her cousin's houses, the Villa Isola Bella. Even on the journey, Mansfield was considering the differ-

---

51   Alpers recounts how, 'On St. Joseph's Day [...] Miss Fullerton inscribed to Katherine a leather-bound copy of *The Imitation of Christ*, which proved a false move. A note in the margin shows that Katherine recoiled from the opening of Chapter 5: "It is a very great thing to be in state of obedience, to live under a superior, and not to be one's own master." Beside those words she scribbled, "Nonsense"' (Alpers, p. 312). Tomalin comments that, 'If Katherine worshipped at any shrines, they were pagan ones' (Tomalin, p. 196).

ences between England and France, as if trying to weigh up her attitude towards them both:

England and France

The great difference: England so rich with the green bowers of the hops and gay women and children with their arms lifted, pausing to watch the train. A flock of yellow hens, led by a red rooster, streamed across the edge of the field. But France: an old man in a white blouse was cutting a field of small clover with an old-fashioned half-wooden scythe. The tops of the flowers were burnt; the stooks (are they stooks?) were like small heaps of half-burnt tobacco (J2, p. 217, September 1920).

With her typically euphemistic approach to life – and sex – she wrote to her old friend Anne Drey (née Rice): 'I believe if I lived in England I could be a eunuch quite cheerfully. But [...] there's something in the air of France – – – which is very *restorative*, lets say' (CL4, p. 153, 26 December 1920). France, the catalyst for so many of her creative endeavours, was enabling her to write again, her personality emerging in quicksilver flashes – human, generous, compassionate and vulnerable. Indeed, in her most fecund period of story writing since 1917, she was to write during this stay no fewer than eight stories [see Appendix B for complete list of stories written in France], 'The Young Girl, and 'Poison' being set in France.

It was also during this period that Mansfield 'discovered' Proust, achieved in a typically duplicitous way. On 1 December 1920, she wrote to Murry:

I had a letter from Schiff today [...] didn't I think that it was a mistake to rate the Russians above de Maupassant? And that Proust is not only the greatest living writer but perhaps (I like the perhaps) the greatest novelist that has ever been!!!!! [...] I will reply I would give every single word de Maupassant and Tumpany ever wrote for one short story by Anton Tchekhov. As to Proust with his Morceaux de Salon (who cares if the salon is 'literary') let him tinkle away. He must be beaten simply. (CL4, p. 130, 1 December 1920).

On the *same day*, however, she wrote to Sydney Schiff: 'It's years since I read de Maupassant: I must read him again. [...] Will you lend me Marcel Proust when you come out this time? I don't feel qualified to speak of him' (CL4, p. 131, 1 December 1920).[52] The above quotations show Mansfield trying to impress, to curry favour, to change her colours, chameleon-like, depending on her correspondent; now being 'clever' with Murry, keeping up with his 'Oxford' brain and his intellectual friends (with whom she often felt uneducated and inferior), by feigning knowledge of Proust and Maupassant, now being deliberately subservient to the wealthy and influential Schiff, whose friendship she sought out for personal reasons. Coincidentally, the following year Murry wrote an article on Proust which necessitated a certain amount of research. Mansfield again wrote to Sidney Schiff:

> I wish you had read J.M.'s real article on Proust. It seems to me not only by far the best thing he has ever done – but really first-chop. We lived Proust, breathed him, talked and thought of little else for two weeks – two solid uninterrupted Swiss weeks. I confess I did not know how important he is until then – I did not feel his importance as I do now, and the marvel is that those books go on breathing after you have put them away; one is never at an end with them (CL4, p. 329, 3 December 1921).

This letter has a ring of truth about it – it probably *was* the first time that Mansfield had really studied Proust and she was impressed. She wrote to Ottoline Morrell a couple of weeks later:

> It has turned me to Proust however at last. I have been pretending to have read Proust for years but this autumn M. and I both took the plunge. I certainly think he is by far the most interesting living writer. He is fascinating! It's a comfort to have someone whom one can so tremendously admire (CL4, pp. 344–45, 20 December 1921).

Mansfield *was* duplicitous by nature. It was part of her character, to act out a role, to be whatever her friends wanted her to be. She always referred to her many selves, recognising this aspect of her personality:

---

52   Sydney Schiff was the pseudonym of 'Stephen Hudson' (1868–1944). A minor novelist and independently wealthy, he is more renowned today for his literary connections. He was the host at a now famous party in Paris, held on 18 May 1922, when he introduced Marcel Proust to James Joyce (other guests included Diaghilev, Stravinsky and Picasso). He had introduced Murry and Mansfield to Joyce in Paris not long before, on 29 March 1922.

> True to oneself! Which self? Which of my many – well really, that's what it looks like coming to – hundreds of selves? For what with complexes and repressions and reactions and vibrations and reflections, there are moments when I feel I am nothing but the small clerk of some hotel without a proprietor, who has all his work cut out to enter the names and hand the keys to the wilful guests (J2, p. 205, May 1921).

She certainly ended up with a connection to Proust, perceived or not. Readings of Proust have always tended to confuse his work with his life, though in his case the author was more than willing to help spread any nascent legend within a literary world ever eager to crystallise rumours into myths. The same confusion over life and fiction is to be found with Mansfield, though in her case it was her bequest of all her papers to Murry that provided the abundant material for the legend he duly devised.

Still in the South of France, on 6 December 1920 Mansfield received from her publishers a copy of the dust jacket for *Bliss*. The publisher's note reads:

> This book of her stories represents her principal work during the last six years. In theme, in mordant humour, and in keen realistic outlook, she is the nearest thing to the modern Russian story writers and to de Maupassant that England has produced.

This was a cruel irony, for Mansfield disliked Maupassant as I have shown and did not welcome the comparison.

Nearing the End

On 2 February 1921, Mansfield wrote to Ottoline Morrell:

> But I mean to leave the Riviera as soon as possible. I've *turned* frightfully against it and the French. Life seems to me ignoble here. It all turns on money. Everything is money. When I read Balzac I always feel a peculiar odious exasperation because according to him the whole of Life is founded on the question of money. But he is right. It is – for the French. I wish the horrid old Riviera would fall into the sea. It's just like an exhibition where every single side show costs another sixpence. But I paid goodness knows what to *come in* (CL4, p. 171, 2 February 1921).

Several things had brought about this typical change of heart. The maid who had seemed so perfect in the beginning had turned out to be dishonest. Her cousin, realising that Mansfield was almost certainly not going to convert to Catholicism had probably cooled in her attitude towards her. Whatever the reasons, the idyll was no more. But there was, however, no talk of returning to England: 'I shall never live in England again. I recognise England's admirable qualities, but we simply don't get on. We have nothing to say to each other: we are always meeting as strangers' (CL4, p. 178, 9 February 1921). On 4 May 1921, therefore, Mansfield left the Villa Isola Bella for Switzerland and a prolonged stay of several months. French influences were still much in evidence, however. Murry in Paris had been to visit Paul Valéry, with whom he had become friendly some years before. He had described the meeting in a letter and Mansfield replied: 'I liked Valéry and his household. It seemed somehow "extremely right" [...] that his mother should be there and that she should be so small. I expect she thought you were a boy. I should like to have been there' (CL4, p. 225–26, 17 May 1921).

Other French influences at this time were often artistic in nature. Manet and Renoir are both mentioned, but her thoughts on Cézanne are of significance, since they shed light on her own particular form of artistry:

> The Cézanne book, Miss, you won't get back until you send a policeman or an urgent request for it. It is fascinating, & you can't think how one enjoys such a book on our mountaintops. He is awfully sympathetic to me. I am absolutely uneducated about painting. I can only look at it as a writer, but it seems to me the real thing. It's what one is aiming at. One of his men gave me quite a shock. He is the *spit* of a man I've just written about – one Jonathon Trout. To the life. I wish I could cut him out & put him in my book (CL4, p. 278, 12 September 1921).

It is no surprise that an artist such as Cézanne should have affected her in this way; they were both experimental and innovative, breaking down barriers and defying the conventions of the past. She spoke in a similar vein about Van Gogh (see CL4, p. 333, 5 December 1921), referring to the famous Post-Impressionist Exhibition in London in 1910, which she had visited and where one of Van Gogh's paintings of sunflowers had caught her eye. Impressionism in art had been a rejection of the principles and practices of the Establishment and from the outset its ideals had engaged the interest of writers as well as artists. Hugo, Zola and Huysmans all championed Impressionism as did Jules Laforgue (admired by Mansfield), who related it to developments in poetry, music and philosophy as well as literature. Many critics have called Mansfield's technique 'impressionistic', there being little in the way of plot or narrative structure.[53] Rather, in Mansfield we find series of 'episodes', glimpses into lives, places, minds – vignettes or sketches, which we are *experiencing* as well as visualising. There is a desire to break down the boundaries between fact and fiction, autobiography and narrative, fantasy and reality. The world according to Mansfield was not fixed or static, but fleeting, elusive, indefinite. Virginia Woolf, via conversations with Mansfield, was to take up her friend's 'stream-of-consciousness' method and transform her own writing, but it was Mansfield who first initiated the experiment.

In the autumn of 1921, Mansfield's stories had come to the attention of the French literary establishment (even though there would be no translations of her work until after her death), when *Bliss* was entered for the 'Prix Femina Vie Heureuse' of 1921. (See Chapter Five for further details). Letters written at this time continued to show her connection with France, via French literature: 'But the "essential moi" as Daudet would say is in Paris sitting in a small darkish room opposite a man called Manoukhine' (CL4, p. 329, 3 December 1921). The ease and fluidity with which she was able to incorporate French authors into her thoughts demonstrates how extensive her knowledge of French literature was, and, indeed, how this knowledge was continuing to expand.

Mansfield remained in Switzerland until 30 January 1922, when she returned to Paris, to see the above-mentioned Dr Manoukhin, who claimed to cure tuberculosis by irradiating the spleen. Mansfield underwent the prescribed treatment, which was of course unsuccessful, and ultimately left her debilitated and suffering from radiation sickness. Her memories of 1918, when she had spent three terrifying weeks in Paris, enduring the German bombardment, undoubtedly contributed to the composition, during this stay, of her short story 'The Fly', a polemic against the inhuman effects of the First World War; it has received more c itical attention than any of her stories. The boss's torturing of the fly, gradually drowning it in ink blots, together with the fly's plucky struggle

---

53   For an in-depth analysis of Mansfield and Impressionism see Julia van Gunsteren, *Katherine Mansfield and Literary Impressionism* (Amsterdam: Rodopi, 1990).

in avoiding suffocation, symbolises the obvious and the not-so-obvious; the destiny of ordinary men, whose lives in war are worth no more than a fly's, together with her own impotent and exhausted condition – dying of tuberculosis – and drowning, literally, in her own blood.

As mentioned above, Sidney Schiff brought James Joyce to tea at the Victoria Palace with Mansfield and Murry (who had joined her in Paris on 9 February). She always had mixed feelings about *Ulysses*, but after the meeting, Joyce recorded that she struck him as having understood the book better than her husband.[54] The only other story written during this stay in Paris was 'Honeymoon', and the last story she set in the south of France which she had come to know so well.

Death in France

On 16 October 1922, Mansfield went to the Prieuré, near Fontainebleau, to Gurdjieff's Institute for the Harmonious Development of Man, initially on a fortnight's trial, but soon becoming a permanent resident. I shall discuss the significance of the Mansfield/Gurdjieff episode, since after her death it became one facet of her life that was either airbrushed out or at the very least distorted by the early French critics attempting to create a myth, for they were never able to square Mansfield's love of living life precociously – and dangerously – with her 'myth' persona.

Gurdjieff was fifty-six when Mansfield arrived at the Prieuré in October 1922. Born in 1866 in Alexandropol, on the Russian-Turkish border, the experiences and special education to which he was exposed, as James Moore explains, imbued him with, an irrepressible striving to understand clearly the precise significance, in general, of the life process

---

54   In a letter to Wyndham Lewis, Sydney Schiff's wife Violet wrote: '[Joyce] told us last night that Mrs Murray [sic] seemed to understand his book better than her husband which would have surprised her'. AM dated 4 April 1922, in Rare Books Dept, Cornell University Library, Ithica, New York.

on earth of all the outward forms of breathing creatures and, in particular, of the aim of human life in the light of this interpretation.[55]

Gurdjieff believed that civilisation had thrown men and women out of balance, so that the physical, the emotional and the intellectual parts had ceased to work in accord. Twenty years of his life, from 1887–1911, were dedicated to a search for traditional knowledge, concentrated in Central Asia. He started teaching in Moscow in 1912, but this work was disrupted by the First World War and the Russian Revolution. Together with the followers he had gathered over these years, who had somehow managed to leave Russia, he arrived eventually in Paris. There had been plans to set up his Institute in London, but these had been cut short by the British authorities, who suspected him of being a spy. He arrived in Paris on 1 October 1922, having leased the Prieuré at Fontainebleau sight unseen.

Gurdjieff spoke very little English or French and his contact with Mansfield was limited. As James Moore states, she, like many others, 'was magnetised not by a system of self-supportive notional abstractions, but by a human being of Rabelaisian stature, by the fine energies at his disposition, and by this empathy, his vision, his humour, and by his sheer quality of "being"' (Moore in Robinson, p. 191). Many Mansfield scholars have speculated as to the reasons why Gurdjieff allowed Mansfield to join his Institute when it was obvious she was dying. In the end it was probably an act of charity for which he received little recognition. There is no other reason to account for his choice in allowing someone with only weeks to live to enter the Prieuré, knowing that the death of a famous English writer at his Institute, so soon after its opening, would certainly not aid his cause in any way – indeed would lay himself and his institution open to denigration. As Ouspensky said, many years later: 'G. was very kind to her, he did not insist upon her going although it was clear that she could not live. For this in the course of time he received the due amount of lies and slanders'.[56] Two of his followers were medically qualified doctors, so there could be no doubt as to the true state of Mansfield's health.

55 George Ivanovitch Gurdjieff, *The Herald of Coming Good* (Angers: Privately Printed, 1933), p.13, quoted by James Moore, 'Katherine Mansfield and Gurdjieff's Sacred Dance', in Robinson, pp. 189–200 (p.190).
56 P. D. Ouspensky, *In Search of the Miraculous* (London: Routledge, 1950), p. 386.

Her initial impressions were mixed: 'Mr Gurdjieff is not in the least like what I expected. He's what one wants to find him, really. But I do feel *absolutely confident* he can put me on the right track in every way' (L2, p. 677, 18 October 1922). Indeed, by November 12 she was writing:

> Here, I confess, after only five weeks, there are things I *long* to write! Oh, how I long to! But I shall not for a long time. Nothing is ready. I must wait until *la maison est pleine*. I must say the dancing here has given me quite a different approach to writing. I mean some of the very ancient oriental dances. There is one which takes about 7 minutes and it contains the whole life of woman – but everything! Nothing is left out. It taught me, it gave me more of woman's life than any book or poem. There was even room for Flaubert's *Cœur Simple* in it (L2, p. 685, 12 November 1922).[57]

At Mansfield's invitation, Murry came out to Fontainebleau to see her on 9 January 1923. That same evening, she suffered a massive haemorrhage and died. She is buried in the communal cemetery at Avon, near Fontainebleau, a few feet away from Gurdjieff himself.

Mansfield was happy at Fontainebleau, that much is clear from her letters, notebooks and the testimonials of many of the other inhabitants of the Prieuré.[58] After her death, and with initial stereotyping by the French critics which thus instigated the process of hagiography, she was assigned, as Moore states, 'the sheepish role of wronged woman to Gurdjieff's predatory male' (Moore in Robinson, p. 199). From all we have learnt of Mansfield and her determined, flamboyant personality, together with Gurdjieff's possible motives, this scenario is impossible to countenance. The whole basis of the Mansfield myth in France is thus a misrepresentation; idolised as a brilliant, romantic figure who battled heroically against illness, her artistic genius her only weapon, and who held a deep

---

57   Moore notes the following: 'Mansfield died at the Prieuré. That is a simple and natural fact – a fact, however, that the European intelligentsia have granted a crepe-edged ascendancy over her entire experience at the institute – at the cost of contradicting every word she herself wrote there' (Moore in Robinson, p. 197).

58   Mansfield wrote to Murry, 'I believe Mr. Gurdjieff is the only person who can help me. It is great happiness to be here. Some people are stranger than ever, but the strangers I am at last feeling near, and they are my own people at last. So I feel. Such beautiful understanding and sympathy I have never known in the outside world' (L2, p. 670, 24 October 1922).

affection for France and her people; we shall see in another chapter how enthusiastically she was taken up by the French critics.

Within her short lifetime Mansfield grew markedly in intellectual discernment, aesthetic accomplishment, and emotional maturity. Her experiences in France would leave indelible marks on these accomplishments, so that when considering her life and her body of work we can see the osmosis of these experiences in France creeping into her thoughts and filtering through to her work. What this chapter reveals is how much Mansfield needed France. Owing to her temperament she required this constant journeying and sense of instability in order to bring her creative temperament to the surface. Indeed, this was one of the ways Mansfield was to demonstrate Modernism – through her commitment to experimentation, which allowed her to move in directions not previously thought of.

Concerning her knowledge of French literature, she was certainly influenced by French authors, and Murry was a constant source of new ideas in this regard. Her relationship with Carco fuelled her creative endeavours, leading directly to the composition of two stories, and indirectly to an assimilation of certain French writers, all of which contributed to the formation of her own distinctive narrative techniques.

Mansfield's brother died in France – she died in France. These are important facts seized on after her death by the French critics anxious to make Mansfield 'theirs'. The attitude she expressed towards France and the French developed into a pattern, dependent on the vacillations of her illness, whether she was lonely and depressed, whether she was happy and content. This contiguity with France shows in her creative life where we see how some of her finest stories would not have come into being without the French experience, this Gallic lens which so often coloured and shaped what she was writing and feeling. A critical analysis of this use of a French 'filter' gives us a much finer understanding of the complex well-spring of Mansfield's creativity.

Life was seen from a different perspective when Mansfield was in France and her work is always informed by her own experience. Spending time in Bavaria inspired her to write her first collection of short stories, *In a German Pension*, but she never sought to return. France was like a sort of love affair for Mansfield in a very similar way to her love for Murry, especially in the latter years – judgemental and denigrating on the one hand – joyful and enthusiastic on the other.

Chapter Three
Specific French Literary Influences

'There is a title which the amateur novelist shares (but how differently!) with the true artist: it is that of experimentalist. However deep the knowledge a writer has of his characters, however finely he may convey that knowledge to us, it is only when he passes beyond it, when he begins to break new ground, to discover for himself, to experiment, that we are enthralled. The "false" writer begins as an experimentalist; the true artist ends as one'.

Katherine Mansfield, *Novels and Novelists* (London: Constable, 1930), p. 119.

In the field of Mansfield studies, scant attention has been paid to the literary influences, together with the historical and literary backgrounds, which would inform Mansfield's fiction. Vincent O'Sullivan, for example, notes how so many aspects of her work have been neglected, such as 'the large question of her reading and her assumptions about life'.[1] This chapter, through specific new readings of Mansfield's writing, reflects on its deep-rooted French literary influences from the earliest stages of her career, thereby corroborating the debt she owed to France, which went beyond the merely superficial one of 'health tourist'. To develop this argument more fully, I examine Colette's *L'Envers du music-hall*,[2] demonstrating how this work remained a constant reference point for Mansfield throughout her writing career, drawing parallels in the texts of both writers which, to my knowledge, have not been alluded to by

---

1   Vincent O'Sullivan, 'The Magnetic Chain: Notes and Approaches to K.M.', in Jan Pilditch, ed., *The Critical Response to Katherine Mansfield* (Connecticut: Greenwood Press, 1996), pp. 129–53 (p. 153).
2   Colette, *L'Envers du music-hall* (Paris: Flammarion, 1913).

other Mansfield scholars. Both thematically and stylistically, Mansfield's use of this early Colettean work is considerable.[3]

In addition, I shall provide evidence for a Baudelairean influence in Mansfield's fiction. From her late teens onwards, when her tastes and preferences started to take shape, Mansfield began, with the Symbolists and the Decadents as her dominant influences, for the most part introduced through her reading of Baudelaire, to write the sort of fiction which was committed to the possibilities of narrative experimentation. Mansfield herself knew that she was searching for the new, the experimental, but did not know what to call it:

> The form I would choose has changed utterly. I feel no longer concerned with the same appearances of things [...] The plots of my stories leave me perfectly cold [...] but especially I want to write [...] perhaps not in poetry. No, perhaps in Prose – almost certainly in a kind of special *prose* (NB2, pp. 32–33, 22 January 1916).

In this chapter I shall demonstrate how the influence of Baudelaire manifested itself in her work and reveal how Mansfield's interest in Decadent theory and practice enabled her to find a way of extending the boundaries of her own prose expression.

Use of *Fin-de-Siècle* Techniques and Themes

The 'Decadent Era' in France, spanning the period between the Commune of 1871 and the Great War, has come to represent a specific literary period, out of whose complexities was to emerge much of twentieth-century European Modernism. This literary climate of innovation allowed experimental writers, like Mansfield, to flourish, yet her own unique form of Modernism was not derivative of other contemporary writers. This chapter will demonstrate how Mansfield's Modernism was partly a product of her early symbiosis of specifically French *fin-de-siècle* techniques and themes.

---

3   There was also a link with Carco, who was a friend of Colette and who had been one of her second husband Willy's ghost-writers.

Antony Alpers describes her in 1908 in London, aged 20, as, 'a girl in a hostel writing things, struggling quite alone to discover a form, with no idea where to turn for the critical guidance that every young writer needs' (Alpers, p. 80). Sydney Kaplan believes that:

Unlike many older writers who had learned their craft through imitation and refinement of traditional narrative conventions, Mansfield – at the very beginning of her career – began, through the dominant influence of the symbolists and decadents, to write fiction committed to the possibilities of narrative experimentation (Kaplan, p. 83).

She was certainly one of the first 'modern' women writers, attempting a writing career in a field dominated by men, and coping whilst living alone in a foreign city at a young age. For Alpers, her main difficulty at this time was precisely this struggle with trying to find a unique form of her own:

She was not by nature a novelist – she had nothing to offer to publishers of books. […] Her aim was something else – to 'intensify the so-called small things, […] so that truly everything is significant'. The short story in that sense did not exist in England yet. There was no place for what […] she wished to do. No place, either, for what young Joyce had been up to, over in Dublin (Alpers, p. 81).

Sixty years previously in his essay, 'Notes nouvelles sur Edgar Poe', Baudelaire had made the following observation, acknowledging his own personal preference for the short story:

Parmi les domaines littéraires […] il en est un que Poe affectionne particulièrement, c'est la Nouvelle. Elle a sur le roman à vastes proportions cet immense avantage que sa brièveté ajoute à l'intensité de l'effet. Cette lecture, qui peut être accomplie tout d'une haleine, laisse dans l'esprit un souvenir bien plus puissant qu'une lecture brisée, interrompue souvent par les tracas des affaires et le soin des intérêts mondains. L'unité d'impression, la totalité d'effet est un avantage immense qui peut donner à ce genre de composition une supériorité tout à fait particulière, à ce point qu'une nouvelle trop courte (c'est sans doute un défaut) vaut encore mieux qu'une nouvelle trop longue.[4]

Elaine Showalter observes, on the *fin-de-siècle* tradition, how, 'In contrast to the sprawling three-decker, the short story emphasised psychological

---

4   Edgar Allan Poe, *Nouvelles histoires extraordinaires*, trans. and intro. by Charles Baudelaire (Paris: Folio, 1972), pp. 18–19.

intensity and formal innovation'.[5] Thus, in writing her short stories, Mansfield was emulating a *fin-de-siècle* convention, which in itself, had been endorsed many years before by Baudelaire; indeed, her early experimental prose poems reveal the influence of the French Symbolists. She also developed a youthful infatuation with the Aesthetic movement and especially the works of Oscar Wilde, which matured into a lifelong admiration; his influence on her writing was considerable. Vincent O'Sullivan, for example, states that, 'Wilde's presence she left behind, but his traces will be in her work for the rest of her life. Her way of describing flowers, for instance; her precision in parodying the language of aesthetes; the brittleness of much of the conversation in her fiction; those inversions which are a mark of her style always' (O'Sullivan in Pilditch, p. 131). *The Picture of Dorian Gray* introduced her to the seminal decadent text *A Rebours* (referred to in Wilde's novel as 'The Yellow Book'), which had been translated into English as *Against the Grain* by Havelock Ellis in 1903. For Enid Starkie, '*The Picture of Dorian Gray*, which was inspired by *A Rebours*, became for England what Huysmans's novel had been for France, its aesthetic bible, the book which gave the most perfect picture of the Decadent. There is no doubt that the 'yellow book' which leads Dorian Gray to perdition is *A Rebours*' (Starkie, p. 105).

Mansfield also read and absorbed the works of Arthur Symons, especially *The Symbolist Movement in Literature*. Symons (1865–1945), the central English Decadent writer and critic of the 1890s, was also a poet of urban life, who found stimulation and metaphor in the music-hall and the city street. He dealt with aspects of London other writers usually avoided – prostitution and casual sex in particular – pursuing fleeting impressions without making moral connections, closely adhering to and therefore derivative of the tenets of Baudelaire, as expressed *in Les Fleurs du mal* and *Le Spleen de Paris*. For Roger Holdsworth, Symons 'both practised and expounded the ideals of the Decadence more energetically than any of his contemporaries'.[6]

---

5   Elaine Showalter, ed., *Daughters of Decadence: Women Writers of the Fin-de-Siècle* (New Jersey: Rutgers University Press, 1993), p. ix. Huge numbers of new periodicals on both sides of the Atlantic were also creating a market for short fiction.

6   Roger Holdsworth, in Symons, *Selected Writings*, p. 19.

Mansfield and Baudelaire

During her stay in Carco's Paris flat in early 1915, Mansfield wrote 'Spring Pictures', published posthumously in *Something Childish* in 1924. With its Parisian backdrop and experimental structure it heralds a new narrative path for Mansfield. Impressionistic description now replaces plotline and narrative, in a brief story separated into three parts, resembling, in Alpers' words, 'three panels in a modern triptych' (CS Alpers, p. 554). On this particular trip she saw at first hand how Paris was changing, leading to an inevitable alteration of her own perception.[7] The constant zeppelin raids were frightening and all her impressions seemed tainted by her fear: 'I wonder if it is the war that has made the people here so hideous or if I am out of joint. They appear to me a nation of concierges. And the women look such drabs in their ugly mourning' (CL1, p. 185, 12 May 1915). In 'Spring Pictures', Mansfield portrays her disgust at those who profiteer from the misery of others: 'There are tables set out with toy cannons and soldiers and Zeppelins and photograph frames complete with ogling beauties' (645). The story moves towards an increasingly poetic prose:

> Hope! You misery – you sentimental, faded female. Break your last string and have done with it. I shall go mad with your endless thrumming; my heart throbs to it and every little pulse beats in time. It is morning. I lie in the empty bed – the huge bed big as a field and as cold and unsheltered. Through the shutters the sunlight comes up from the river and flows over the ceiling in trembling waves (646).

---

7   The changes that Baudelaire espied in Paris during the Industrial Revolution, for example, though not the same as those Mansfield was witnessing decades later, nevertheless give both writers common ground; the sense of seeing an urban landscape shift beyond recognition is visible in the work of both writers. (See in particular Baudelaire's 'Le Cygne' (LXXXIX in *Les Fleurs du Mal*), 'Le vieux Paris n'est plus (la forme d'une ville / Change plus vite, hélas! que le cœur d'un mortel); / Je ne vois qu'en esprit tout ce camp de baraques, / Ces tas de chapiteaux ébauchés et de futs, / Les herbes, les gros blocs verdis par l'eau des flaques, / Et, brillant aux carreaux, le bric-à-brac confus' (*Baudelaire: The Complete Verse, Volume 1*, ed. by Francis Scarfe (London: Anvil Press Poetry, 1986), pp. 174–75. (All subsequent references in French to *Les Fleurs du mal* are taken from this edition.) The similarities between this poem and Mansfield's description of Paris in 'Spring Pictures' as quoted above, are striking.

Alpers claims that, 'If a literary ancestor is to be sought for these products of K.M's quest for modern forms, it must surely be Baudelaire's *Petits poèmes en prose, 'Le Spleen de Paris'* (CS Alpers, p. 554). Mansfield read and admired Baudelaire; in this new and experimental way of writing, she was attempting an innovative form set out by him sixty years before in his 'prose poems'.[8]

In the issue of *Rhythm* for March 1913, Murry had written a five page article on the influence of Baudelaire, reviewing a recently published book on the subject, which Mansfield, as co-editor of *Rhythm*, would certainly have read.[9] The article states:

> The 'Poèmes en Prose' possess a line of lineal descendants in virtue of their form alone, and their influence is at work to-day through Arthur Rimbaud upon one of the most interesting of the younger French literary movements, that of the Fantaisistes' (p. xxv).

Of course, *Rhythm* had its own 'fantaisiste' poet in Francis Carco. Murry concludes:

> The truth is that English aestheticism and the so-called Renaissance of the 'Nineties' derive from sources very different from Baudelaire. The true line of descent is English and insular, from Ruskin through Walter Pater. [...] We should never have

8   In 1907, in one of her first published stories whilst still a teenager in New Zealand, she wrote the following: 'Each day they walked down Bond Street together, between the hours of twelve and one, and turned in at the Bleinheim Café for lunch and conversation. She, a pale, dark girl with that unmistakable air of "acquaintance with life" which is so general among the students in London, and an expression at once of intense eagerness and anticipated disillusion. Life to a girl who had read Nietzsche, Eugene Sue [sic], Baudelaire, D'Annunzio, Georges Barres [sic], Catulle Mendes [sic], Sudermann, Ibsen, Tolstoi, was, in her opinion, but a trifle obvious' (NB1, pp. 171–72) – first published in *Native Companion* (Australia), no. 5, 2 December, 1907. Obviously autobiographical, this excerpt demonstrates how well-read Mansfield was for a 'young colonial' of nineteen.

9   John Middleton Murry, 'The Influence of Baudelaire', in *Rhythm*, 2.14 (March 1913), xxiii–xxvii. In this article Murry discusses Gladys Turquet-Milnes, *The Influence of Baudelaire in France and England* (London: Constable, 1913). For Con Coroneos, Murry's use of the word 'modernism' in this article implies, 'something deeply hostile to the Wildean aestheticism which first attracted Mansfield'. Con Coroneos, 'Flies and Violets in Katherine Mansfield' in *Women's Fiction and the Great War*, ed. by Suzanne Raitt and Trudi Tate (Oxford: Clarendon Press, 1997) pp. 197–18 (p. 211).

heard so much of the so-called French influence upon our literature of the nineties if Oscar Wilde had not been able to take advantage of the abysmal ignorance of French literature then prevailing. Wilde treated the French as a professional secret, a privately printed book of pornography which he did not really understand, but yet vaguely felt was beautifully written [...] Even the French did not quite assimilate Baudelaire. [...] 'Baudelaire may be a cynic or mad; he is never gross; there is never a wrong fold in the impressions with which he clothes himself. He is always courteous with ugliness. He behaves well...' said Laforgue. The English Baudelairians [sic] never behave. There is a world of difference (p. xxvii).

Wilde was an early and important influence on Mansfield; indeed, his influence can be detected throughout her literary career. I contend that this article may well have fostered a desire in Mansfield to reinvigorate her own Baudelairean experiments, initially in tentative pieces such as 'Spring Pictures', moving on to the more mature and innovative techniques of 'Prelude', and eventually extending to later stories such as 'Carnation' and 'The Doll's House'. As mentioned previously, the working title of 'Prelude' was 'The Aloe' – a symbolist–inspired title, which, as Stephanie Pride states, had, amongst others, the themes of a dismantling of, 'the opposition between man and nature, the separation of the senses and the distinction between prose and verse'.[10] Mansfield's story upholds all these tenets, and even the title she would finally settle on, 'Prelude', a word defined as a self-contained piece of music, a fore-taste, hints at the musicality of the prose it contains and its experimental nature; the story itself was finished in Bandol, nearly a year later.[11]

In *The Symbolist Movement in Literature* (a well-thumbed text for Mansfield in her youth, as I indicated in Chapter One), she would have read Arthur Symons, quoting a translation from Gérard de Nerval:

Everything in nature assumed new aspects, and secret voices came to me from the plants, the trees [...] All things live, all things are in motion, all things correspond; the magnetic rays emanating from myself or others traverse without obstacle the infinite chain of created things (Symons, *Symbolist Movement*, p. 17).

10 Stephanie Pride, 'Mansfield's "Leves Amores", French Symbolism and Gender Politics' in *Worlds of Katherine Mansfield*, ed. by Harry Ricketts (Palmerston North: Nagare Press, 1991), pp. 85–101 (p. 86).
11 It was at this time that Mansfield wrote about her search for a new prose expression – see NB2, pp. 32–33, 22 January 1916.

The origins of the specific symbolism she attributes to 'The Aloe' will be discussed in Chapter Four, but its origins were inspired by the French symbolists and her assimilation of French literature, introduced through her reading of Symons. Mansfield even went so far as to copy the title of one of Symons' own poems, 'Leves Amores' – ('Casual Love') and use it as the title for a youthful prose poem:

> Come this Old Age, I have forgotten passion, I have been left behind in the beautiful golden procession of Youth. Now I am seeing life in the dressing-room of the theatre [...] Yes, even the green vine upon the bed curtains wreathed itself into strange chaplets and garlands, twined round us in a leafy embrace, held us with a thousand clinging tendrils.[12]

Mansfield deliberately omits any reference to the gender of the narrator, thus rendering the text sexually ambiguous, at a time when she herself was experimenting with lesbian relationships, producing, as Pride points out, 'a very differently structured discourse from that displayed in the texts of the male Symbolist writers' (Pride, in Ricketts, p. 98). Indeed, in modern-day terminology, the title might be translated more aptly as 'Casual Sex'. This youthful vignette has never been mentioned before as a precursor to other more mature 'prose-poem' works influenced by Baudelaire, such as 'Spring Pictures'.

With 'Prelude', Mansfield, writing in France, discovered her 'special prose', in a story which delineates the 'prelude' to the birth of her now-dead brother, a homage to the natural world, steeped in plant and nature symbolism. Towards the end of her life, in 1921, she wrote the following, in a letter to her cousin Elizabeth:

> This afternoon John [...] has been reading aloud Swinburne's Ave Atque Vale, which did not sound fearfully good. I suspect those green buds of sin and those gray fruits of shame. And try as one may, one can't see Baudelaire [sic] (CL4, p. 300, 23 October 1921).

---

12 'Leves Amores' (*Poems 2*, pp. 14–15). A slightly different version of this prose-poem can be found in NB1, pp. 160–61. This latter version however, reads more as 'prose-story' rather than 'prose-poem'. Strikingly, it is immediately preceded in the notebooks by a French quotation from Flaubert: 'Nous ne suivons plus la même route, nous ne navignons [sic] plus dans la même nacelle. Moi je ne cherche pas le port, mais la haute mer' (NB1, p. 160). The inference of new paths to be trod, new directions to take, immediately preceding the penning of such a vignette, cannot be coincidental.

It is doubtful whether these experiments in form and content would have occurred in Mansfield's work to such an extent, without the catalyst of being in France itself. Indeed, 'Spring Pictures' could not have been conceived without her knowledge of French literature and of Paris; this is a story wholly immersed in the culture of France and Mansfield's response to it.[13]

'Carnation' and *Les Fleurs du mal*

Plants, and especially flowers, are constantly recurring symbols in Mansfield's stories; Sam Hynes, for example, comments that: 'It is not strange that Miss Mansfield chooses to state this theme [of lost innocence] most frequently in flower imagery; flowers are beautiful, delicate, and transitory – like the innocence of childhood'.[14]

A short piece written in 1917, 'Carnation' (published posthumously in *Something Childish*), reads on the surface as Mansfield reminiscing on her school days, in a semi-jocular, quasi-innocent fashion. In fact, it is one of Mansfield's most sexually charged stories, convincingly read as a Baudelairean intertext, taking a shard of time in an adolescent's summer and producing a polished meditation on an evolving self. The carnation referred to in the title is a 'deep, deep, red one that looked as though it had been dipped in wine and left in the dark to dry' (664). It is brought into a French class by a school girl named 'curious Eve'. The story is recounted by another girl – Katie – Mansfield's own name.

The day is hot – too hot to work. M. Hugo decides that instead of taking notes, the girls will listen to him reading some French poetry.

---

13 As to what her other influences may have been, we know from her notebooks and letters during this period 1914–15, that she was reading Stendhal: 'I have adopted Stendhal. Every night I read him now & first thing in the morning' (CL1, p. 168, 25 March 1915). Other French authors mentioned in her notebooks and letters at this time [see Appendix D for full list], include Paul Deroulède, Jean Tharaud, Balzac, Colette, Rachilde and, of course, Carco.

14 Sam Hynes, 'Katherine Mansfield: The Defeat of the Personal', in Pilditch, pp. 66–70 (p. 68).

Mansfield prepares the reader for what is to come with a sexually charged description of how M. Hugo read to the girls:

> He would begin, softly and calmly, and then gradually his voice would swell and vibrate and gather itself together, then it would be pleading and imploring and entreating, and then rising, rising triumphant, until it burst into light, as it were, and then – gradually again, it ebbed, it grew soft and warm and calm and died down into nothingness (666).

This may be plausibly read as a covert description of a male orgasm, exposed through the characterisation of M. Hugo, and preceding a female orgasm experienced by Katie. The latter is overwhelmed by the scent of the carnation: 'Oh, the scent! It floated across to Katie. It was too much' (666). Her eyes wander out of the window to the stable yard below, where a workman is cleaning some carriage wheels, pumping water into a bucket: 'as he worked the pump [...] a great gush of water followed' (666).

The burgeoning sexual references now become more and more obvious, as the young girl is overcome by the heat, the smells (even the French room 'always smelled faintly of ammonia' (666)),[15] and the scene in front of her eyes:

> She saw him – simply – in a faded shirt, his sleeves rolled up, his chest bare, all splashed with water – and as he whistled, loud and free, and as he moved, swooping and bending, Hugo-Wugo's voice began to warm, to deepen, to gather together, to swing, to rise – somehow or other to keep time with the man outside (Oh, the scent of Eve's carnation!) until they became one great, rushing, rising, triumphant thing, bursting into light, and then –
>
> The whole room broke into pieces (667).

The orgasmic nature of the writing, the building up to a crescendo, the rhythmic pattern of the words and phrases, the repetition of 'bursting into light' from the previous description, together with the connotations of the words themselves – all this leads the reader towards an understanding that Katie has undergone a sexual experience – an 'orgasm'. And Mansfield, underlining this covert sexual explanation, terminates the story with the following sentence: 'And, "Keep it, dearest," said Eve, "*Souvenir*

15   Ammonia has a smell sometimes associated with bodily emissions such as sweat and urine.

tendre," and she popped the carnation down the front of Katie's blouse' (667). Eve – the archetypal sinner, is here responsible for the metaphorical 'deflowering' of her friend, and this notion is carried through in the choice of flower in the title itself, since through the use of a carnation, Mansfield is underlining the almost mystical/religious experience which Katie undergoes. According to Christian legend, the Virgin Mary shed tears at the plight of Jesus on the cross and carnations grew where her tears fell; Jesus is also perceived as the 'incarnation' of God made flesh. The carnation is, of course, the paradigmatic *fin-de-siècle* symbol for homosexuality, used repeatedly by Wilde, Huysmans and others and here by Mansfield herself. Indeed this story is 'Decadent', in its immorality, its symbolism, its repeated reference to France and French and the fact that it is whilst the teacher is reading aloud *French* poetry that the 'orgasms' occur. The girls are in a 'French Room' (665), M. Hugo speaks French to the girls, 'Un peu de silence, s'il vous plaît' (665), he reads them, 'a little French poetry' (665); the word 'French' occurs five times in a story barely three pages long, and it is Eve who closes this story with the French words '*Souvenir tendre*'.[16] Though this is only conjecture, I believe Mansfield leaves enough clues – even to the title itself – for us to come to an understanding that M. Hugo is reading out poems from *Les Fleurs du mal* to his female pupils as one of them undergoes an involuntary sexual experience.

Indeed, Baudelaire's poem, 'Parfum exotique', from *Les Fleurs du mal*, has uncanny similarities with Mansfield's story, replicating identical vocabulary and themes.[17] Firstly, the all-pervading sense of smell: 'je respire l'odeur', 'ton odeur', 'le parfum des verts tamariniers, / Qui circule dans l'air et m'enfle la narine'. The sense of smell in Baudelaire's poem is heady with sexual connotations. In Mansfield's story we find, 'Katie turned away to the dazzling light outside the window', 'the dazzle outside'; in Baudelaire we find, 'Qu'éblouissent les feux d'un soleil monotone'. The effect of 'Des hommes dont le corps est mince et vigoureux', is similarly reproduced in Mansfield's story by the half-naked

16   This was the title of a popular waltz in the early part of the last century composed by Thomas J. Hewitt. Ironically it also conjures up the title of one volume of Apollinaire's letters published in 1952 under the title *Tendre comme le souvenir* (Paris: Gallimard, 1952).

17   Charles Baudelaire, XXII 'Parfum Exotique', *Les Fleurs du mal*, pp. 82–83.

workman, 'his chest bare, all splashed with water [...] as he moved, swooping and bending'. Similarly, 'Et des femmes dont l'œil par sa franchise étonne' is partly recalled in Mansfield's story by the calculated look of Eve, 'her eyebrows raised, her eyes half veiled, and a smile that was like the shadow of her cruel little laugh'. Even Baudelaire's nautical theme and water symbology, 'la vague marine', finds its way into Mansfield's story: '[a] whistling that skimmed over the noise of the water as a bird skims over the sea'. There is also the obvious Baudelairean connection with the idea of 'ennui' or 'spleen', encapsulated in the stifling boredom of the French class, the ensuing 'spleen', culminating in an epiphanic moment of sexual release. The entire last verse of 'Parfum exotique' epitomises the essence of the story 'Carnation': the perfume of a plant fills the air, intoxicates, and has a subconscious effect, whilst the poetic reading of the French teacher ebbs and flows in a deliberately musical fashion.

This lyricism of the words in 'Carnation', owes much to the Symbolists and Decadents, with their notion of expressing the inexpressible. Baudelaire himself writes, in his introduction to *Le Spleen de Paris*:

> Quel est celui de nous qui n'a pas, dans ses jours d'ambition, rêvé le miracle d'une prose poétique, musicale sans rythme et sans rime, assez souple et assez heurtée pour s'adapter aux mouvements lyriques de l'âme, aux ondulations de la rêverie, aux soubresauts de la conscience?[18]

Even the title of her story pays homage to the French Decadent movement, since a dyed-green carnation, the preferred lapel-flower of Oscar Wilde, was the French symbol of Decadence and homosexuality. The fact that at the end, 'curious Eve' presents the carnation to her female friend, 'Katie': 'she popped the carnation down the front of Katie's blouse' (667), is a covert reference to the lesbianism which Mansfield experimented with in her youth, some critics maintaining that she was sexually attracted to other women throughout her life.[19] Sydney Kaplan also notes the Wildean influence in Mansfield's work, which for her is epitomised through her use of 'symbolism, epigrammatic phrasing, and

18   Charles Baudelaire, *Le Spleen de Paris: petits poèmes en prose* (Paris: Flammarion, 1997), p. 5.
19   See Alison J. Laurie, 'Queering Katherine' (AWSA 2001 conference proceedings), http://www.socsi.flinders.edu.au/wmst/awsa2001/pdf/papers/Laurie.pdf

exaggeration to highlight its undercurrent of half-suppressed lesbian sexuality' (Kaplan, p. 32). Yet it is only in the last few years that lesbian references in Mansfield's narrative art have been brought forward for discussion.

Mansfield's interest in Decadent literature, her experiments with various writing techniques and styles, and certainly the content of some of her stories, would have placed her firmly in what many outraged male critics of the time termed 'literary degenerates' (Showalter, p. ix). Showalter continues:

> New Women and decadent artists were linked together as twin monsters of a degenerate age, sexual anarchists who blurred the boundaries of gender. Thus, decadent art was unmanly and effeminate, while New Women's writing was unwomanly and perverse (p. x).

Mansfield however, deliberately conceals the subversive undercurrents of 'Carnation', so that the reader is therefore not immediately alerted to its risqué themes.

Alison Fairlie observes that: 'Baudelaire does not start from philosophical theories or mystical beliefs, but from observing human experience'.[20] With a sharply observant eye, Mansfield too catches a moment and within that moment, encapsulates a host of themes and undercurrents. Baudelaire comments on those moments of intensity, 'when we feel our vitality intensified so that any object we look at, however trivial, seems to hold delight and meaning, strikes our senses strongly and suggests a train of ideas' (Fairlie, p. 9). In the following quotation from Mansfield, where she discusses just such an intensity of 'seeing', it is almost as if Baudelaire's words were in front of her:

> I've *been* this man, *been* this woman. I've stood for hours on the Auckland Wharf. I've been out in the stream waiting to be berthed – I've been a seagull hovering at the stern and a hotel porter whistling through his teeth. It isn't as though one sits and watches the spectacle. That would be thrilling enough, God knows. But one IS the spectacle for the time (CL4, p. 97, 3 November 1920).

Claire Tomalin describes this technique of Mansfield's as encapsulating 'the isolation in which each character dwells' (Tomalin, p. 6), and like

---

20   Alison Fairlie, Baudelaire: *Les Fleurs du mal* (London: Edward Arnold, 1960), p. 9.

Mansfield, Baudelaire has a sharply observant eye, continually transforming the everyday into something more powerful and universal.

Mansfield and Colette

Joanne Banks is one of the few critics to recognise that several of Mansfield's stories are based on an experimental form used by the ancients and Theocritus in particular, perceiving that they are 'startlingly like the "dialogues for one voice" by Colette, a writer whose lifestyle Mansfield admired, and whose work was currently being published in *Le Matin*'.[21] She maintains however that, 'the experimental stories disappointed Mansfield [...] so she had no encouragement to continue in this vein', adding that 'in some mysterious way, when good writers are writing badly, they are often on the eve of writing better' (Banks, p. 71). I demonstrate in this section, that not only was Mansfield 'not writing badly', but she in fact returned to the techniques of Colette throughout her writing career, generating, in the process, some of her finest work.

During the period of her life when Mansfield enjoyed associating herself with Colette, Ruth Parkin-Gounelas recognises that both writers seemed to be re-enacting their childhoods through the medium of literature:

> In 1915, at the very time references to Colette occurred in the journal and letters, Mansfield was reunited with her brother in London and was on the lookout for a

---

21 Joanne Trautmann Banks, 'Virginia Woolf and Katherine Mansfield', in *The English Short Story 1880–1945: A Critical History*, ed. Joseph M. Flora (Boston: Twayne, 1985), pp. 57–82 (p. 70). Antony Alpers also makes the connection, stating: 'Someone on the *New Age*, probably Orage, must have handed her a volume of Theocritus and suggested that she might make an amusing pastiche of the XVth Idyll by applying it to the Coronation. The result, a mere skit dashed off at speed, led to her learning, from Theocritus and not from Chekhov, the method which she later made her own' (Alpers, p. 125).

discursive model to apply to the childhood experiences Chummie had helped her recall. Colette's novels provided just such a model.[22]

Parkin-Gounelas is right to stress Mansfield's attraction to Colette, the similarities in their past, and the inspiration she drew from her life at this time, but this section reveals just how far this discursive model would infiltrate Mansfield's fiction and remain there.[23]

In a 'Lettre de Paris' from the July 1912 edition of *Rhythm*, Carco writes: '*La Retraite Sentimentale* suffisait a classer Colette Willy. De puis elle a donne *La Vagabonde* qui'a bouché le grand public lettré' [all sic]. In November 1912 he mentions Colette once more, stating, 'Colette Willy chérit l'impressionnisme le plus éclatante' [sic].[24] Mansfield, now co-e..itor of *Rhythm* with Murry, would have noted these references to Colette, indeed they may have instigated her initial reading of the French author, since there is no reference to Colette prior to this date in any of her extant writing. Claire Tomalin briefly notes Mansfield's connection with Colette in her biography, stating:

> Colette's success on stage, her bisexuality and her acquaintance with the demi-monde were all likely to have interested her, and her vision may have played its part in Katherine's falling in love with France itself, although none of this was shared with Murry (Tomalin, p. 124).[25]

The first reference to Colette in Mansfield's notebooks dates from November 1914: 'Colette Willy is in my thoughts tonight' (NB1, p. 284, 3 November 1914). *La Vagabonde* and *L'Entrave*, which had first appeared

---

22 Ruth Parkin-Gounelas, 'Katherine Mansfield Reading Other Women: The Personality of the Text', in Robinson, pp. 36–52 (p. 38).

23 In his preface to Mansfield's *Œuvre romanesque* from 1955, André Maurois had made a connection between Mansfield and Colette: 'Colette, chez nous, serait souvent assez proche de ce que cherchait Katherine Mansfield et celle-ci le savait bien' (OR, p. xiv).

24 Francis Carco, 'Lettre de France: le roman français, introduction', *Rhythm*, 2.10 (November 1912), 269–76 (p. 275).

25 Jeffrey Meyers also briefly notes that, 'Katherine liked to identify herself with George Sand and Colette, who were independent, impulsive, and imaginative women, proud of their desire for love and passion for art' (Meyers, p. 75). Conversely, Alpers, in his biography of 1980, makes no such connection.

in 1910 and 1913 respectively,[26] were certainly known to her: 'I've reread L'Entrave. I suppose Colette is the only woman in France who does just this. I don't care a fig at present for anyone I know except her' (NB1, p. 284, 15 November 1914). This particular entry coincided with a period of turbulence in Mansfield's life – her disaffection for Murry and burgeoning feelings for Carco – which for some reason made her think of Colette. On 18 December 1914, analysing her misery over Murry, she wrote: 'I submit, that's true. But I'm not Colette' (NB1, p. 286, 18 December 1914). I believe it is no coincidence that at the very moment in her life when she is infatuated with Carco and disaffected by Murry, she uses Colettean terms of reference to portray her emotional state. I contend that she was reading Colette because Carco had spoken about her on Mansfield's and Murry's first trip to Paris together. In the knowledge that Colette was his friend, perhaps reading her books was a way for the young, impressionable and infatuated Mansfield to feel closer to the new-found object of her affection. The dates in her notebooks and letters indicating her interest in Colette, tie in with this hypothesis.

Colette was the first woman in France to report from the front lines of the First World War, in the autumn of 1914. The similarities between Colette's experience and Mansfield's infamous escapade to Gray (though minor by comparison), are striking and, to my knowledge, have not been remarked on before. Carco was Colette's friend. She had started reporting from the front. Carco may well have been encouraging his English girlfriend to follow in the footsteps of the author she so admired, Mansfield herself being only too keen to emulate her favourite writer of the moment. The connection may certainly have given her the impetus to act in the way she did, and then subsequently to write about her experiences in her fiction – both writers were particularly adept at delineating the landscape of rootlessness. It would also explain the profusion of references to Colette at this stage in Mansfield's life, such as we find here:

---

26   Colette, *La Vagabonde* (Paris: Ollendorff, 1910) and *L'Entrave* (Paris: Ollendorff, 1913).

I am longing for my Colette books (CL1, p. 225, 23 December, 1915).[27]

What will you think of Colette, I wonder [...] and will you find her 'sympathetic'. For me she is more real than any woman I have ever known (CL1, p. 282, early October 1916).

Colette as a personality therefore, remains yet another protagonist in the saga of Mansfield's emotional connection with France. However, on a literary level the connection ran earlier, was deeper, and its influence extended throughout Mansfield's writing career.

In *The Blue Review* for June 1913 (the new name for *Rhythm*, still edited by Murry and Mansfield, based on the French *Revue bleue*), Marcel Boulestin reviews *L'Envers du music-hall*:

Colette Willy can see and she can describe, and through the medium of her talent, we can see them too, those artists of the music-halls, 'off' without their make-up, their graceful gestures and their fine clothes – as they really are. These sketches are sometimes very amusing, often very pathetic, and always admirably done. For Colette Willy has a sharp and fresh vision and that wonderful gift which is typical of great French writers, for describing a thing in a few decisive lines, for discovering the right and sometimes unexpected adjective, for pointing out the one essential and exceptional detail in a character – where lesser writers would write pages of dull, obvious and almost meaningless disquisitions. [28]

Mansfield's mature fiction bears an uncanny resemblance to this description of Colette's literary technique. A comparison of this review with later critical appraisals of Mansfield's work highlights the similarities of both writers, as here in the following analysis of Mansfield's writing by Katherine Anne Porter, where she too notes the use of a deceptively simple technique:

With fine objectivity she bares a moment of experience, real experience, in the life of someone human being; she states no belief, gives no motives, airs no theories, but simply presents to the reader a situation, a place, and a character, and there it is;

27   This was written whilst Mansfield was alone in France; she had asked Murry to send her some books by Colette. Two days later she wrote, 'Colette has come – thank you love' (CL1, p. 231, 25 December 1915).

28   Marcel Boulestin, 'Recent French Novels', *Blue Review: Literature, Drama, Art, Music*, 1, 2 (June 1913), 138–40 (pp. 138–39).

and the emotional content is present as implicitly as the germ is in the grain of wheat.[29]

C. K. Stead also concurs with this notion when he states:

> Quite a number of her shorter fictions do have something of the character of a 'story', though few rely primarily on narrative for their effect. They develop around a single image, scene or situation, and they move towards the recognition, or realisation (in the French sense of making real) of something latent there.[30]

Both Stead and Porter emphasise the lack of conventional plot in Mansfield's stories, the simplicity of her presentation, belying the complexity of the underlying themes. I believe that this similarity is no mere coincidence, and that just as Mansfield was famously influenced by Chekhov, she was no less influenced by this young French writer, whose risqué life had particular appeal for the reckless Mansfield of 1914. Perhaps Boulestin's comments gave her an early push in formulating the direction she wished her own prose to move towards and her relationship with Carco at this time, initially as Murry's friend and subsequently as a lover, would only have enhanced and encouraged her further reading of Colette. Mansfield's youthful work had already provided ample evidence of her linguistic virtuosity and penetrating intelligence. Now, with Colette as role-model, she had found a narrative structure to contain those gifts.

In 1902, a play had appeared in France entitled *Claudine à Paris*, based on one of Colette's schoolgirl novels – a racy read, spiced with lesbian antics, which had become a bestseller – with the young actress Polaire in the female lead.[31] Its success encouraged Willy, Colette's pub-

29   Katherine Anne Porter, 'The Art of Katherine Mansfield', in Pilditch, pp. 45–48 (p. 47).
30   C. K. Stead, 'Katherine Mansfield and the Art of Fiction', in Pilditch, pp. 155–72 (p. 159).
31   Colette's husband had claimed authorship for the original stories: 'Willy had trouble making ends meet [...] He used hacks of all kinds whose books he signed. It occurred to him that he could make something by using his young wife as a hack too [...] The result was *Claudine à l'école* which Willy signed [...] Willy deployed all his advertising genius to promote the book. He made Colette pose as schoolgirl Claudine for photographs; he encouraged her to put in spicy bits, developing the peasant nymphette, compliant pupil and budding lesbian act. He made her play the Claudine part, dressed up as Claudine, on stage and in town [...] Three sequels were [all] signed "Willy"'. Catherine Portuges and Nicole Ward Jouve, 'Colette', in

licity-seeking husband at that time, to have both his wife and Polaire appear in public dressed as identical twins. Colette herself notes:

> De par sa décision nous eûmes, Polaire et moi, trois 'tenues' identiques, trois seulement, et c'était bien assez, et c'était bien trop: un costume tailleur écossais vert, noir et marron; une robe blanche, une 'charlotte' en tulle blanc et bouquets de cerises; un autre tailleur gris-bleu à bandes gris-blanc, piqûres, pattes, et je ne sais plus quelles nervures appelées 'straps' [...]

> Mettez vos robes blanches, conseilla M. Willy. J'aurai l'air de balader mes deux gosses [...]

> [Polaire] se cramponnait des deux mains à la porte de la loge, s'effaçait: 'Non...non... Jeu ne veux pas... Jeu vous en prie... J'entends ce qu'*ils* pensent, c'est laid, c'est haffreux...'.[32]

On 14 December 1915, Mansfield wrote the following from Bandol to Murry:

> I should like to be at a large circus tonight, in a box – very luxurious, you know, very warm, very gay with a smell of sawdust and elephants. A superb clown called Pistachio – white poneys, little blue monkeys drinking tea out of Chinese cups – I should like to be dressed beautifully, beautifully, down to the last fragment of my chemise, and I should like Colette Willy to be dressed just exactly like me and to be in the same box. And during the entr'actes while the orchestra blared Pot Pourri from The Toreador we would eat tiny jujubes out of a much too big bag and tell each other all about our childhood (CL1, pp. 212–13, 14 December 1915).

She was obviously familiar with the Colette story when writing the above; it is probable that it was Carco who related the tale to her. During

---

French Women Writers, ed. by Eva M Sartori and Dorothy W Zimmerman (Westport: Greenwood Press, 1991), pp. 78–89 (p. 79). Jennifer Waelti-Walters explains how influential the Claudine stories became: 'The attitudes and assumptions inscribed in the *Claudine* novels, represent a shift in the portrayal of lesbians in French literature from the totally male perspective of the previous hundred years [...] Colette and Willy enlarge the possibility for female identification with their characters, while at the same time maintaining the traditional androcentric underpinnings that structure the presentation of female sexuality within their texts'. Jennifer Waelti-Walters, *Damned Women: Lesbians in French Novels* (Montreal: McGill-Queen's University Press, 2000), p. 65.

32   Colette, *Mes Apprentissages* in *Œuvres de Colette*, vol. 3 (Paris: Flammarion, 1960), p. 434.

this period of her life Mansfield enjoyed associating herself with Colette, having recognised that they both seemed to be re-enacting their childhoods in adulthood, through the medium of literature, an aspect discussed by Ruth Parkin-Gounelas:

> In 1915, at the very time references to Colette occurred in the journal and letters, Mansfield was reunited with her brother in London and was on the lookout for a discursive model to apply to the childhood experiences Chummie had helped her recall. Colette's novels provided just such a model (Parkin-Gounelas in Robinson, p. 38).

It is no coincidence that during this period, when Colette seemed never far from her thoughts, Mansfield, in Paris, ensconced in Carco's flat on the Left Bank, was beginning 'The Aloe', describing scenes from her childhood in New Zealand, through the medium of fiction.

The fascination with Colette had become so ingrained that over a year later, Murry still found himself applying Colettean references when referring to Mansfield:

> You are [...] the eternal woman [...] (You is a type – the wonderful type from Aspasia to B.B. Colette Vagabonde, and you above all moderns) naturally the tendency is to be extravagant and outrageous, retaliating against the hostility that puts up right and wrong against you.[33]

And *three* years on, Mansfield would use the same reference in a letter to Murry, thereby supporting my hypothesis that Colette as a creative inspiration remained long after her affair with Carco had been consigned to dust: 'I feel extraordinarily better and stronger with no pain at all, but I can't write you the letters I should like to because my "vagrant self" is uppermost – and you don't really know her or want to know her' (CL2, p. 188, 23 May 1918).

For Parkin-Gounelas, both Mansfield and Colette employed a compensatory, nostalgic tone in their reminiscences, the idea of belonging to a land long since abandoned. In so doing, as she notes, 'both writers were conforming to a turn-of-the-century tradition, sentimentalizing childhood as redemptive' (Parkin-Gounelas in Robinson, p. 38). Both Mansfield and Colette, however, were far too clear-eyed about the ways of the world to

---

33   C. A. Hankin, ed., *The Letters of John Middleton Murry to Katherine Mansfield* (London: Constable, 1983), pp. 53–54.

sugar-coat their stories and they both share a disconcerting habit of pulling their readers up short through situations, actions and dialogue. There was always a sense of intimacy whenever Mansfield mentioned Colette, as exemplified in this quotation mentioned earlier: 'What will you think of Colette, I wonder [...] and will you find her "sympathetic". For me she is more real than any woman I have ever known' (CL1, p. 282, early October 1916).

Colette's novels *L'Entrave*, and *La Vagabonde*, though very different from her more famous *Claudine* series of books, contained much for Mansfield to identify with, namely the predicament of how a bourgeois woman survives and develops in the environment of urban bohemia; the phrase 'femme seule' is a constant leitmotif. It is no coincidence then, that throughout 1915 the words 'femme seule' or 'dame seule' occur frequently in Mansfield's own writing, culminating in the story 'The Little Governess', written during this time in Paris:

> The little governess shrank into her corner as four young men in bowler hats passed, staring through the door and window. One of them, bursting with the joke, pointed to the notice *Dames Seules* and the four bent down the better to see the one little girl in the corner (177–78).

Thus, Colette's depictions of sexually burgeoning young girls finds its echoes in Mansfield; 'The Little Governess' is an uncomfortable depiction of a young girl, journeying alone through Europe, at the mercy of predatory males. The notion of 'dame seule' persisted till the end of Mansfield's life on both a physical and emotional level. It must be remembered that for most of Mansfield's time in France she *was* 'une femme seule' – reliant on writing letters for conversation which she could not obtain elsewhere; she even conducted her own personal 'dialogue for one' within her notebooks and diaries. On an emotional level, she would leave Murry increasingly behind, ultimately demonstrated by her decision to go to Fontainebleau and enter Gurdjieff's community alone. After her death, the French critics who were so swift in building the myth of Mansfield, may have in part been reacting against writers such as Colette, with her perceived immorality and excesses, the irony being that Mansfield was far more like her than they ever dared to realise.

L'Envers du music-hall

An analysis of *L'Envers du music-hall* reveals striking and hitherto un-acknowledged similarities with certain of Mansfield's stories and I believe shows how Colette's influence remained with her throughout her literary career. First published in 1913, it takes the form of various inter-connected vignettes, combining to create an exposé of the general sor-didness of French music-hall life, written heterogeneously as intimate first-person monologues, dialogues for one voice, or third person ac-counts.

Mansfield's own story, 'Pictures',[34] centres on just such a run-down squalid theatrical world, focusing on Miss Ada Moss, a middle-aged, down-at-heel contralto singer who, virtually penniless, moves from one theatrical/film agency to another in the hope of finding any sort of paid work which will enable her to pay her rent and buy food:

> 'Oh, dear,' thought Miss Moss, 'I am cold. I wonder why it is that I always wake up so cold in the mornings now. [...] It's not as if I was skinny – I'm just the same full figure that I used to be. No, it's because I don't have a good hot dinner in the evenings.'
>
> A pageant of Good Hot Dinners passed across the ceiling, each of them accompan-ied by a bottle of Nourishing Stout... (119).

Colette's vignette, 'L'Enfant de Bastienne', recounts similar experiences:

> [...] poussées par une rage d'estomac vide, Bastienne et sa campagne de chambre – une plate petite fille blonde – dépensent parfois leurs derniers sous dans la brasserie du Grand-Théâtre, après minuit, pour payer une canette de bière [...]
>
> Moi, si j'avais de l'argent, je me paierais bien un bon sandwich au jambon! [...]
>
> Moi, j'aimerais encore mieux une choucroute, avec beaucoup de ronds de sau-cisse...

---

34   First written in dialogue form in 1917 for *The New Age*, Mansfield rewrote 'Pic-tures' as straightforward narrative in 1919, and included it in *Bliss* in 1920.

118

Il arrive que la choucroute et le boudin grillé, qu'elles évoquent si fiévreusement, descendent, providentiels, entre les deux petites danseuses (57–58).[35]

The unusual image of the floating food, replicated in Mansfield's later story, is notably similar in both extracts. In addition, both protagonists are down-at-heel female performers in need of sustenance, dreaming of what they would eat if they had the money. Both Mansfield and Colette are adept at evoking the dismal nature of cheap lodgings, together with the general grime and sordidness of early-twentieth-century London and Paris. These few facts delineate for the reader more about the situation of Bastienne and Miss Moss than paragraphs of regular plot-driven narrative. The appearance of a bottle of beer in both extracts only serves to highlight the similarities of tone, content and form.

In Colette's story, 'L'Ouvroir', we find the following description: 'Maria Ancona chante, en défaisant ses jarretelles qui tiennent par des épingles anglaises, son corset au lacet rompu. Elle rit de voir sa chemise crevée sous le bras' (22). Miss Moss, in Mansfield's story 'Pictures', is portrayed in a similar fashion: 'Miss Moss [...] could not get out of bed because her nightdress was slit down the back [...] Still keeping on her nightdress she began to drag on her clothes [...] She went over to the chest of drawers for a safety pin' (121). The poverty inherent in both descriptions, the underwear and nightdress held together with safety pins, the hidden nature of this seediness implying the need to keep up appearances, the fact that Maria Ancona sings and Miss Moss is a singer – the similarities are once more striking.

One of Colette's favourite devices is the 'dialogue for one voice' – the second voice is reduced to a series of ellipses, as here, in the vignette, 'Nostalgie':

C'est moi, madame, c'est l'habilleuse. Madame a tout ce que Madame a besoin?
…!
Hein? n'est-ce pas qu'en voilà d'une surprise? [...] Et ça va? Toujours contente?
…
Moi de même, quoiqu'il y ait bien à dire là-dessus…
…
Oui, oui, je vous habille, bien entendu (70–71).

35   Colette, 'L'Enfant de Bastienne' in L'Envers du music-hall (Paris: Flammarion, 1913), to which all subsequent page references refer.

Mansfield first attempted a similar format in 1915, in a little-known piece entitled 'Stay-Laces', published in the *New Age* on 4 November 1915:

> MRS BUSK: [...] The man said today he had never seen longer or thicker hair.
> MRS BONE: ...!
> MRS BUSK: On the contrary. Good heavens! I'd give anything on earth to get rid of it [...] I'm awfully observant, as you know. .... New hat, too, isn't it?
> MRS BONE: ...?
> MRS BUSK: Oh, sweet! [36]

This technique suited Mansfield's theatrical nature, having had experience of being both a music-hall performer and silent movie 'extra' – indeed she would return to it in several more stories. The structure of these stories draws the reader in as if events are happening in front of one's eyes, so that sensations and emotions appear to be shared with the fictional characters portrayed. It is also a technique which allows for a certain comic effect, which both authors are always keen to exploit. However, Colette is not afraid of addressing social issues in her vignettes, for example how the poor are frequently too fearful to change their situation, as in 'L'Accompagnatrice', a dialogue for one, discussing the benefits of marriage:

> Ma place, ma place, mais c'est celle qui me convient! Qu'on m'y laisse, c'est tout ce que je demande. J'ai fait un peu la bête, dans mon jeune temps, mais j'en ai été si corrigée!... J'en suis restée craintive [...]
>
> ...?
>
> Me marier? Oh! non, j'aurais peur, à présent [...] Non, non, je vous assure, je suis bien comme je suis, je veux rester comme ça (66–67).

This vignette closely resembles Mansfield's 'The Lady's Maid' (written in France in December 1920, returning once more to Colette's technique), where a servant is depicted talking to a friend of her employer on the subject of marriage. This time the second person's silent 'speech' is incorporated into the monologue of the main character:

---

36   'Stay-Laces' (CS Alpers, p. 195). She returned to the format again in 1917, in a piece entitled, 'Two Tuppenny Ones, Please', printed in *The New Age* on 3 May 1917 and eventually published in *Something Childish*.

... No, madam, never now. Of course, I did think of it at one time. But it wasn't to be [...]

... Oh dear, I sometimes think ...whatever should I do if anything were to ... But, there, thinking's no good to anyone – is it madam? Thinking won't help. Not that I do it often (379–80).

Both protagonists are 'companion-servants', who have subjugated their own wishes for the comfort of others. This sacrifice extends even to their long-term prospects of marriage, which they have both passed over. Of course this leaves them fearful of the idea of change and vulnerable to the vagaries of an old age when they will no longer have the patronage of an employer. Once more, all the above notions are expressed in a few 'simple' sentences. A close reading of both stories reveals masterly control of pace and structure, pitch-perfect capturing of voice, a simple humane pleasure in the small satisfactions life has to offer, whilst all the time overshadowed by an awareness of the ways in which they can be jeopardised.

Colette enjoyed impersonating accents in her writing, as here, in 'Le Laissé-pour-compte': 'La mère Schmetz, qui raccommodait au promenoir les maillots de ses fils, en a failli quitter la place. Ça, une ardisde! ça, une tanzeuse! Ach! c'est une femme de drodoir, oui!' (83). Mansfield herself is particularly effective at writing dialogue, being constantly alert to the way people reveal themselves by their use of language. Both writers obviously enjoyed the comic effect which the imitation of accents produced in their work,[37] such as we find here in 'Prelude', commenced in Carco's flat on the Quai aux Fleurs, in 1915, with the work of Colette fresh in her mind:

Mrs Samuel Josephs [...] waddled down the garden path.

'Why not leave the chudren with be for the afterdoon, Brs. Burnell? They could go on the dray with the storeban when he comes in the eveding. Those thigs on the path have to go, dod't they?' (11).

37 Joanna Woods notes how 'Anne Estelle Rice describes Katherine at a party, which must have been around this time [1915], giving impersonations of Hollywood stars "with great success" and "repeatedly sliding down an ironing board, gallantly assisted by D. H. Lawrence"'. Joanna Woods, *Katerina: The Russian World of Katherine Mansfield* (Auckland: Penguin, 2001), p. 126.

Indeed, as I shall demonstrate in my chapter on the translations of Mansfield's work into French, the seeming inability of her translators to replicate the accents of Mansfield's original characters leads to a serious diminution of the comic effect of her writing, and possibly contributes to the fact that the influence of Colette on Mansfield's writing has, until now, been underestimated.

From the examples outlined above, it is clear that Mansfield had not only read Colette, but had assimilated various ideas and techniques and incorporated some of them into her own fiction.[38] Both writers were searching for a new mode of expression, capturing the transitory nature of life, bringing 'ordinary' moments and 'commonplace' people into sharp relief, whilst at the same time rejecting the literary conventions associated with an intricately plotted narrative, and instead relying on direct and indirect narrative, producing constantly shifting focuses of perspective. This

---

38 Little snippets from Colette's vignettes resurface continually in Mansfield's own stories:

[Colette] Elle se repose, avant de recrépir sa figure à l'aide de la grosse houppe et du tampon de coton carminé. (37)

[Mansfield] 'Mr. Bithem here yet?' asked Miss Moss, taking out an old dead powder-puff and powdering her nose mauve. (124)

[Colette] Je voudrais sortir d'ici. Mais dehors, c'est la pluie, la déprimante, la noire et désolante pluie méridionale [...] (45–46)

[Mansfield] Outside it is raining. I like to think of that cold drenched window behind the blind, and beyond [...] And all at one and the same moment I am arriving in a strange city [...] (433).

[Colette] Je ne connais, de la caissière, que son buste, incliné en avant par l'habitude d'écrire et le désir d'être aimable... Elle arrive aux Folies-Gobelins bien avant moi et s'en va à minuit. Marche-t-elle? a-t-elle des jambes, des pieds, un corps de femme? Tout cela a dû fondre, depuis vingt-quatre ans, derrière le petit bureau râpé. (68)

[Mansfield] I do not know why I have such a fancy for this little café [...] When she is not serving, she sits on a stool with her face turned, always to the window. Her dark-ringed eyes search among and follow after the people passing, but not as if she were looking for somebody. Perhaps, fifteen years ago, she was; but now the pose has become a habit. You can tell from her air of fatigue and hopelessness that she must have given them up for the last ten years, at least. ... (61)

notion leads both writers to lean towards a theatrical – and at times almost cinematic – quality in their work, via the use of monologue and dialogue.

Mansfield's contiguity with the French Symbolist and Decadent movements shows in her creative life where we see how some of her finest stories would not have come into being without her knowledge of Decadent and Symbolist texts. Sydney Kaplan confirms this viewpoint in concluding that:

> Mansfield's devotion to the '90s went deeper than fashionability and had a permanent effect on her literary career. [It] provided her with an ideal of the city which became linked with her own intensifying sense of sexual ambivalence and urge toward sexual experimentation. She had perceived that the world of the decadents was one of sexual ambiguity, a place where sexual boundaries broke down for the pure artist, where experience led to artistic creation (Kaplan, p. 72).

This world of sexual ambiguity and the breaking down of sexual boundaries is encapsulated in the three brief pages that comprise her story, 'Carnation'. Vincent O'Sullivan points to the fact that, 'One of the important matters biographers have approached too cautiously is the extent to which lesbianism touched Mansfield's adult life. Criticism also might find its presence more marked in her work than has yet been conceded' (O'Sullivan in Pilditch, p. 144). O'Sullivan argues that sexuality and sexual issues are, 'a feature of Mansfield which any perspective must include' (p. 145), though most do not. A 'Decadent' reading of Mansfield brings this issue to the fore in the story 'Carnation'.

The practical aesthetics of Symbolism include fluidity of rhythm, repetitions, echoes, and delicate evasions, all of which become trademarks of Mansfield's Modernist, narrative technique,[39] demonstrating, as Julia van Gunsteren notes, 'how Mansfield's imagery is faithful to Pound's dictum for poetry; that the poet should reject discursive analysis

---

39   See Symons, *Symbolist Movement*, p. 20. Kaplan also discusses this notion: 'Symons had defined symbolism as "a form of expression, at the best but approximate, essentially but arbitrary, until it has obtained the force of a convention, for an unseen reality apprehended by the consciousness". Katherine Mansfield translated this conception from its metaphysical frame of reference to a psychological one. The "unseen reality" loses its occult and spiritual dimensions for the most part with Mansfield, but it takes on, instead, those of psychic alienation and problems in communication between human beings, as well as the dimension of the *social* construction of reality' (Kaplan, pp. 64–65).

in favour of the poetic image – "that which presents an intellectual and emotional complex in an instant of time"' (Gunsteren, p. 171). Mansfield's use of symbols increases the emotional and intellectual capacity of a story, working on the reader in a powerful yet subliminal way. This story and others like it never harden into anything as clear-cut as allegory, but nevertheless, they resonate with suggestiveness. Melanie Hawthorne notes how:

> Modernism is characterised, not only by experimentation in form, but by its expression in both theme and form of reactions to the new gender configurations that resulted from nineteenth-century reforms (legal, educational, and electoral) as well as the social upheavals wrought by the Great War.[40]

Lisa Downing postulates that for certain commentators, 'Baudelaire is best remembered as a pioneer of poetics, experimenting with subject matter and prosody, giving birth to Symbolism, and developing the prose poem form'.[41] I would extend this notion and claim for Baudelaire a place as a primary stimulus of the twentieth-century Modernist short story, as exemplified in Mansfield's narrative technique.

---

40   Melanie Hawthorne, *Rachilde and French Women's Authorship: From Decadence to Modernism* (Lincoln: University of Nebraska Press, 2001), pp. 209–10.
41   Lisa Downing, *Desiring the Dead: Necrophilia and Nineteenth-Century French Literature* (Oxford: Legenda, 2003), p. 67.

Chapter Four
Translating Katherine Mansfield

> '*Mit Wölfen muss man heulen* seems to be a
> straightforward statement and a translator may
> write "Among wolves one must howl". The critic
> then says, "That is nonsense, isn't it? You should
> have written 'When in Rome, do as Rome does'."
> The translator replies, "But that is not what the
> author wrote." "No," says the critic, "but it is
> what he meant". And so the translator faces the
> question as to whether his function is to record
> the words of his original author or to give their
> meaning'.
>
> Theodore Savory, *The Art of Translation*
> (London: Jonathan Cape, 1968), p. 18.
>
> 'The translation of language is an exercise in
> comparison, the translation of texts, an exercise in
> interpretation'.
>
> Jean Delisle, *Translation: An Interpretive
> Approach* (Ottawa: University of Ottawa Press,
> 1988), p. 76.

Following Katherine Mansfield's death in 1923, critical reviews of her work started to appear in France, fuelling an interest which concentrated primarily on her life and personal writing, and only secondarily on her fiction. This thirst for biographical detail gave impetus to the translations of the *Letters* and *Journal* in 1931 and 1932 (which had first appeared in English in 1928 and 1927 respectively). (See Appendix F for a chronological list of Mansfield's primary works in English and French.) Within the space of a few years, translations of various volumes of her stories were also published. It was *Bliss* and *The Garden Party* which received most of the critical attention lavished on the stories in France, yet not even their fame could compete with the immediate and enduring popularity of the *Journal* and *Letters*.

In this chapter, I shall determine how the translations of her personal writing, together with her fiction, have influenced Mansfield's reputation in France, and highlight how her narrative technique (together with her personality), revealed in the original texts, has been diluted and even censored during the translation process. I shall highlight the fundamental problems of translating writing such as Mansfield's and determine, via the use of in-depth analysis of the translated texts, whether Mansfield's narrative and personal ideologies, together with literary nuances, survive translation from English to French. I shall provide examples of how her writing was edited, manipulated and mistranslated in order to aid the creation of the 'French' Katherine Mansfield. An examination will also be made of more than one translation of the same text, where such translations exist, to determine whether these newer translations help to demystify or promote the legend. Finally, I ask whether any of the translations, or the inadequacies of the translation process itself, contribute to the method of hagiography.

Of course, the issues to be discussed here extend beyond the remit of a single author. Translation theory inevitably encompasses a wide area of study, which can only be touched on in this chapter. Theories abound as to the 'correct' way to translate, what rules should be followed, what ideologies adhered to. (See Appendix G for Jean Delisle's summary of the characteristics of a literary text, with reference to the art of translation.) For Susan Petrilli: 'To translate is neither to "decodify" nor to "recodify". Such operations are doubtlessly part of the translative process, but they do not exhaust it. *In the first place to translate is to interpret*'.[1] Jeremy Munday considers that translation studies encompass the 'central recurring theme of "word-for-word" and "sense-for-sense" translation'.[2] Editorial manipulation notwithstanding, this chapter will highlight how difficult Mansfield's particular form of writing is to translate, and how with her fiction, French translators have consistently sought to replicate her words rather than interpret their meaning, thus diluting her artistic philosophy. For Jeremy Munday, the work of a translator may be summed up as follows:

1   Susan Petrilli, 'Translation and Semiosis. Introduction' in *Translation, Translation* (Amsterdam: Rodopi, 2003), ed. by Susan Petrilli, pp. 17–37 (p. 17).
2   Jeremy Munday, *Introducing Translation Studies: Theories and Applications* (Abingdon: Routledge, 2001), p. 18.

Translating is an intellectual process that consists in re-articulating a thought expressed in a context. Just as knowing how to write is not enough to make one a writer, knowing two languages is not enough to make one a translator (Munday, p. 28).

Margherita Ulrych concurs with the notion of having a 'flair' for translation, which goes beyond the notion of merely being a 'competent' translator and adds:

A translation is the same as an independent text, as far as the receiving culture is concerned, and a derivative text insofar as it is a reconstruction or recreation of another text and the result of the translator's mediating presence.[3]

In the nineteenth century a 'good' translation was, on the whole, perceived to be a literal translation; Mary Snell-Hornby declares that, 'the process of translating literature was seen to be one of reverbalising a written text in another language'.[4] In the first half of the twentieth century, this rigid adherence to the original text is challenged by the advent of Modernist movements, which, according to Lawrence Venuti, 'prize experiments with literary form as a way of revitalising culture. Translation is a focus of theoretical speculation and formal innovation'.[5] Several commentators, including Venuti, also note the advent of translation as manipulation, in other words using translation as a means to an end:

Yet the effects of translation are also social, and they have been harnessed to cultural, economic, and political agendas: evangelical programs, commercial ventures, and colonial projects, as well as the development of languages, national literatures, and avant-garde literary movements (Venuti, p. 5).[6]

---

3   Margherita Ulrych, 'Diversity, Uniformity and Creativity in Translation', in Petrilli, pp. 133–52 (p. 133).
4   Mary Snell-Hornby, 'Literary Translation as Multimedial Communication: On New Forms of Cultural Transfer', in Petrilli, pp. 477–86 (p. 477).
5   Lawrence Venuti, ed., *The Translation Studies Reader* (London: Routledge, 2000), p. 11. For Susan Bassnett: 'Much of the discussion in English on translation in theory and practice in the first half of the twentieth century notes the continuation of many of the Victorian concepts of translation – literalness, archaizing, pedantry and the production of a text of second-rate literary merit for an élite minority'. Susan Bassnett, *Translation Studies* (London: Routledge, 1991), p. 73.
6   Theo Hermans also notes the manipulatory aspect of translating: 'The practice of translation comprises the selection and importation of cultural goods from outside

No commentator, however, underestimates the *difficulties* of translating; for Lačesar Stančev:

> L'art de traduire est souvent un art plus difficile que celui d'écrire, car l'auteur a le droit de choisir des mots et des images pour donner forme à son idée initiale, tandis que le traducteur doit chercher dans un matériel nettement fixe une idée déterminée avec précision.[7]

Finally we arrive at an extreme viewpoint, noted by Susan Petrilli, where the translation may be perceived as a superior artistic creation to the original:

> Borges maintains that a translation never catches up with the original chronotopically, but may surpass it in terms of artistic rendition. Understanding 'fidelity' as creativity, and not imitation, repetition, a literal copy in another language, the translating text must establish a relation of alterity with the translated text.[8]

Here, we are far-removed from the literal translation of the nineteenth century and earlier and have arrived at an 'artistic reinterpretation' of an original literary text, in order to convey best the stylistic nuances and

a given circuit, and their transformation into terms which the receiving community can understand, if only in linguistic terms, and which it thus recognises, to some extent at least, on its own'. Theo Hermans, 'Paradoxes and Aporias in Translation and Translation Studies', in *Translation Studies: Perspectives on an Emerging Discipline*, ed. by Alessandra Riccardi (Cambridge: Cambridge University Press, 2002), pp. 10–23 (p. 17). Venuti also points out: 'Other theories have assumed a hermeneutic concept of language as interpretation, constitutive of thought and meaning, where meanings shape reality and are inscribed according to changing cultural and social situations' (Venuti, p. 6).

7   Lačesar Stančev, 'Traducteurs, Semeurs de Rêves', in *The Nature of Translation: Essays on the Theory and Practice of Literary Translation*, ed. by James S. Holmes (The Hague: Mouton, 1970), pp. 175–81 (p. 180). This dichotomy vis à vis the origins of a translated work is also noted as a duality of *purpose* by Cees Koster: 'A translation is a strange phenomenon, because it is always two things: on the one hand the status of a translation is that of an independent text: once produced, a translation, in its own cultural environment, functions in a way similar to that of any other text in that environment; on the other hand its status is that of a derivative text: a translation is a representation, or a reconstruction, or a reproduction, of another text'. Cees Koster, 'The translator in between texts: on the textual presence of the translator as an issue in the methodology of comparative translation description', in Riccardi, pp. 24–37 (p. 25).

8   Susan Petrilli, 'Translating with Borges', in Petrilli, pp. 517–30 (p. 517).

meaning of the original. I shall highlight in a later part of this chapter which translational methods are used for the works of Mansfield and which of these translational styles seem to be the most effective in conveying Mansfield's artistic technique and philosophy.

Initial Editorial Bias

The French critic Louis Gillet, a Catholic, an anglophile, and a reader of *The Adelphi* (the English periodical which Murry edited at this time), was the first to draw attention to the dead artist in France. As an 'antidote' to the notoriety of such home grown writers as Rachilde and Colette, the veneration of an 'innocent', feminine, child-like writer, was encouraged by the overwhelmingly male, reactionary, literary and critical establishment in France (see Chapter Five). Jeremy Munday cites André Lefevere in order to underline how this type of literary manipulation is not uncommon:

> Lefevere focuses particularly on the examination of 'very concrete factors' that systematically govern the reception, acceptance or rejection of literary texts; that is, 'issues such as power, ideology, institution and manipulation'. [...] The people involved in such power positions are the ones Lefevere sees as 'rewriting' literature and governing its consumption by the general public (Munday, p. 128).

Lefevere writes that translation is the most obviously recognisable form of rewriting and is potentially the most influential since 'it is able to project the image of an author and/or those works beyond the boundaries of their culture of origin'.[9] The time was ripe for a Mansfield figure to be launched by the French critical establishment, and the tide of this new critical process would carry her reputation to the limits of subjective, interpretative criticism. If one then adds to this critical distortion the *presentation* of her writing to the French reading public through the translations – the subject of this chapter – then we begin to understand how little of the essential Mansfield, both as a personality and an author,

9   André Lefevere, *Translation, Rewriting and the Manipulation of Literary Fame* (London: Routledge, 1992), p. 9.

actually survived the journey to France. My argument in this chapter therefore, contends that, in the case of Mansfield, the translation of the written word is less important than an assessment of editorial principles – a prism through which her personal writing is deflected and distorted.

As I outlined in the previous section, translations are frequently manipulated to serve a specific function. For Ulrych:

> [Translators] are always present as a mediating and manipulating force and are called upon to activate creative strategies. The degree of and type of manipulation and creativity depends on the socio-cultural circumstances in which the act of translation takes place, the genre of the ST [source text], the function or functions of the translation, the mode of transmission as well as on the translation strategy adopted (Ulrych in Petrilli, p. 149).

The fact that Mansfield was so well received in France is due in no small part to the anti-intellectualist climate prevalent at the time (discussed in Chapter Five); Ulrych underlines this notion of exterior forces governing the translation process:

> The most far-reaching development in the field of translation studies has been the 'discovery' of the historical, cultural and social dimensions of translation which involve socio-political forces such as ideology and power. [...] Taking account of socio-political, ideological and cultural components offers a means to understand the complex, manipulative textual processes that take place in translation: how a text is selected for translation, what role the translator plays in that selection, what role an editor or publisher plays, what criteria determine the strategies that the translator employs, how a text is received in the target system (pp. 133–34).

So far as the *Journal* and *Letters* were concerned, the critics had decided that Mansfield was an essentially spiritual writer, seeking hidden truths to explain the meaning of life. As Ulrych points out:

> The translated discourse can exert a subliminal effect on the recipients of the TT [target text], particularly when it appears to be at its most latent. Since the receiving culture tacitly accepts that the translator is 'invisible', and is generally unaware of his or her discursive presence, it has no power to withstand or be alert to any manipulation that is being exerted through the process of translation. The more transparent the text, the more willing the TC [target culture] audience are to suspend their disbelief and accept the interpretation offered by the TT (p. 143).[10]

---

10   Susan Bassnett concurs with this argument: 'Translation [is seen as] one of the processes of literary manipulation, whereby texts are rewritten across linguistic

In turn, I shall reveal how the reader of Mansfield in French is being manipulated without his or her knowledge.

Translating the *Letters*

The first French edition of the *Letters* is an abridged version of the English original which appeared in two volumes in 1928. The French version is condensed into one volume; nearly all the letters in the second English volume are reproduced, compared with only about half the letters in the first volume, containing earlier letters where Mansfield is at her most sarcastic, youthfully humorous and condemnatory. With maturity and the consciousness of her impending death from tuberculosis, Mansfield's personal writing becomes more philosophical in tone, and *these* are the letters that make up the bulk of the French edition.

Two of the most common reasons for the omission of certain letters are either because of translational difficulties (Mansfield is as fond of impersonation and the use of colloquialisms in her letters and personal writing as she is in her fiction), or more importantly, because what she has written does not correlate with the incipient French critical perception of her character. Detailed textual examination also reveals an editing out of passages, sentences, sometimes merely phrases, from some of the translated letters themselves.

Most surprising of all is the stance taken in the preface to this first edition, written by Gabriel Marcel, which is hagiographical in both tone

boundaries and that rewriting takes place in a very clearly inscribed cultural and historical context [...] A reflection involves a mirroring, a copy of an original; a refraction involves changes of perception, and this is an image that is useful to describe what happens when a text crosses from one culture to another. Moreover, refraction theory necessarily involves a consideration of literary evolution and thus places translation in a time continuum, rather than being an activity that happens in a vacuum' (Bassnett, p. xvii).

and content.[11] On her decision to enter Gurdjieff's esoteric community at Fontainebleau shortly before her death he remarks:

> J'ai entendu des admirateurs non-chrétiens de Katherine Mansfield déplorer qu'elle ne se soit pas réfugiée de préférence dans un couvent; mais précisément, la caractère arbitraire, discordant, et pour tout dire inesthétique de cette résolution dernière me paraît justement souligner de la façon la plus poignante ce qu'il y eut d'intenable, de désespéré dans l'attitude de cet être si manifestement visité par la Grâce, mais si étranger en même temps à toute conscience de cette Visitation qu'il lui fallut fuir jusque dans les bras d'une pauvre hérésie mort-née Celui qui sans relâche l'appelait par son Nom éternel:

> Ah! fondest, blindest, weakest,
> I am He whom thou seekest!
> Thou drawest love from thee, who drawest Me! (FL1, pp. xvii–xviii).

The religious tone of this introduction, together with its attempt to re-define, in Christian terms, Mansfield's decision to enter Gurdjieff's theo-sophical colony at Fontainebleau, gives some clue as to the translational and editorial stance of this volume of her personal writing in translation.

Defining the editorial principles for translation is not difficult, for many of the letters and passages omitted can be categorised. My first category of omissions in French, contains anything deemed particularly distasteful or shocking: 'Paris looked exactly like anywhere else: it smelled faintly of lavatories' (L1i, p. 8, 19 March 1915). In the French translation, the last phrase is omitted entirely, with suspension points re-placing the offending words: 'Paris avait exactement le même aspect que tout le reste...' (FL1, p. 23). Similarly, letters containing unsuitable mater-ial as quoted below are more often missed out entirely:

> He got behind the man and suddenly thrust his hand between the man's legs. You should have heard the yell he gave (L1i, p. 31-32, 23 May, 1915).

> Sailors, who spend their time half in the urinals, half flirting with the girls (L1i, p. 100, 14 January 1918).

11   Gabriel Marcel (1889–1973), philosopher, editor and critic, converted to Catholi-cism at the age of 40, about the same time as he was writing his articles on Mans-field.

The following passages from translated letters, where Mansfield attacks the French, disappear from the first French edition:

Two dirty little froggies [...] the most hideous touts (L1i, p. 20, 27 March 1915).

I wonder if it is the war that has made the people here [in Paris] so hideous or if I am out of joint. They appear to me a nation of concierges (L1i, p. 32, 24 May 1915).

Yet I am very sincere when I say I hate the French. They have no heart – no heart at all (L1i, p. 114, 27 January 1918).

Another thing I hate the French bourgeoisie for is their absorbed interest in evacuation. What is constipating and what not? [...] Also the people of the village have a habit of responding to their serious needs (I suppose by night) down on the shore round the palm-trees [...] The other day one palm-tree had a placard nailed on it 'chiens seulement' (L1i, p. 124, 6 February 1918).

Translational difficulties also give rise to omissions in the French translation. Mansfield's love of imitating spoken colloquialisms in the written word, her lapses into verse, in fact most of the essential ingredients of her comic writing are simply removed from this first French edition:

Injections, chère
In my derrière
Driven into a muscular wad
With a needle thick
As a walking stick
How can one believe in God! (L1i, p. 223, 13 January 1919).

Words such as 'effugions', 'furrin', 'umberellar', 'bin and gone', 'pignig', 'sangwiches', 'bregglechick', are all swallowed up and either disappear completely or are normalised into gramatically correct words, e.g. 'umberellar' – 'parapluie'. Anything risqué in her comedy is axed; the letter in which the following quotation appears is omitted entirely: 'My laundry [...] there was a bill for 3.15 [...] I shall have to cut myself a little pair of football shorts out of Le Radical, I can see that' (L1i, p. 41, 12 December 1915). Her most overtly political statements are censored out of the translated letters:

I arrived at Paddington to find the station crowded with Sinn Feiners who had just arrived from Wormwood Scrubs (...) I very nearly joined them, and I rather wish I had (L1i, p. 71, 16 May 1916).

What did my son die for, Sir? To keep the war going or, to end it, Sir? To keep it going, Sir, until everybody else's son is as dead as he! (L1i, p. 215, 27 October 1918).

[...] and then the loathsome press about Germany's cry for food (L1i, p. 218, 13 November 1918).

Though neither an outright pacifist nor a feminist, she brought political realism to her fiction, though often in a covert manner. In her personal writing however, she was much more forthright in her views – and this is one aspect of her personality denied to the French reader in this initial translation of the *Letters*.

The biographical evidence available today clearly portrays the love-hate relationship between Mansfield and her adoring, self-effacing companion, Ida Baker. In the letters she is frequently referred to as 'the Mountain', in reference to her size. Accounts of 'the Mountain's' actions result in comically vituperative statements, which, since they were never translated, the French knew nothing about.

However – let her go. And I shall never shoot her because the body would be so difficult to dispose of after. One couldn't make it into a neat parcel or put it under a hearth stone, and she would never burn (L1i, p. 251, 12 October 1919).

When the Mountain brought me my early-morning tea this morning she whispered, tenderly: 'Do you think it would be a good idea to change one ton of coal for two of large anthracite?!' (L1i, p. 224, February 1919).

My final category of translational difficulties in the *Letters* involves Mansfield's blasphemous statements. She was not a practising Christian, and in fact her search for the spiritual was of a much more esoteric nature, leading her ultimately to join Gurdjieff and his followers at Fontainebleau, where she died. The reactionary Catholic critics who so swiftly claimed her (see Chapter Five), ignored this aspect of her personality, and the French editors of her work removed offending items such as these from the translations:

Yes, I know that God is a monster and there are moments when one realises the war (L1i, p. 163, 12 May 1918).

Just as I left I said out loud: Thank you very much, it's been lovely – But to whom? To the Lord who gave me consumption? (L1i, p. 163, 12 May 1918).

The translator of the *Letters*, Madeleine T. Guéritte (who also translated *Something Childish*), translates 'Oh dear' as 'Oh Seigneur' on at least two occasions, when no religious connotation need be present at all, adding to the religious and spiritual tone of the French version.

In 1951, a new edition of the *Letters* appears in England. It is in no way a revision of the earlier edition, but to all intents and purposes a completely new version. The jacket notes state:

We have been allowed various small glimpses of this story previously. But only now for the first time, in one of the most remarkable series of unexpurgated love letters ever printed, is substantially the whole of this great and tender and moving story revealed [...] Mr Murry has also restored all passages omitted from those letters previously published in part (L2, inside cover notes).

Immediately, in the use of the term 'love letters', the reader can discern Murry's altered editorial stance from the original, more general edition, published twenty years previously. There are also two inaccuracies in the above quotation; firstly in the word 'unexpurgated' which, since Murry's death and the subsequent publication of the five-volume *Collected Letters of Katherine Mansfield*, we now know to be false; secondly in the phrase, 'restored all passages', for exactly the same reason – omissions still remain. Thus, an English reader would be forgiven for concluding that they were reading a version free from editorial manipulation, which I shall demonstrate was not the case.

The translation of this edition, *Lettres à John Middleton Murry*, comprising three volumes published from 1954–57, is viewed not as a replacement for the earlier French edition however, but rather as an *addition*. The original translation remains in print, entitled *Lettres 1915–1922*, with no apology for the expurgations which are obvious when letters appearing in both volumes are compared. In the preface to this new French edition, André Bay, Mansfield's French editor, writes:

De la part du mari, publier cette correspondance amoureuse, n'est-ce pas, comme l'ont prétendu certains critiques anglais, faire preuve d'une grave indélicatesse?

[…] C'est un acte d'humilité et une preuve supplémentaire du dévouement […] On a reproché à J. Middleton Murry de nous donner qu'un aspect de cette correspondance. Il manque, dit-on, ses propres lettres, comme s'il était vraiment impossible d'en imaginer le contenu en lisant celles de Katherine. On peut faire confiance à J. Middleton Murry. Il n'a pu agir que pour de justes motifs. Au lecteur d'en être digne (FL2i, pp. 4–5).

Murry's editorial stance – obviously questioned in England – is thus vindicated by the person responsible for publishing Mansfield's works in France. Christiane Mortelier notes that, 'André Bay, the general secretary of Stock Publishers, Paris, met John Middleton Murry and acknowledged his help when drafting his prefaces and notes to the French Editions of K.M.'s works'.[12] Collusion, or at least misinformation, seems an obvious outcome, since Murry was providing biographical information subsequently used by André Bay. Mortelier continues:

The romantic elements of the legend were strengthened into melodrama as the result of the publication of personal and previously unpublished material, the *Letters to John Middleton Murry* […] These letters, relating her impossible search for a completely satisfying love-relationship with her husband, were now read as a tragic 'roman d'amour' (Mortelier, p. 256).

More surprising still, this later French edition of the *Letters* is no longer in print and the only version readily available today in France is the one volume edition originally published in 1931, with no letters earlier than 1915.

The translation itself is a literal rendering of the original. Comments and criticisms against the French are all now translated, as are many of Mansfield's more cutting and incisive remarks. I shall demonstrate in the next chapter how certain French critics viewed this 'new' Mansfield as a threat to the woman writer they had thus far idolised, which perhaps explains why this much 'franker' edition of Mansfield's personal writing was abandoned in favour of the earlier, more severely edited, less vituperative Mansfield, who corresponds more favourably with the legend-

12   Christiane Mortelier, 'The Genesis and Development of the Katherine Mansfield Legend in France', *AUMLA*, Nov. 1970, 252–63 (p. 262, n. 40). This collaboration did not end with the *Journal*, for in the endnotes to OR, André Bay states, 'Il reste que les dates de composition sont des points de repère quand une œuvre est, comme celle-ci, indissociable de la vie. Avec l'aide de John Middleton Murry, nous avons dressé une table aussi précise que possible' (p. 717).

a *y* character now firmly entrenched in people's minds. Yet the most r.oticeable aspect of Mansfield's writing style missing from this translation is once more the humour:

> I sent your toospeg cream after you today. What an awful man on this p.c.! […] After that I say no more, Betsy (L2, p. 658, July 31, 1922).

> Je vous ai envoyé tout à l'heure votre dentifrice. Quel affreux bonhomme, sur cette carte! […] Bon, je me tais (FL2iii, p. 321).

The formality of the 'vous' form, adds a completely different tone to the letter which, in English, is intimate and colloquial. The comedic value of 'toospeg' is lost, as is the use of the nickname 'Betsy' which Mansfield frequently used when addressing Murry. Another example of Mansfield's typically jocular, light hearted style including yet another childish nickname for Murry appears here:

> The idle time of year is coming, Jaggle, when you can sit outside with a piece of bread and butter on your knee and watch it fristle – frisle. (How do you spell that?) (L2, p.18, March 20, 1915).

> Voici venir le temps de la paresse, cette époque de l'année où on peut rester assis, dehors, une tartine sur les genoux, à écouter le beurre grésiller (FL2i, pp. 34–35).

The letters make compulsive reading *because* of the irony, the jocular tone, the playfulness. The French perceived a very different Mansfield, more serious in character, much less playful – a grown woman, with the *innocence* of a child, writing to her lover in a more or less serious tone. In the following sentence, Mansfield's wit, always pithy, pared down and to-the-point, is transformed into two lines of dull French:

> My work is snapping at my heels but I have to Down Rover it, so far (L2, p. 13, March 13, 1915).

> Mon travail est comme un chien qui jappe méchamment à mes talons, mais il me faut le laisser faire, pour le moment (FL2i, p. 28).

Mansfield the mimic and gifted raconteur peppers so much of her correspondence with the accents and colloquialisms of those around her, as here retelling a conversation with a Cornish maid:

As I wrote that I have kept up a running fire with Mrs Honey. *She* says I ought to have children. 'It might maäke eë a deal stronger, and they do be such taking little souls.' I agreed and asked her to order me a half-dozen. The other night her husband 'waited' for her outside, and she asked me to 'come and look at him on the bal-*coney*'. A fine, neat old man, walking a bit shaky. She said, 'He don't look his age, do eë? He wur a rare *haändsome* lad' (L2, p. 286, 6 June, 1918).

Après avoir écrit ces mots, j'ai subi un feu roulant de la part de Mrs. Honey. Elle dit que je devrais avoir des enfants. 'Cela vous rendrait plus forte, et ces petites créatures, cela vous prend le cœur.' Je lui ai répondu que j'étais bien d'accord, et qu'elle veuille bien m'en commander une demi-douzaine. L'autre soir, son mari l'attendait, dehors ; elle m'a demandé d'aller le regarder du balcon. C'est un beau vieillard soigné, qui marchait d'un pas un peu chancelant. 'Il ne porte pas son âge, n'est-ce pas ? Il était si beau garçon' (FL2ii, p. 68).

There is no attempt made in the French to mimic the rural accent of the maid, no comedy in the mispronunciation of the word 'balcony', no attendant meaning in the emphasising of the word 'waited', implying the actions of a much younger man waiting to escort his sweetheart; the deep seated affection between the elderly couple, brought to life in the use of the words 'a rare *haändsome* lad', deliberately emphasised by Mansfield to show how much she herself had been captivated by them – all of this is lost in translation. The underlining of the word *she*, also implies some sort of friction in her life with regards to the possibility of having children. All these nuances are lost in translation.

The first volume of the *Collected Letters of Katherine Mansfield* appears in England in 1984, followed over the next twelve years by three more volumes (with a projected fifth and final volume still to appear). These unexpurgated editions are invaluable to any Mansfield scholar, since, in many cases, they reveal what Mansfield actually wrote as opposed to what Murry wanted us to believe she had written, especially when compared to the earlier editions of her work; they have been a critical factor in bringing a true sense of Mansfield's personality to the reader. And yet, more than twenty years after the original publication of the first volume in English, a French translation has yet to appear, once more leaving the French reader with incomplete and incorrect reference points for Mansfield, brought about by old, inaccurate translations. As Lawrence Venuti points out:

> A translation participates in the 'afterlife' [...] of the foreign text, enacting an interpretation that is informed by a history or reception ('the age of its fame'). This interpretation does more than transmit messages; it recreates the values that accrued to the foreign text over time (Venuti, p. 11).

If a French reader wants to read the *Letters* of Mansfield today, then the only edition currently still widely available is the original, incomplete edition of 1931, heavily edited by Murry, with many more 'offending' or difficult passages removed by the translator. This old, incomplete edition has reinforced the false perception of Mansfield as a writer and as a personality, in France. Augusto Ponzio reflects on this idea of translations becoming barriers to the original texts:

> The stiffening, the ossification of words, that codify, block and paralyze thought, this is but one aspect of the general sclerotization of human signs which must be restored by the forgotten resources of language understood as an infinite modelling process, as writing.[13]

Since Mansfield's death, there has been, in England, a steady issue of Mansfield's works, each edition fuller than the last, shedding light on her persona and aiding our understanding of her complex character. In France, the reader is stranded with an ossified literary figure, purporting falsely reactionary ideas through deliberately sabotaged works.

One particularly striking detail concerning the four volume definitive collection of the *Letters*, is that the first one hundred or so pages of the first volume contain letters never previously published, for the most part having been written by Mansfield to various correspondents prior to her relationship with Murry, and only collected after his death. They form an interesting glimpse into Mansfield's early life, containing letters to her first husband George Bowden, and youthful suitors such as William Orton and Garnet Trowell: 'A man is coming to spend the evening with me. I don't feel entirely responsible for my actions. I want to smile mysteriously and to run away' (CL1, pp. 100–01, to William Orton, autumn 1910). However, further evidence is found of Murry's editorial bias, for deliberately omitted from both his editions of the *Letters* is a letter written to him in May 1913 from Mansfield, where she discusses divorcing her first husband: 'My letter from G. [George Bowden] says

---

13   Augusto Ponzio, 'The Same Other: The Text and Its Translations' in Petrilli, pp. 55–68 (p. 63).

divorce papers will be served in a day or two. No damages and no costs for us to pay' (CL1, p. 122, 13 May 1913). Even in 1951, until Murry's revised edition of the letters was published, it was still not common knowledge that Mansfield was a married woman when she met Murry and that they merely acted out the role of man and wife for several years until they could be legally married.[14] Murry briefly discusses this state of affairs in a note to the 1951 edition of the *Letters*, but chooses not to include any letter which mentions the divorce.[15] Removing letters which confirms this state of affairs thus lessens the impact and in part masks the truth regarding their marital status.

Translating the *Journal*

The *Journal* of 1927 meets with almost identical treatment in translation as the *Letters*.[16] The first French edition of 1931 is remarkable because of the items missed out of a seemingly *unexpurgated* version, since there is no obvious difference in size, as was the case with the *Letters*. The French reader has no idea that his version is not identical to the English original, and a certain deception is therefore being undertaken by the editor and translator of the work. Every aspect of Mansfield's personal writing deemed unsuitable in the *Letters* and omitted, receives similar treatment in the translation of the *Journal*. Details which might sound

14   The promised divorce papers cited above never materialised, as George Bowden withdrew his petition and in fact Murry and Mansfield weren't married until 3 May 1918, the divorce papers having finally come through the day before.

15   The note reads: 'After a few weeks we recognised our love for one another. We became lovers, and expected to be married soon. But, for some reason, Katherine's husband, whom she had left shortly after their marriage three years before, delayed divorcing her for six years. We were not actually married until May 3, 1918' (L2, p. 1).

16   Philip Waldron notes that: 'The [manuscript] material consists of four diaries which, like most diaries, are copious in early January but quickly peter out; some thirty notebooks and exercise books; and several hundred loose sheets of paper. There is no evidence whatsoever that Mansfield ever had publication in mind'. Philip Waldron, 'Katherine Mansfield's Journal', *Twentieth-Century Literature*, 20, 1 (January 1974), 11–18 (p. 11).

shocking and especially any mention of sex, physical descriptions of illnesses, sarcasm or evidence of moral laxity, are censored:

[On sexual attraction:]

Heaven knows what memories she had of taking M. Roué his hot water, of being found by M. Paul, looking for his shirt stud on his bedroom floor, on her charming little hands and her still more delicious knees! (J1, p. 31, May 1915).

[On the illness of her kitten:]

It had gastric trouble, acute constipation, with a distended belly, and canker in both ears (J1, p. 97, 20 September 1918).

[On telling falsehoods:]

When he asked any young lady in the room to hold up her hand if she had been chased by a wild bull, and as nobody else did I held up mine (though of course I hadn't) (J1, p. 55, February 1916).

Omissions of comic writing includes the following description of childbirth:

The young woman blushed and lowered her voice. 'I got her to...' And she paused to find a very *medical, private* word to describe washing… 'To *navigate* with a bottle of English water,' she said, 'but it isn't all away yet' (J1, p. 129, September 1919).

Colloquialisms abound in the *Journal* and the translation makes no attempt to convey them; 'awful crool' becomes 'des misères terribles' , 'grownupedness' – 'Quand on est grand', 'It has all been mush of a mushness' – 'C'était toujours à peu près la même chose'. The comic, light-hearted tone of the words in English is straitjacketed into normality in French.

One feature of Mansfield's personal writing which is not present in the *Letters* but which is frequently found in the *Journal* is the mention of personal details, such as 'I decided to faire les ongles de mes pieds' or 'washed my hair'. The majority of these details are painstakingly removed in the French translation. Other examples of omissions include:

I feel a bit more cheerful today because I don't look quite so revolting as I have done (J1, p. 23, 2 February 1915).

A vague stomach ache in my bath (J1, p. 86, 21 June 1918).

Had my hands done (J1, p. 22, 26 January 1915).

These interesting snippets of ordinary life tucked in between more serious writing, are a constant reminder to the reader of Mansfield's down-to-earth nature. Since the French were obsessed with the *spiritual* aspect of her persona, these commonplaces would have detracted from the saint-like image. They also refer to her appearance – her body – so their suppression contributes to an erasure of the physical Mansfield in favour of this perceived spiritual persona.

A particular translational problem attending this personal writing is that it is Mansfield herself who is speaking; no excuses can be made, nothing couched in other terms. Yet for the French editor, what she says has to ring true with the publicly created persona. It is an easy task, therefore, eradicating the moments when she does not fit into this image, and it is far simpler to omit them rather than attempt to justify them.

In 1954, a new edition of the *Journal* appears in England. Murry's preface states: 'In this edition of Katherine Mansfield's *Journal*, passages have been restored which for various reasons were suppressed in the original edition of 1927' (J2, p. ix). As with the *Letters*, careful editing had resulted in a severely expurgated first version, which in no way fully reflected what the author had written. The 1954 edition is intended to restore the balance. The French translation, which appears in 1956, is a literal rendering of the original, although many translational difficulties are still presented by poems, colloquial peculiarities of language, and generally humorous language. However, rather than resorting to suppression, as in the earlier version, any problematical phraseology now resurfaces as straightforward French prose – much of the verve and vitality of the original disappears. 'Verses Writ in a Foreign Bed', omitted from the first French edition, perhaps because of its perceived 'blasphemous' content, as well its peculiarities of style, is now reinstated and transformed into the following:

Verses writ in a Foreign Bed.
Almighty Father of All and Most Celestial Giver
 Who has granted to us thy children a heart and lungs and liver;
If upon me should descend thy beautiful gift of tongues

Incline not thine Omnipotent ear to my remarks on lungs (J1, pp. 74–75, February 1918).

Prière composée sur un lit étranger.
Dieu tout-puissant et éternel, qui dans votre miséricorde avez donné à vos enfants un cœur, des poumons et un foie; daignez, s'il m'arrivait jamais de recevoir le don des langues, détourner votre Oreille toute-puissante de la phrase que j'ai dite sur les poumons (FJ2, p. 233).

Not only does the French version omit the humorous tone of the original, but by turning Mansfield's rhyme into prayer-like prose, the French version appears much more serious and even religious in tone, categorically opposite to the effect Mansfield must have intended. Perhaps, in the French version, other ways could have been found to bring out the comical, tongue-in-cheek tone of this particular passage; as Susan Bassnett points out, 'Equivalence in translation […] should not be approached as a search for sameness, since sameness cannot even exist between two TL [target language] versions of the same text, let alone between the SL [source language] and TL version' (Bassnett, p. 29).

The beginning of the draft of a letter to Frederick Goodyear, edited out of both the English and French first editions, is translated as follows:

Never did cowcumber lie more heavy on a female's buzzum than your curdling effugion which I have read twice and won't again if horses drag me (J2, p. 108, March 1916).

Jamais bombe n'est tombée plus lourdement sur un cœur de femme que cette chaude effusion glacée que j'ai lue deux fois; je ne la relirais pas trois, même si l'on m'y forçait (FJ2, p. 202).

The witty, colloquial style of the English original is here converted into dull, lacklustre French.

Murry's introduction to the original edition of 1927, is included in the French definitive edition of 1956, once more vindicating, nearly thirty years later, all the falsehoods contained within it. Thus, while in England a fuller appraisal of Mansfield's personal writing could now take place, in France, however, the presuppositions surrounding the 'French' Mansfield are merely strengthened by this latest translation

One of the most significant episodes in Mansfield's adult life, and well documented by her in her notebooks, is her brief love affair with

Francis Carco, in February 1915, as discussed in Chapter Two. In her notebooks of the time, Mansfield, having temporarily ended her love affair with Murry, recounts the journey she undertook to the occupied war zone at Gray, to visit Carco, using the pre-arranged excuse of an aunt's illness to get her through the checkpoints. She made use of these notes in her semi-autobiographical story 'An Indiscreet Journey', written in May 1915, published posthumously in 1924 in *Something Childish*; in France, the story is not translated until 1950.

In the 1927 English edition of the *Journal*, the Carco episode fills four pages, in the form of a couple of unposted letters together with a long description of her arrival in Gray and initial meeting with Carco. The first French *Journal* of 1931 contains a translation of these pages with several omissions, including a whole paragraph outlining the dangerous and foolhardy nature of the expedition, the duplicity involved and the connection with another man. It was not until 1954, when the *Definitive Journal* was published (the 'Carco' episode now extending to six larger-formatted pages), that it was possible to see how much had been expurgated from the original *English* edition, notwithstanding the further removal of various passages in the French edition.

Details of a sexually explicit nature, anything which would have revealed that Mansfield had journeyed illegally to a war zone for a brief sexual liaison with a Frenchman she barely knew, the calculating tone of this 'experience', all this had been removed from the original English edition, including the following:

> Beside me on a chair is a thick leather belt and his sword. He left at nearly eight o'clock. I am just up. [...] We spent a queer night [...] F. quite naked making up the fire with a tiny brass poker – so natural and so beautiful (J2, p. 75, February 20, 1915).

> We stayed together a little, but always laughing. The whole affair seemed somehow so ridiculous, and at the same time so utterly natural. There was nothing to do but laugh (J2, p. 77).

> The sword, the big ugly sword, but not between us, lying in a chair. The act of love seemed somehow quite incidental, we talked so much. It was so warm and delicious lying curled in each other's arms (J2, p. 78).

A misrepresentation of words occurs when the *Journal* of 1954 states 'where he had taken a room for me' (J2, p. 75) – a case of Murry restoring his original expurgation. In the original 1927 edition, Murry had written 'where *they* had taken a room for me' (J1, p. 25, my italics). The use of the word 'they', implies a much more impersonal, innocent reason for a journey and is much less difficult to explain than the word 'he', with its attendant notion that Mansfield is a 'femme seule'. I contend this was no mere typing error on Murry's part, but was, rather, a deliberate misrepresentation and falsification of what Mansfield had actually written, in order to protect her posthumous 'reputation'.

In the second French edition of 1956, the above episode is accurately translated, including the reinstatement of the word 'he' (FJ2, p. 157). Because Mansfield's original description is so matter-of-fact in tone, written almost as a form of 'reportage' – there is little to determine her personal style in these pages – it is not difficult for the French translator to render accurately both the tone and content of the episode, even though it is still possible to distinguish a very slight watering down of this matter-of-fact attitude of the original into something vaguely more romantic:

> L'épée, cette grosse épée si laide, mais pas posée entre nous. J'ai été à lui, mais cela paraît une chose d'une importance assez secondaire, nous avions tant à nous dire! Nous étions délicieusement bien, blottis l'un contre l'autre (FJ2, p. 161).

The phrase 'j'ai été à lui', when compared with 'the act of love', sounds more passive and submissive than the forthright and impersonal English version.

Francis Carco would, after her death (and once she had become famous), become one of the upholders of the Mansfield legend in France, penning a number of articles and discussing his relationship with her in various chapters of his autobiography, as I shall demonstrate in the next chapter. Everything that he published, however, was done so *prior* to the second edition of the *Journal* in the fifties. Thus, the general French reader is unaware of the sexual aspect of Carco's relationship with Mansfield, and he is therefore able to talk of a relationship, 'folle d'ailleurs, mais absolument pure' between the two of them and in words of a similar vein contribute to the hagiography of Mansfield's personality in France (Carco, *Montmartre*, p. 190).

Another example of the prudishness of both Murry and the French translators occurs over the use of the word 'urine'. This is what Mansfield wrote about her taste for different mineral waters, in a light-hearted note, whilst living in Switzerland:

> Saint-Galmier is superseded by Montreux, which the label says is saturated with carbonic acid gas. But my physiology book said this was deadly poison & we only breathed it out – never unless we were desperate, took it in. However, according to Doctors Ritter, Spingel and Knechtli it's marvellous for gravel and makes the urine sparkil like champagne. These are the <u>minor</u> mysteries (NB2, p. 269, June 1921).

Murry included the passage in his first edition of the *Journal*, but substituted the word 'water' for 'urine' (J1, p. 180). Yet again, the earthy, witty personality of Mansfield disappears, to be replaced by the 'sanitised' version. Needless to say, 'water' is translated as 'eau' in the first French edition (FJ1, p. 189). In the 1954 definitive edition of the *Journal*, Murry makes the editorial decision to replace his own word, 'water', with the original 'urine' (FJ2, p. 250). Not so, the French translator of this newer edition however, who persists in translating 'urine' as 'eau' (FJ2, p. 392), thus perpetuating the 'sanitising' of Mansfield's writing in French translation.

In 1997, *The Katherine Mansfield Notebooks* are published in two volumes. In nearly seven hundred pages of text, Margaret Scott has painstakingly transcribed all the original notebooks and loose manuscripts from which Murry created his editions of the *Journal*. Mansfield scholars are now able to ascertain how disparate these various documents are, and how false is the sense that Mansfield had ever really written a 'journal' as such, intended for publication. It is to Murry's credit as an editor that he was able to create such a seemingly fluid text from so many bits of paper, but this should not detract from the essentially duplicitous nature of his endeavours, which allowed for a false impression of the legacy of Mansfield's personal writing for nearly three quarters of a century.

These manuscripts were also used by Murry to create the volume known as *The Scrapbook of Katherine Mansfield* in 1939, an 'intermediary' edition of the *Journal*. In the introduction, he writes:

> It is possible that I attach an exaggerated importance to these [fragments]. But [...] European opinion has received her [*Journal*] as a minor classic [...] There are now many people in many different countries – In France, perhaps, above all others – who take a peculiar personal and loving interest in all that pertains to Katherine Mansfield. In their eyes, I know, this book needs no apology (SB, pp. v–vi).

Translated as *Cahiers de notes* in 1944, the editorial stance remains unchanged from the volumes already discussed. Much of the book consists of extracts of unfinished stories which would have no place in a journal. However, previously unpublished journal-type extracts are included here, with the same prudish omissions as before; for example, the phrase: 'The stockings like snakes in the back room' is omitted from the *Scrapbook* in 1939 (SB, p. 239), yet is reinstated into the definitive edition of the *Journal* in 1954 (J2, p. 296, 8 February, 1922), and prudishly translated in the 1956 French *Journal* as '*Les chaussettes*, comme des serpents, dans le débarras' (FJ2, p. 455, my italics).

Since these translations – dating from the fifties – of the *Letters* and *Journal*, no new French versions have appeared. Today's French edition of the *Journal* dates from 1956 and contains the introductions by Murry from both the 1932 edition as well as the 1956 edition, thereby giving credence to his editorial stance. And, as mentioned earlier, the edition of the *Letters* which can be bought today in France, is the one volume edition originally published in *1931*, with no letters earlier than 1915. The larger, three volume edition published in the fifties is now out of print. Nor does a French reader have access to the *Katherine Mansfield Notebooks*, a volume which collates all Mansfield's extant writings from which the two editions of the *Journal* were derived, since this has never been translated.

Narrative Technique in Translation

I shall now turn my attention to the translational style of the stories, only one collection of which has had two different translations published – *The Garden Party*.[17] The 'Folio Classique' edition of 2002 represents the only new translation of any of Mansfield's work since the fifties. Clive Scott contends that new translations of the same work offer a valuable contribution to the life of an author abroad:

17   The recently published new edition of Mansfield's collected stories in France, is, in fact, a re-worked compilation of old translations. *Katherine Mansfield: Les nouvelles*, pref. by Marie Desplechin (Paris: Stock, 2006).

Translation needs ever to be started afresh, not because available translations are wrong, have avoidable infelicities, misunderstand, but because all ages, as all individuals, want to say things differently, have different ways of projecting a self into a response.[18]

Susan Petrilli takes this argument further and talks of the 'translatability' of a text, whereby no translation can ever be perceived as being definitive or incapable of being superseded:

['T]ranslatability' does not only signify the possibility of translation. It also indicates an open relation between a text in the original and its translation. As the general 'interpretability' of a text – with respect to which 'translatability' is a special case – translatability also indicates that the translation of a text remains open, that a translated text may continue to be translated, in fact may be translated over and over again, in the same language into which it has already been translated.[19]

In this section I shall be looking therefore, for signs which demonstrate a different approach to an understanding of Mansfield's work, as well as searching for evidence to show whether the themes and philosophy encoded in the original stories have been diluted – or indeed misrepresented – in translation.

As outlined in my introduction, in any assessment of a literary translation the fundamental technique of the translator soon becomes apparent as being a choice between two different approaches. The translator must decide on the one hand, whether his role is to faithfully record the words of the original author, denying his own literary style and artistic judgement the right to colour the text, although for Eugene Nida, even this is, in fact, impossible:

Since no two languages are identical, either in the meanings given to corresponding symbols or the ways in which such symbols are arranged in phrases and sentences, it stands to reason that there can be no absolute correspondence between languages. Hence there can be no fully exact translations. The total impact of a translation may be reasonably close to the original, but there can be no identity in detail.[20]

18   Clive Scott, *Translating Baudelaire* (Exeter: University of Exeter Press, 2000), p. 3.

19   Petrilli, 'Introduction', in Petrilli, p. 31

20   Eugene Nida, 'Principles of Correspondence', in Venuti, pp. 126–40 (p. 126).

On the other hand, perhaps the role of the translator should really be that of an *interpreter of meaning* – to make a subjective decision upon his/her own interpretation of the text, and then to convey this in translation to the non-indigenous reader. For Georges Mounin, this task is however, fundamentally impossible: 'On ne peut pas traduire parce qu'on ne parle jamais tout à fait de la même chose, même quand on parle du même objet, dans deux langues différentes'.[21] A similar thought leads Justin O'Brien to conclude that:

> Sometimes such an experience may even lead to the conclusion that certain works had best *not* be translated. Raymond Guérin, writing in *La Parisienne* of January 1954, wondered why Maupassant is so exaggeratedly admired outside of his native country and concluded that the very banality of his thought and poverty of his style had facilitated his credit abroad.[22]

I shall therefore be determining the ease with which Mansfield's fiction can be translated and discussing whether her narrative style always survives the translation process.

Use of the Action Verb

The earliest comprehensive study of Mansfield's narrative technique undertaken in France appeared in 1937.[23] May Lillian Muffang provides a detailed assessment of Mansfield's use of language and stylistic tech-

21 Georges Mounin, *Les Problèmes théoriques de la traduction* (Paris: Gallimard, 1963), p. 53.
22 Justin O'Brien, 'From French to English', in *On Translation* ed. by Reuben A. Brower (New York: Oxford University Press, 1966), p. 81. The author Vladimir Nabokov however, takes an extreme view on this argument: 'The term "free translation" smacks of knavery and tyranny. It is when the translator sets out to render the "spirit" – not the textual sense – that he begins to traduce his author. The clumsiest literal translation is a thousand times more useful than the prettiest paraphrase'. Vladimir Nabokov, 'Problems of Translation: "Onegin" in English', in Venuti, pp. 71–73 (p. 73).
23 May Lillian Muffang, 'Katherine Mansfield: Sa vie, son œuvre, sa personnalité' (unpublished thesis, University of Paris, 1937).

niques, focusing especially on her use of the verb. The extraordinarily wide range of action verbs which Mansfield employs, highlights a specific stylistic technique, utilised in order to suggest a whole body of actions, moods and thought, within a single word. As Muffang states:

> Ces verbes si évocateurs, si variés, et dont nous n'avons malheureusement pas le pendant dans notre langue: to hobble, to wobble, to waddle, to paddle, to patter, to clatter, to scuttle, to scurry, to skim, to flop, to lollop, to flick [...] tous verbes qui se passent de prépositions, étant assez expressifs en eux-mêmes (Muffang, p. 111).

The phrase 'et dont nous n'avons malheureusement pas le pendant dans notre langue', speculates upon the translational difficulties the use of these verbs pose, a theme echoed generally by Jose Ortega y Gasset, when he states: 'Of all the European languages, the one that least facilitates the task of translating is French'.[24]

Within three short sentences of 'The Daughters of the Late Colonel', are to be found eight action-verbs:

> She snatched away their plates of mock something or other and slapped down a white, terrified blancmange.
> 'Jam please, Kate,' said Josephine kindly.
> Kate knelt and burst open the sideboard, lifted the lid of the jam-pot, saw it was empty, put it on the table and stalked off (265–66).

Apart from 'lifted', the verbs are all monosyllabic and reflect the sharp, impatient movements of the rude, petulant serving girl. Marthe Duproix translates this passage as follows in the original translation:

> Elle enleva violemment les assiettes où elles avaient mangé je ne sais quel fade ragoût et plaqua sur la table un entremets pâle et tremblant.
> 'La confiture, s'il vous plait, Kate,' lui dit gentiment Josephine.
> Kate s'agenouilla, ouvrit le buffet avec fracas, souleva le couvercle du pot de confiture, vit qu'il était vide, le mit sur la table, et s'en fut à grands pas (281).

The abruptness of the language in the original, mirroring the actions of the servant girl, is not produced in translation, and consequently a French reader does not understand Kate as a character in the same way that she

---

24   Jose Ortega y Gasset, 'The Misery and the Splendour of Translation', in Venuti, pp. 49–64 (p. 63).

is understood in the English original. The 2002 edition reproduces the same passage thus:

> Elle fit disparaître les assiettes où elles avaient mangé un soi-disant ceci ou cela, et flanqua sur la table un blanc-manger visiblement terrorisé.
> 'La confiture, Kate, s'il vous plaît', demanda gentiment Josephine.
> Kate se mit à genoux devant le buffet, en ouvrit brutalement la porte, souleva le couvercle du pot à confitures, vit qu'il était vide, le posa sur la table et sortit, raide comme la justice (FGP2, p. 134).

This most recent edition is longer than the original translation, and even though different verbs have been chosen in some places, the violence and speed of the original remains elusive to the French reader. The English is difficult to translate – the economy of Mansfield's prose cannot easily be transported to the French language. However, 'un blanc-manger visiblement terrorisé' is a closer rendering of the tone of the original than 'un entremets pâle et tremblant', as is 'en ouvrit brutalement la porte', and therefore the more recent is, I believe, the more successful of the two translations.

In 'Sun and Moon', Mansfield writes, 'he did so hate being sent stumping back to the nursery' (154), and again in the last line of the story, 'And wailing loudly, Sun stumped off to the nursery' (160). The translator, J. G. Delamain, proposes the following French version: 'Sun détestait tellement être renvoyé, clopinant, à la nursery!' (151), and 'Et pleurant très fort, Sun retourna à la nursery d'un pas lourd' (158). The action encapsulated in the English is that of a stubborn little boy almost *marching* defiantly back to the nursery, whilst the French participle 'clopinant', conjures up a picture of a boy who – perhaps after some sort of corporal punishment – is almost physically unable to return to the nursery. There is also an absence of homogeneity in the French version which translates 'stumping' in two different ways. In the English version there is an echo and an emphasis in Sun's action, implying stultification in the little boy's life. The image in translation is not at all the same as the original.

'The Doll's House' provides a further example of the difficulties in translating Mansfield's action verbs: 'Kezia thieved out at the back' (399) – an image of a child tiptoeing quietly, eyes everywhere, in an attempt to evade detection; the word 'thieved' encompasses all these notions and more. Marguerite Faguer translates the same phrase as follows

– 'mais Kezia sortit par la porte du fond, à la dérobée' (429). The need in French to elongate phrases in order to arrive at the meaning of the original detracts from the simplicity and economy of the English, a particular hallmark of Mansfield's narrative technique.

One final striking and famous example of action verbs employed by Mansfield to remarkable effect, occurs in 'Life of Ma Parker':

> People went flitting by, very fast; the men walked like scissors; the women trod like cats (308).

> Des gens passaient, filant très vite; les hommes marchaient en ciseaux; les femmes posaient le pied à la façon des chats (331).

There is no attempt to translate the word 'flitting', and the last phrase of the sentence is twice as long in French as in English; a French translator is faced with concise and difficult modes of expression in the English source text.

Style of language is an important aid to characterisation for Mansfield, and the action verbs form part of the process of characterisation. In 'Honeymoon', a waiter is presented as follows in the original, and then in the translation:

> The sleek manager who was marvellously like a fish in a frock-coat, skimmed forward (404).

> Le gérant luisant, qui ressemblait étonnamment à un poisson en redingote, se glissa en avant (435).

This translation is successful on two levels. Firstly, using the technique of the free translation, any problems which might have arisen over the translation of the words 'sleek' and 'skimmed forward' have been overcome. The 'slippery' quality of the words, emphasised in the image of the fish, are as emphatically evoked in translation as in the English version. Secondly, it is clear that an attempt has been made to imitate the alliteration found in the original with the repetition of the 's', 'm' and 'f' sounds. In French, the alliteration within the sentence centres more openly on the 's' sound and, to a lesser extent, 'r'. Thus, it is possible to see how an interpretative translation approximates the original far more than the more literal translations featured above.

I do not discern, however, as with Mansfield's personal writing, the translator deliberately seeking to redefine Mansfield's personality through the written word. Rather, so far as the fiction is concerned, it is the *quality* of the translation which diminishes Mansfield's perceived narrative techniques and consequently the understanding of her personal artistic and philosophical aesthetic.

Translating Mansfield's Punctuation

For David Daiches, writing as early as 1939, Mansfield's style of writing is intrinsically tied to its content:

> The nature of the medium reflects back on, and to a large extent determines, the nature of the content. It is, like lyrical poetry, a type of writing where conception unites instantaneously subject (matter) with style (form). If we asked ourselves what is the story of *The Daughters of the Late Colonel*, for example, we should find it very difficult to express even the idea behind it, the conception underlying it, in any other terms than those employed by the author herself in telling it.[25]

Mansfield's use of punctuation and syntax when examined reveals further problematical uses for the translator. In a letter written in 1921, she writes of having finished 'Miss Brill':

> I choose not only the length of every sentence, but even the sound... After I'd written it I read it aloud – numbers of times – just as one would play over a musical composition [...] If a thing has really come off, it seems to me there mustn't be a single word out of place (CL4, p. 165, 17 January 1921).[26]

---

25 David Daiches, *The Novel and the Modern World* (Chicago: University of Chicago Press, 1939), p. 76.

26 For O. F. Babler, a good translation needs to be worked on in a similar fashion: 'The translation, if it wishes to succeed, must have firm formal relations to the original, to its rhythms and cadence. The translator, his sensibility profoundly rooted in his mother tongue, must hear other languages comparatively, testing their rhythms and modes of expression against the background of his own. Translation exploits all the resources of language with the primary purpose of creating the closest possible analogy to the contents and form of the original structure'. O. F.

The above quotation demonstrates the *exactness* of Mansfield's art. Here again surfaces the problem of the free or the literal translation – the rigid adherence to the structure and vocabulary of the original, contrasted with a 'looser' translation which aims to capture the essence of tone and meaning of the original.

The brief investigations into the use of the action verb in the previous section, demonstrate how a translator of Mansfield requires an unfettered medium with which to reproduce both tone and meaning. Nevertheless, the right to alter the essential *structure* of her writing needs careful scrutiny. For Eugene Nida, it is the quality of any given source text which determines its ease of translation:

> It must be recognized, however, that it is not easy to produce a completely natural translation, especially if the original writing is good literature, precisely because truly good writing intimately reflects and effectively exploits the total idiomatic capacities and special genius of the language in which the writing is done. A translator must therefore not only contend with the special difficulties resulting from such an effective exploitation of the total resources of the source language, but also seek to produce something relatively equivalent in the receptor language (Nida in Venuti, p. 133).[27]

Punctuation anomalies in translation can sometimes lead to a weakening, a minimising of tone and meaning.

J.-G. Delamain, the translator of *Bliss*, only loosely recreates the original punctuation in 'Mr Reginald Peacock's Day', within the confines of the paragraph. The original story contains twenty-nine hyphens, used both within the narrative, which help to convey the workings of Reginald Peacock's inner consciousness, and also in his speech, as a device which he employs constantly. Within Mansfield's stream-of-consciousness narrative, the hyphen intensifies the notion of thought processes at work, together with the general air of conversational 'intimacy',

Babler, 'Poe's "Raven" and the Translation of Poetry', in Holmes, pp. 192–200 (p. 194).

27 Babler continues his argument thus: 'An easy and natural style in translating, despite the extreme difficulties of producing it – especially when translating an original of high quality – is nevertheless essential to producing in the ultimate receptors a response similar to that of the original receptors. In one way or another, this principal of "similar response" has been widely held and effectively stated by a number of specialists in the field of translating' (p. 133).

which pervades this form of presentation. The French translation contains eleven hyphens – a significantly smaller amount. This absence explains a perceived absence in the intimate tone of the narrative in translation.

The use of suspension points in this story also creates problems in translation. There are seventeen cases in the original and twenty in the translation. In the latter, however, they are used indiscriminately and frequently not in the same places as the original:

> even the bath tap seemed to gush stormy applause... (145).

> et que le robinet de la baignoire sembla faire jaillir un impétueux applaudissement (142).

The suspension points reflect the use of the word 'seemed'. It is an image that the reader is presented with; the finality of the full stop concretises the essential fluidity of the image. In the following example suspension points are *added* in the translation:

> 'They fade so soon – they fade so soon', played Reginald on the piano (150).

> 'Elles se fanent si vite... – se fanent si vite...', jouait Reginald (147).

The use in the translation of both the hyphen and the suspension points complicates – and essentially occludes – the meaning of the original text. The difference in nuance is small but noticeable, for the tone is being irrevocably altered.

The problem of the narrator's voice itself will be discussed shortly, but the use of punctuation does play a role within it. In the third paragraph of the story, consisting of thirty-one lines of what are essentially internal thought processes, the French version has thirteen major punctuation differences. One full stop is used instead of a comma; two semic.lons replace two commas; a full stop replaces suspension points; five l.yphens are omitted; one exclamation mark is omitted; finally two question marks and one colon are added. One sentence reads as follows:

> He rolled over in the big bed, his heart still beating in quick, dull throbs, and with every throb he felt his energy escaping him, his – his inspiration for day stifling under those heavy blows (144).

Il se retourne dans le grand lit, son cœur bat encore à coups rapides et sourds. Il sent son énergie lui échapper à chaque pulsation; son inspiration pour la journée étouffée sous le martèlement de ces coups (141).

The unnecessary alterations in punctuation – unnecessary, that is, for an understanding of the text, detract from the tone of the original through the inevitable breakdown of Mansfield's syntactic technique, which relies on simple punctuation and the constant use of hyphens and suspension points to imitate the thought processes of her characters. There is a sense of rhythm, a sense of urgency to the English version – we can hear Reginald talking, hesitating over the choice of a word; we can almost hear him breathing, since his voice is indirectly that of the narrator's. In the French version an added full stop, a missed hyphen, turn an individual's thought processes into a considered, impersonal narrative. A few minor differences in punctuation can thus significantly alter both the mood and understanding of a text.

Finally, no attempt is made to translate the name 'Peacock', carefully and deliberately chosen by Mansfield, full of connotation, association and integral to the meaning behind the story. As Luca Manini points out:

> Proper nouns, which have a special status within the language system as opposed to common nouns, can be used as characterizing devices in literary texts and so become a meaningful element in the texture of such works. Names can in this way be endowed with an extra semantic load that makes them border on wordplay. The presence of meaningful literary names is likely to cause problems when the text is to be translated, the question being not only whether the transposition of such names in the target language is technically possible, but also to what extent this would be viewed as an appropriate procedure.[28]

I contend it is essential to translate the word 'Peacock', since that sense of the 'cocky' proud male, constantly presenting a colourful, if ultimately vacuous and meaningless display, precisely defines Reginald Peacock in the mind of the English reader. For a French reader, who may not even understand the word 'peacock', the translation of the title as 'La journée de M. Reginald Peacock' is worthless. 'La journée de M.

---

28   Luca Manini, 'Meaningful Literary Names. Their Forms and Functions, and their Translation', in *The Translator: Wordplay and Translation*, ed. by Dirk Delabastita (Namur: St Jerome Publishing, 1996) 161–78 (p. 161).

Reginald Paon', however, would bring an instant understanding of the character to a French reader.

When the original punctuation is altered via translation in 'Life of Ma Parker', especially concerning the use of suspension points, it is again the 'stream-of-consciousness' narrative which suffers. There are fourteen uses of suspension points in the original, compared with eleven in the translation. In this story they constitute a flashback device, as Ma Parker the character, shifts her thoughts from the present to the past, from memories of her husband and grandson, back to the realities of her present life as a cleaner to the 'literary gentleman':

> But he was gran's boy from the first .... 'Whose boy are you?' said old Ma Parker (306).

> Pourtant, depuis le commencement, il avait été le chouchou de grand'mère. 'A qui tu es?' dit la vieille Maman Parker (329).

In the above quotation, the suspension points constitute the equivalent, in a film, of 'mist' or 'waves' in the picture whenever the storyline retreats into the past. Their absence here – and elsewhere – in the French text, minimises any intended effect.

The painful conclusion to this story, together with the seriousness of Ma Parker's plight, is destroyed in the French by the introduction of exclamation marks, which lend the French version almost an air of gaiety to one of the bleakest scenes in the whole of Mansfield's fiction:

> Even if she broke down [...] she'd find herself in the lock-up, as like as not (308).

> Même si elle perdait courage [...] on la conduirait au poste, il avait des chances! (331).

Obvious syntactical changes are also evident in Marguerite Faguer's translations in *The Dove's Nest*, an example of which can be found in 'The Doll's House', where the children see the doll's house for the first time and are overwhelmed with excitement:

> 'Oh-Oh!' The Burnell children sounded as though they were in despair (394).

> Les petites Burnell poussèrent un 'oh!' prolongé qui ressemblait à un cri de désespoir (424).

The immediacy of the 'Oh-Oh!' in the English, which precedes any explanation, is lost in this translation by the 'oh!' placed midway in the sentence.

Idiolects, Modes of Expression and Humour

Differences in the translation of speech patterns can lead to a serious reduction of artistic effect. Mansfield is recorded by many of her contemporaries as having a gift for impersonation, which she incorporated into her work through the myriad of characters presented there. Ida Baker, Mansfield's school-friend and companion remarks:

> There was a bell-like quality in her rich low voice and her singing was a high, pure soprano [...] She was a born actress and mimic, and even in her ordinary everyday life took colour from the company she was in.[29]

Leonard Woolf concurs with this opinion of Mansfield, though is perhaps less sentimental in his description:

> By nature, I think, she was gay, cynical, amoral, ribald, witty. When we first knew her she was extraordinarily amusing. I don't think anyone has ever made me laugh more than she did in those days. She would sit very upright on the edge of a chair or sofa and tell at immense length a kind of saga, of her experiences as an actress [...] [T]he extraordinary funniness of the story was increased by the flashes of her astringent wit. I think that in some abstruse way Murry corrupted and perverted and destroyed Katherine both as a person and a writer [...] Her gifts were those of an intense realist, with a superb sense of ironic humour and fundamental cynicism.[30]

This description of Mansfield, by a contemporary who knew her well, reiterates firstly, how far removed Mansfield's 'French' persona was from reality, and secondly, underlines how her humour was perhaps the foremost quality Woolf remembered about her. The almost complete ab-

29 Baker, *The Memories of LM*, p. 233.
30 Leonard Woolf, *The Autobiography of Leonard Woolf* (London: Hogarth Press, 1964), p. 204.

sence of Mansfield's humour in translation, both in her personal writing and in her fiction, is, I contend, one of the primary reasons for the prolongation of the legend surrounding her personality in France.

Ján Ferenčík contends that, 'l'emploi de mots dialectaux caractérise le personnage avant tout sur le plan spatial (local, horizontal), mais dans une large mesure aussi du point de vue social (c'est-à-dire verticalement)'.[31] I agree with this notion but also believe that Ferenčík's statement does not go far enough; Antoine Berman moves the argument forward thus:

> Every novelistic work is characterised by linguistic superimpositions, even if they include sociolects, idiolects, etc. The novel, said Bakhtin, assembles a *heterology* or diversity of discursive types, a *heteroglossia* or diversity of languages, and a *heterophony* or diversity of voices.[32]

In Mansfield's narrative technique, idiolects play an essential role; they are used as a vehicle primarily for her satire or humour and through the use of accents she reveals status and social position, without the need for detailed analysis for which there is no space in a short story. Verisimilitude is a constant factor – she always makes the language of her characters appropriate to their personality and status. Again, the difficulties this poses for the translator are evident, as Munday explains:

> A semiotic function is also performed by idiolect and dialect [...] The systematic recurrence of this purposely functional feature of the speech of certain characters is identified by Hatim and Mason [...] as 'a noteworthy object of the translator's attention'. The peculiarities and connotations of the dialect are unlikely to be replicated easily in any TT [target text] culture (Munday, pp. 100–01).[33]

---

31   Ján Ferenčík, 'De la spécification de la traduction de l'œuvre dramatique', in Holmes, p. 141.

32   Antoine Berman, 'Translation and the trials of the Foreign', in Venuti, pp. 284–97 (p. 296).

33   Dušan Slobodník also emphasises the comic aspect which the use of an idiolect invariably introduces: 'L'écrivain emploie des éléments dialectaux dans le discours direct pour caractériser ses personnages exclusivement du point de vue social. L'emploi du dialecte dans le discours direct d'un tel personnage doit exprimer avant tout la mesure dans laquelle il ne se conforme pas au milieu. Le texte de l'auteur vise à produire, dans la plupart des cas, un effet comique. Je crois qu'en traduisant les éléments dialectaux ainsi employés, on peut recourir aux éléments

However, a novelist is not necessarily a dialectologist. We are not entitled to assume either his ability or his intention to record the speech of his contemporaries. Nevertheless, I contend that a translator should make the effort to record some sort of accent in order to provide his readers with at least a part of the richness of the original. Eugene Nida concurs with this opinion, making the following point on idiolects in translation:

> [I]t is essential that each participant introduced into the message be accurately represented. That is to say, individuals must be properly characterized by the appropriate selection and arrangement of words, so that such features as social class or geographical dialect will be immediately evident. Moreover, each character must be permitted to have the same kind of individuality and personality as the author himself gave them in the original message (Nida in Venuti, p. 139).

Every walk of life is portrayed in Mansfield's stories, from 'down-and-outs' like Ada Moss, through to the Burnell's servant girl Alice, on up to the very middle class Sheridan family, through to the extremely wealthy Rosemary Fell in 'A Cup of Tea', each with their own distinctive 'voice'; Mansfield's translators however, ignore most idiolects presented to them in the original text.

Mistakes made by foreigners in their use of English have frequently been used with comic effect by novelists. In 'The Man Without a Temperament', Mansfield plays with the accent of the foreign waiter – the characterisation adding another dimension of richness to the story. No accent appears in translation:

> 'Just this moment, Signora,' grinned Antonio. 'I took-a-them from the postman myself. I made-a the postman give them for me' (132).

> 'A l'instant, Signora', ricane Antonio, 'je les ai prises moi-même au facteur, j'ai forcé le facteur à me les donner' (129).

In 'Honeymoon', another foreign waiter appears; again his idiolect is absent in translation:

> 'Dis way, sir. Dis way, sir. I have a very nice little table,' he gasped (404).

> analogues du dialecte de la langue de but. [...] L'élément local (la couleur locale) n'étant pas d'importance, le traducteur peut s'orienter vers la solution équivalente, il peut chercher un effet analogue, par exemple un effet comique'. Dušan Slobodnik, 'Remarques sur la traduction des dialectes' in Holmes, pp. 139–43 (p. 143).

'Par ici, Monsieur! Par ici, Monsieur! J'ai une très bonne petite table', disait-il, tout haletant (435).

Frequently, Mansfield utilises an 'affected' accent, when one or other character attempts a genteel mode of expression, which always introduces a note of humour. Nowhere in the stories is this type of idiolect more ruthlessly or more humorously portrayed than in the ridiculous self-importance bestowed upon Nurse Andrews in 'The Daughters of the Late Colonel'. Neither the original translation of 1929, nor the more recent 2002 version, reveals any idiolect as such:

'When I was with Lady Tukes,' said Nurse Andrews, 'she had such a dainty little contrayvance for the buttah. It was a silvah Cupid balanced on the – on the bordah of a glass dish, holding a tayny fork. And when you wanted some buttah you simply pressed his foot and he bent down and speared you a piece. It was quite a gayme' (265).

'Quand j'étais chez Lady Tukes, disait Nurse Andrews, elle avait une petite machine si coquette pour servir le beurre. C'était un petit Amour en argent qui se tenait en équilibre sur le...sur le bord d'un plat de cristal avec une fourche en miniature à la main. Et quand on voulait du beurre, eh bien, on appuyait tout simplement sur son pied, il se penchait, piquait un morceau et vous le donnait. Ça faisait un véritable amusement, quoi!' (280–81).

'Quand j'étais chez Lady Tukes, dit Miss Andrews, il y avait un petit présentoir à beurre tout à fait ravissant. C'était un petit Amour en argent, en équilibre sur le...sur le bord d'un récipient en cristal et qui tenait à la main une minuscule fourchette. Et quand on voulait du beurre, on n'avait qu'à appuyer sur son pied et il se penchait pour vous en piquer un morceau. C'était amusant comme tout!' (FGP2 133).

The differences between the two translations are small but significant, though neither of the translators has attempted to capture Nurse Andrews's affected idiolect which so absolutely and immediately defines her character for an English reader. This is the first time she speaks – the impact of these words is therefore all the more important. The title 'Nurse Andrews' obviously poses a problem for both translators since no French word is deemed suitable; 'Miss' seems to lead further away, however, from the true meaning, since by prefixing her name with the word 'Nurse', Mansfield is according her a certain position, is fixing her in our minds' eye with her role in life which 'Miss' simply does not fulfil.

Concerning the use of idiolects in writing, Lavinia Merlini Barbaresi is of the opinion that 'the translator cannot overcome the difficulty of extreme richness in lects, registers and styles and tends to standardize and unify the expression: he chooses stability instead of variety'.[34] The idiolects need not be present in translation for a reader to understand the plot of any given story, but in the difficult task of trying to understand Mansfield's art in a foreign language, their absence leads to no less than a bowdlerisation of the original. Nida endorses this view when he states in the following general comment:

> It is essential not only that a translation avoid certain obvious failures to adjust the message to the context, but also that it incorporate certain positive elements of style which provide the proper emotional tone for the discourse. This emotional tone must accurately reflect the point of view of the author. Thus such elements as sarcasm, irony, or whimsical interest must all be accurately reflected in […] translation (Nida in Venuti, p. 139).

It is Mansfield's wicked humour which is lost, her ability to impersonate – and occasionally ruthlessly expose – stock types; precisely the side of her personality which the French edit out completely from both the early editions of the *Letters* and *Journal*. The image of a satirical humorist, obvious signs of which permeate *all* her writing, could only with difficulty be affiliated to the persona of a quasi-saint.

In Charles Dickens' work, references to upper class speech are generally uncomplimentary;[35] an examination of Mansfield's usage reveals a similar prevalence. All the examples examined above incorporate the role of status and social class with idiolect. In England, and especially in the class-conscious England of the 1920s, a colloquial accent would mark a person for life, and the middle and upper classes employed a very different sort of vocabulary to those beneath them in the social scale. France, however, has not been as conscious of accent as a delineator of social class to the same extent, so that obvious stylistic difficulties not-

---

34   Lavinia Merlini Barbaresi, 'Text Linguistics and Literary Translation', in Riccardi, pp. 120–32 (p. 132).

35   See G. L. Brook, *The Language of Dickens* (London: Deutsch, 1970).

withstanding, this might indicate another minor reason why Mansfield's translators omit translating the myriad of idiolects present in her stories.

There are also stories where particular modes of expression are employed to reveal the entire persona of a major character, without the need for further character delineation – for example Stanley Burnell in 'Prelude':

> 'Well, you might just give me five-eighth's of a cup,' said Burnell [...] 'Tip-top meat, isn't it? [...] By Jove, this is a pretty pickle' (19).

> 'Tu pourrais bien m'en donner les cinq-huitièmes d'une tasse,' répondit Burnell [...] 'Viande parfaite, n'est-ce pas? [...] Nom de nom, c'est un joli fourbi eh, Beryl?' (9–10).

The evident pomposity of the translation mirrors the original, instantly revealing Stanley's character. Another example occurs in the story 'The Lady's Maid'. The story takes the form of a monologue by a servant, recounting incidents from the long history of service she has given her 'lady' – gentle comedy is blended with the eventually more insistent note of blank resignation to old age and loneliness. The modes of expression in her speech reveal her origins, but she attempts to upgrade her speech, not through affectation, but rather in a conscious effort to 'improve' herself. It is an ironical situation, for the light-hearted comedy of her words is contrasted with the sadness of her situation, as she describes a life selflessly devoted to the service of her mistress:

> 'It fidgets me something dreadful to see her [...] When I tucked her up just now and seen – saw her lying back [...] A ducky little brooch' (375–76).

> 'Ça me fait un souci terrible de la voir comme ça [...] Quand je l'ai bordée dans son lit, tout à l'heure, et que je l'y ai vue couchée [...] Une mignonne petite broche' (412).

The French translation does not register the correction of the colloquialism 'seen' to the grammatically correct 'saw', emphasising the servant's self-imposed decision to better her speech and therefore her station. It is a glimpse of the character's make-up which has been lost for the French reader. The story itself is a bitter indictment of how servants are frequently made to feel guilty for wanting to lead a different life, and highlights the difference between rich and poor, between those who wield power and those who submit.

George's mode of speech in 'Honeymoon' is inherent to the plot of the story:

> 'Topping villa,' said George [...] 'Well you'd need a crowd of people if you stayed there long. [...] Deadly otherwise. I say, it is ripping' (403).

> 'Chic villa,' dit Georges [...] 'Évidemment il faudrait être très nombreux pour y séjourner longtemps [...] Ce serait mortel autrement! Mais c'est épatant' (435).

George is an upper-class fool, a fact which his young and innocent new bride has yet to discover, though throughout the story Mansfield hints at a burgeoning awareness. His buffoon-type language *has* to be brought out in translation in order to make any sense of this underlying meaning. The above quotation shows how an attempt has been made to capture this verbal nincompoopery in French, with some degree of success.

Social awareness emerges in the general tone of a story, the use of accents being one of the instruments for its portrayal. The tone can vary greatly, depending on the notions being put forward by the author; sarcasm is normally used by Mansfield as a means of condemnation. In 'Bliss', her sarcasm reveals itself in the characters of the Norman Knights and the poet Eddie Warren. Portrayed as apparently witty, young literati, the words Mansfield puts into their mouths force us to laugh at them, not with them:

> 'Isn't she very *liée* with Michael Oat?'
> 'The man who wrote *Love in False Teeth*?'
> 'He wants to write a play for me' [...]
> 'What's he going to call it – 'Stomach Trouble?'
> 'I *think* I've come across the *same* idea in a lit-tle French review, *quite* unknown in England' (100).

> 'N'est-il pas très liée avec Michael Oat?'
> 'L'homme qui a écrit L'Amour en fausses dents?'
> 'Il veut me faire une pièce'. [...]
> 'Comment va-t-il l'intituler? *Troubles digéstifs?*'
> 'Je crois que j'ai rencontré la même idée dans une petite revue française toute à fait inconnue en Angleterre' (93).

The stupidity of the conversation can be just as much appreciated in French as in English, although the mock sophistication of the French loan-word 'liée', cannot be perceived in translation. Eddie Warren has a peculiarly pedantic way of emphasising every other word; its absence in French is a lost source of comedy which also takes the edge off the author's sarcasm in her portrayal of these characters.

A similar exposé of sham personalities is to be found in 'Marriage à la Mode':

> 'I do wish, Bill, you'd paint it.'
> 'Paint what?' said Bill loudly, stuffing his mouth with bread.
> 'Us' said Isabel. [...]
> Bill screwed up his eyes and chewed. 'Light's wrong,' he said rudely, 'far too much yellow,' and went on eating. And that seemed to charm Isabel too (317).

> 'Je voudrais tant, Bill, que vous peignez tout ça.'
> 'Que je peigne quoi?' demanda Bill, d'une grosse voix en se remplissant la bouche de pain.
> 'Nous' dit Isabel. [...]
> Bill roula des yeux et mastiqua. 'Mauvaise lumière,' répliqua-t-il sans amabilité, 'trop de jaune.' Et cela aussi parut enchanter Isabel (342).

> J'aimerais tant Bill, que tu peignes ça.
> 'Peindre quoi?' demanda Bill d'une voix forte en se bourrant de pain.
> 'Nous', dit Isabel. [...]
> Bill plissa les yeux en mastiquant son pain.
> 'La lumière est pas bonne', jeta-t-il avec brusquerie, 'beaucoup trop de jaune', et il se remit à manger. Cela aussi sembla charmer Isabel.
> (FGP2 174).

Idiolects and general speech patterns are intimately connected with the narrative process. Mansfield's gift for impersonation – and her ability to transpose this gift to the written page – is one way in which her characters are so acutely brought to life. The brilliance of her writing, combining the vivacity of her wit, the sharpness of her tongue, the concerns of her mind, is, on the whole, achromatised and enfeebled in translation. I contend that the newer translation above is even weaker in its effect than the older version, with the heavy-handed repetition of the word 'pain' and the unnecessarily lengthy 'La lumière est pas bonne'.[36] It is just possible to perceive in the French version Mansfield's obvious satire against so-called 'artists', who, under the guise of Art, are able to while away their lives whilst living off the money of some generous benefactor. However, the words 'rudely' and 'stuffing his mouth' indicate the narrator's viewpoint, and 'sans aimabilité' and 'se remplissant la bouche' are dilutions of the original, disparaging, innuendoes. In addition, there is not enough movement and renewal in either translation to break down the ossification of the hagiography. Itamar Even-Zohar seeks to clarify this idea:

> A highly interesting paradox manifests itself here: translation, by which new ideas, items, characteristics can be introduced into a literature, becomes a means to preserve traditional taste. This discrepancy between the original central literature and the translated literature may have evolved in a variety of ways, for instance, when translated literature, after having assumed a central position and inserted new items, soon lost contact with the original home literature which went on changing, and thereby became a factor of preservation of unchanged repertoire. Thus, a literature that might have emerged as a revolutionary type may go on existing as an ossified *système d'antan*, often fanatically guarded by the agents of secondary models against even minor changes.[37]

Susan Bassnett and Harish Trivedi also reiterate this sense of translation as manipulation:

> Translation does not happen in a vacuum, but in a continuum; it is not an isolated act, it is part of an ongoing process of intercultural transfer. Moreover, translation is a highly manipulative activity that involves all kinds of stages in that process of transfer across linguistic and cultural boundaries. Translation is not an innocent, transparent activity but is highly charged with significance at every stage; it rarely, if ever, involves a relationship of equality between texts, authors or systems.[38]

36   On the subject of the expansive tendency of translation, Antoine Berman notes: 'Every translation tends to be longer than the original. George Steiner said that translation is "inflationist". This is the consequence, in part, of the two previous tendencies. Rationalising and clarifying require expansion, an *unfolding* of what, in the original, is "folded". Now, from the view point of the text, this expansion can be qualified as "empty"' (Berman, in Venuti, p. 290).

37   Itamar Even-Zohar, 'The Position of Translated Literature within the Literary Polysystem', in Venuti, pp. 192–97 (p. 195).

38   Susan Bassnett and Harish Trivedi, eds., *Post-Colonial Translation: Theory and Practice* (London: Routledge, 1999), p. 2.

Near the end of her life, Mansfield wrote in one of her notebooks:

> To be wildly enthusiastic, or deadly serious – both are wrong. Both pass. One must keep ever present a sense of humour. It depends entirely on yourself how much you see or hear or understand. But the sense of humour I have found true of every single occasion of my life. Now perhaps you understand what to be indifferent means. It's to learn not to mind, and not to show you mind (J1, p. 247).

The first edition of the French *Journal* did not contain this quotation, though it was present in the first English edition. It is not translated into French until the second edition of 1956. Thus the emphasis that she herself places on humour in both her life and her work was not a factor for consideration by early French scholars studying her work. In the preface to the 2002 French edition of *The Garden Party*, Françoise Pellan notes:

> [Mansfield] n'était pas source d'un apaisement total et définitif. L'humour, autre instrument de distanciation et de libération, ne pouvait l'être davantage [...] *Lettres, Journal* et nouvelles en font foi, l'humour de Katherine Mansfield connaissait d'inévitables éclipses. Il l'a néanmoins grandement aidée, dans sa vie comme dans son écriture, la préservant le plus souvent de l'apitoiement sur soi, et sauvant presque entièrement *La Garden Party* du pathos et du mélodrame (FGP2, p. 30).

The humour is therefore noted, if not always brought out in this most recent of translations, and in general appears to be one of the qualities hardest to reproduce. Wit is frequently conveyed through the use of idiolects (and especially those of the minor characters), as I have indicated, as well as through situations or comical characters such as Nurse Andrews in 'The Daughters of the Late Colonel', or Miss Moss's landlady, Mrs Pine (curiously translated as 'Mistress Pim' in French), in 'Pictures'. In fact, the story 'Pictures' abounds in caricatures of types that are easily recognisable, as in the aforementioned Mrs Pine:

> 'My sister Eliza was only saying to me yesterday [...] She may have had a college eddication [...] but if your Lizzie says what's true,' she says 'and she's washing her own wovens and drying them on the towel rail, it's easy to see where the finger's pointing' (120).

> 'Ma sœur me le disait pas plus tard qu'hier au soir [...] Miss Moss peut avoir reçu une éducation au collège, [...] mais si ta Lizzie dit vrai,' dit-elle, 'et qu'elle lave elle-même ses flanelles et les fait sécher sur le porte-serviettes, il est facile de voir de quel côté le vent tourne' (116).

There *is* some indication of an idiolect in the French version, although the comic accent perceived in the use of the word 'eddication', receives no attention whatsoever.

All these idiolects and general modes of expression remain the proof of Mansfield's awareness of every walk of life – each one encapsulates an undertone which describes the inner psychology of a character. Their absence in translation leads to a further sterilisation of her work.

Use of the Narrator as Stylistic Technique

In the majority of Mansfield's stories – and certainly in the most accomplished ones – the narrator is not an emotionally neutered entity, but rather one or other of the characters. Stories are presented through the thoughts of someone experiencing the events taking place. This is a crucial aspect of her artistic technique – a direct, provocative way of writing – and one which lends itself to a high degree of reader-participation. And in the same way that the mind shifts its focus from one thought to another, so the focus shifts within a single story. Occasionally there are two or more narrators, but mostly there is just one – a single character around whose thought-patterns, words and actions the storyline is attached. In order to fully appreciate Mansfield's artistry, this technique *must* be rendered in translation, since its absence would lessen the emotional effect, the originality and even the understanding; it is precisely through the glimpses of the characters' minds during the narration that the reader arrives at a fuller understanding of the message the author wants to convey.

The story 'Life of Ma Parker' provides an example of this technique, which takes the form of Ma Parker's thought patterns. She moves around the literary gentleman's flat, cleaning and polishing, but it is not her actions which are important but rather her thoughts, her inner life. In Delamain's translation the conversational tone of the narrative is diluted and consequently much of the intimacy of the story is lost. In the dialogue itself, some attempt has been made at converting a cockney accent into French – 'Beg parding, sir?' – 'Mande pardon Monsieur?' Yet within the interior monologue, Ma Parker's idiolect is not retained – kitching maid/fille de cuisine; arsking her/on lui en parlait; beedles/cafards; chimley/cheminée; 'ad 'er side of ham 'anging/avait toujours son quartier de porc qui pendait. In not attempting to recreate these colloquialisms, the reader's notion of being intimately connected to Ma Parker and her story is lost, for she is talking to the reader and recounting her life in her own words. It is a story she has told many times, evident from such phrases as:

> 'A baker, Mrs Parker!' the literary gentleman would say (304).
> 'Un boulanger, Mme Parker!' dit le monsieur auteur (327).
>
> Here Ma always gave a little laugh (304).
> A ce point, Maman Parker poussait toujours un petit éclat de rire (327).

The 'would say' of the first sentence merely translates as 'dit', and the nuance of the oft-told story is weakened.

In the whole of this story only one colloquialism within the interior monologue is preserved: 'émigrimé' for 'emigrimated'. Yet in the French version, the translator sees fit to italicise it, thereby according it undue prominence; in the English it is perceived as nothing more than an idiosyncrasy of the idiolect. Any intimate liaison between Ma Parker and the narrator is destroyed by this form of distancing from the subject. Idiolects and general speech patterns are intimately connected with the narrative process. Mansfield's gift for impersonation – and her ability to transpose this gift to the written page – is one of the major factors which bring her characters so acutely to life.

The narrator in 'Sun and Moon' is a small boy – the language is therefore simple and abundant in child-like images and vocabulary:

> real things and not real ones / les choses vraies et pas vraies
> goldy chairs/chaises dorées
> a cap like a blancmange / un bonnet comme du blancmanger
> it wasn't real night yet / Bien que ce ne fût pas encore la vraie nuit
> funny, awfully nice hats nodding up the path / des drôles de chapeaux très beaux qui dodelinaient le long du sentier

None of the French equivalents constitutes child-speak to the same degree as the English originals do. In the translation of the story as a whole, the essential naivety of the storyteller, together with the underlying theme of the adult's sham world is barely discernable, in the same way that the different speech registers (the little boy's 'queryings' contrasted with the adult's commands and exclamations), are ill-defined.

A similar pattern emerges in 'The Doll's House'. Here the reader inhabits the mind of the little girl Kezia, and adults are presented through the speech and thoughts of the children. The translation of the early paragraph describing the doll's house, lacks the child-like charm of the original vocabulary:

> There stood the doll's house, a dark, oily spinach green, picked out with bright yellow. [...] The door was like a little slab of toffee (393).
>
> La maison de poupées se dressait donc dans la cour. Elle était d'un vert épinard, sombre, huileux [...] La porte [...] ressemblait à un caramel (423).

If a combined assessment is made of all the points discussed so far – the vocabulary, punctuation, idiolects, tone and handling of the narrator – it becomes difficult to distinguish between the overall successes and failures of each individual translator. However inadequate these translations are for their reader-public, they are still, with one exception, in use today, in some cases nearly *eighty* years after they were first published.

Translating *In a German Pension*

Mansfield's first collection of short stories, *In a German Pension*, cannot profitably be integrated into a discussion of the other three collections. It is the least well-known of her books in France, and was only translated after the other collections had been received and digested by the French reading public. First published in English in 1911, when Mansfield was twenty-one (and which she never allowed to be published again during her lifetime), the stories in this book represent a youthful vision, with no clearly definable artistic technique. The translator of these stories, the distinguished French critic Charles Mauron,[39] does not employ methods

---

39 See Chapter Five for a discussion of the importance of Mauron as a literary translator.

used by the preceding Mansfield translators, yet overall, the technique he chooses to employ results in the finest French translations of her fiction to date.

In Mauron's translation, which first appeared in 1939, meaning is constantly interpreted rather than words literally rendered, and the total effect is one of close harmony with the original – a general feeling of 'rightness', which Mansfield's other translators fail to achieve. Examples abound from 'The-Child-Who-Was-Tired', for example, of 'free' translations, which appear wholly successful:

> Staring out of the window at the bruised sky, which seemed to bulge heavily over the dull land (759).
> Considérant par la fenêtre un ciel malade, lourdement gonflé, au-dessus d'une terre morne (679).

> 'Stop sousing about the water while I'm here' (759).
> 'Tu ne vas pas tout tremper pendant que je suis là?' (679).

The two passages of English are expressive pieces of writing, difficult to translate, yet Mauron does not opt for a dilution in meaning. Instead, he recreates the sense of the original, which I believe is what is required. Here is another example from 'Germans at Meat':

> He turned up his eyes and his moustache, wiping the soup drippings from his coat and waistcoat (697).

> Il leva vers le ciel les yeux et la moustache, en essuyant des gouttelettes de soupe sur sa veste et son gilet (613).

> 'Wonderful,' said the widow contemptuously, replacing the hairpin in the knob which was balanced on the top of her head (699).

> 'Merveilleux?' dit la veuve avec mépris en repiquant l'épingle cheveux dans le chignon en équilibre au sommet de son crâne (615).

The sarcasm and comedy present in the English version, so frequently lost in the translations of the other collections is clearly distinguishable here. For the most part unread and forgotten, and receiving little critical attention, an analysis of these stories reveals them as leading the field in the harmonious capturing of the essence of Mansfield's narrative aesthetic.

Translating the *Poems*

Although not translated into French until 1946, *Poems by Katherine Mansfield* was the second volume of her work that Murry brought out posthumously in 1923 (after *The Dove's Nest*), collected from the manuscripts left in his possession after her death. The French edition comprises a selection from the original. Vincent O'Sullivan speculates that:

> *Poems by Katherine Mansfield* [...] was perhaps the single volume that would have caused her particular disquiet. Although she returned to writing verse at different times during her life, Mansfield made no claims to be a poet. Murry was determined to establish her as one. He brought together the twenty-odd poems she had published mostly under pseudonyms, and another fifty from manuscripts that very often were the sketchiest of drafts. He presented as finished or considered work which was not only occasional, but also extremely casual (*Poems 2*, p. ix).

As a result – within the literary community in England at least, this volume only served to enhance the general scorn for Murry, which, as I shall demonstrate in the next chapter, eventually became the default setting of the majority of critics in England.

As mentioned, this was Murry's second foray into creating a book from Mansfield's manuscripts. *The Dove's Nest* had been a relatively simple gathering together of finished stories for a volume which Mansfield herself had been working on in the months prior to her death. But as O'Sullivan points out, this volume of poetry now took Murry on a completely different editorial journey, creating the first volume of work in Mansfield's name which she had never envisaged whilst alive. It is not difficult to see why Murry started his editorial journey in the way he did; *The Dove's Nest* was more or less a 'fait accompli', Mansfield herself having discussed with Murry the stories for her new book, and completed most of them before she died. The poems too, would have been simple to locate within the hundreds of manuscripts he inherited after her death, and easy enough to arrange by date into a volume which could be got to the printers as quickly as possible after the initial success of *The Dove's Nest* (published in June 1923, five months after Mansfield's death and so popular that it went to two reprints in the same year). *Poems by Katherine Mansfield* appeared in November of the same year, containing sixty-eight poems, spanning Mansfield's early childhood verse, through to poems written as a mature writer.

Already, Murry's desire to edit and recreate is becoming evident. As a result of Vincent O'Sullivan's definitive edition of the *Poems*, we are now aware that not all of the poems Mansfield wrote were published in Murry's original edition; there is already a selection process at work, though the reader is not told of the criteria for selection. Murry also sees fit to omit certain verses of the poems he selected, though again this is not made clear in the text presented to the reader. Of the verses written at the Villa Pauline in France, O'Sullivan notes that, 'He does not mention that the verses made no pretence to being finished poems and that the manuscripts are the roughest of drafts' (*Poems 2*, p. 89). Of 'Voices of the Air!' in particular, O'Sullivan continues: 'He printed only four of the poem's six stanzas, implying a completed poem which in fact was not the case' (p. 89). In 1930, Murry brought out a second edition of poems, similar in content to the first edition but with the addition of two extra poems, 'Sunset' and 'Old-Fashioned Widow's Song'.

Only twenty of the sixty-four poems are translated for the French edition of 1946. In his introduction and condensed biography of Mansfield, the translator, Jean Pierre Le Mée, does not restrict himself to factual biographical material concerning Mansfield, to the detriment of his credibility as a critic. He commences his introduction thus: 'Il est assez curieux de constater qu'aucun des biographes de Katherine Mansfield, ne mentionne ses poèmes. C'est un de ces mystères comme il en existe en littérature' (*Poèmes*, p. 9). He talks of her having had her first story 'published' at the age of nine (in reality only in a school magazine), of her badgering her parents to send her to school in England (in fact an English education was her father's idea and all three of his daughters were educated in England), followed again by the continually recurring myth of her returning to England, 'nantie d'une faible pension' and struggling to survive. He continues, 'Cette existence d'aventure n'est pas faite pour un être aussi frêle et aussi sensible'. Of her known miscarriage, he merely states, 'A la suite d'une maladie, elle doit partir en convalescence et échoue dans une petite ville d'Allemagne' (p. 10). Mansfield returned to London in January 1910, eventually marrying Murry in 1918, once her divorce had come through; Le Mée, however, deliberately ignoring all the known facts about Mansfield at that time, chooses instead to present the following version: 'Katherine Mansfield revenue à Oxford en 1915, épouse son écrivain, John Middleton Murry' (p. 11). The tone of his eulogy becomes ever more religious, finally ending thus: 'Comme elle avait raison Katherine Mansfield d'écrire dans son journal: 'Seigneur, rends-moi pareille au cristal pour que la lumière brille à travers moi' [...] Votre œuvre est là pour témoigner que Dieu vous a exaucée' (p. 16).

A dual examination of the poems Murry omitted from his selection together with those omitted by Le Mée in *his* selection, reveals the extent to which in France, as with the *Letters* and the *Journal*, Mansfield both as a personality and a writer is misrepresented. The most obvious omissions from the English version are the poems Mansfield wrote to Murry during their long separations. Towards the end of her life Mansfield became more and more disillusioned and dismayed by Murry's perceived abandonment of her, whilst she sought relief from the symptoms of her ever-worsening tuberculosis by spending more and more time abroad in a constant shuttling between Swiss mountain and Mediterranean sea. In December 1919, Mansfield sent him the following seven stanza poem (and two others in a similar vein), from Ospedaletti on the Riviera, following a turbulent period in their relationship, fuelled by Murry's encounters with other women in England, his penny-pinching nature, her own fears for her health and their future together:

The New Husband

Someone came to me and said
Forget, forget that you've been wed
Who's your man to leave you be
Ill and cold in a far country
Who's the husband – who's the stone
Could leave a child like you alone. [...]

I had received that very day
A letter from the Other to say
That in six months – he hoped – no longer
I would be so much better and stronger
That he would close his books and come
With radiant looks to bear me home.

Ha! Ha! Six months, six weeks, six hours
Among these glittering palms and flowers
With Melancholy at my side

For my old nurse and for my guide
Despair – and for my footman Pain –
I'll never see my home again […] (*Poems 2*, p. 77).

This poem was written not merely as an artistic exercise but also as a personal attack on the recipient. Its overt message was certainly received loudly and clearly by Murry, who packed his bags for the Mediterranean and was with Mansfield within a couple of weeks of its receipt. He eventually published the poem in the second edition of the *Letters* in 1ᴖ51, where it was duly translated into French.[40]

Other criteria for omission from the original English version are verses which do not correlate with Murry's re-creation of Mansfield's personality – for example, references to sexual matters or those with political implications, together with instances of her sarcastic or ironic humour. The following are all extracts from poems Murry chose *not* to include in his selection:

[…] O'er her loosened hair
The firelight spins a web of shining gold
Sears her pale mouth with kisses passionate
Wraps her tired body in a hot embrace […]
(Poems 2, p. 19, extract from 'The Winter Fire').

Out in the fog-stained, mud-stained street they stand
Two women and a man . . . Their draggled clothes
Hang on their withered bodies. It is cold
So cold the very rain and fog feel starved
And bite into their scarcely covered bones
(p. 23, extract from 'The Trio').

Sleeping together . . . how tired you were! . . .
How warm our room . . . how the firelight spread

40   L2, pp. 427–28, 4 December 1919. The poem was translated as 'Le Nouvel Epoux' in FL2iii, pp. 282–83. Murry wrote the following editorial note below the poem: 'The effect of these verses upon me was shattering. At that time I did not fully understand how uncontrollable is the mood of despair which engulfs the tubercular patient, or how Katherine was from time to time possessed by it as by an alien power' (L2, p. 428). Murry's self-centred response, concluding that his wife had been rendered angry and fallible by depression and medication, goes some way to eliciting sympathy from the reader towards Mansfield, notwithstanding the maudlin, sentimental tone of the poem itself.

On walls and ceiling and great white bed!
(p. 28, extract from 'Sleeping Together').

The man in the room next to mine
Has got the same complaint as I
When I wake in the night I hear him turning
And then he coughs
And I cough
And he coughs again
This goes on for a long time –
Until I feel we are like two roosters
Calling to each other at false dawn
From far away hidden farms
(p. 66, poem entitled 'Malade').

Which was Judas' greatest sin
Kiss or gold?
Love must end where sales begin
I am told.
We will have no ring, no kiss
To deceive.
When you hear the serpent hiss
Think of Eve
(p. 80, extract from 'The Ring').

The French version with some forty less poems than the English edition
and therefore only a third its size, can best be defined by what it includes
rather than that which is excluded. For reasons of space and typesetting,
no poem longer than around twenty lines is included and this appears to
be the principal editorial selection criteria. The French edition is a slim,
'artistically' presented volume with short, easily digestible poems. The
'Villa Pauline' poems are present, originally a series of six written in
Bandol in the south of France during the winter of 1915/1916, sentimental in both tone and content, and now reduced to four because
'Waves' and 'The Town Between the Hills' are simply too long for this
slim-line French edition. They contain the poem 'To L. H. B. (1894–
1915)' in memory of Mansfield's dead brother, with its mawkish sentimentality and the religious overtones of its final lines:

By the remembered stream my brother stands
Waiting for me with berries in his hands . . .

176

'These are my body. Sister, take and eat'
(Poems 2, p. 54, extract from 'To L. H. B. (1894–1915)').

Près du ruisseau retrouvé mon frère
se tient
M'attendant avec des baies dans ses mains . . .
'Celles-ci sont mon corps. Sœur, prends et manges'
(*Poèmes*, p. 35).

The rest are, for the most part, youthful poems written either expressly for or about children, such as 'The Opal Dream Cave', 'Butterflies', 'Little Brother's Secret' and 'Out in the Garden', all of them insubstantial and with little literary merit:

In an opal dream cave I found a fairy:
Her wings were frailer than flower petals –
Frailer far than snowflakes
(Poems 2, p. 33, extract from 'The Opal Dream Cave').

Dans une cave opale de rêve j'ai découvert une fée
Ses ailes étaient plus frêles que les pétales d'une fleur.
Encore plus frêles que des flocons de neige
(*Poèmes*, p. 47).

The *Poems* did little to enhance Mansfield's reputation in England, and only served to reinforce the legend in France. As a result of the 'avant-propos', the familiar biographical myths relating to Mansfield are deliberately reproduced, with no attempt at corroboration, and deftly supplemented with newly invented details.

On the subject of translation as manipulation, Susan Bassnett writes:

Translation, like criticism, editing and other forms of rewriting, is a manipulatory process. It was suggested by some that the manipulation approach focussed too closely on the fortunes of a text in the target culture, and that by examining what took place during the processes of reading, rewriting in another language and subsequent reception, attention was being directed away from the source text and its cultural background (Bassnett, pp. xii–xiii).

I contend that subjective editorial decision-making controls Mansfield's personal writing in translation. The editor and translators were giving the public what it wanted and the public did not want a whimsical creature at all. When the *Journal* and *Letters* are assessed together with the short stories, perhaps the most overriding feature which seems to be lost in translation is her humour. There is sadness and philosophising too, but they do seem to be able to make the journey from English into French, whereas the humour almost *never* does. The sharp-witted, sarcastic, comedienne perceived in her original writing becomes a dull, sober 'thinker' in translation. The reintroduction of this humour into the translations of her personal writing would do much to introduce a saner, more down-to-earth, comical writer to the French reading public.

In 1970, Christiane Mortelier wrote:

> With new editors free from personal involvement, the distance brought by the years, and the outlook of a new generation, the Katherine Mansfield legend will probably alter. However, until a new [French] edition of the *Journal* and a really complete edition of her *Letters* are made, the Legend will survive (Mortelier, p. 260).

We are still waiting. On the other hand, Philip Waldron takes a more pessimistic stance:

> The distortion of the text by Murry has in turn distorted the personality of the writer herself as we know it, and is to some extent responsible even now for the myth still current in France of a temperamentally ethereal figure. Mansfield's *Journal* could never again arouse the interest it commanded in the years when it was something of a best seller, and I cannot see that a more adequate edition would result in a radical revision of her status (Waldron, p. 18).

Having discussed the editions of Mansfield's work currently available in France, both Waldron's and Mortelier's hypotheses, written over thirty years ago, appear to have been prophetic. There have been no new French editions of the *Journal*, and the *Mansfield Notebooks*, an enormous feat of scholarship and diligence, transcribing all the documents and manuscripts from which Murry derived Mansfield's *Journal* and all the other non-fiction editions of Mansfield's work, although of great interest to serious Mansfield scholars, is more or less unknown outside of this scholarly community and has never been translated.

Mansfield's personal writing – especially in the early years after her death – has undergone progressive fragmentation and refiguration, through highly subjective editing. It is not always possible to discern the original character of the writer from the cleverly crafted myth, thereby making the case for remapping these texts against the grain of the accumulated mistranslations all the more urgent. Falsification, distortion and omission are key themes in what we might call the repertoire of normative Mansfieldian hagiography and anyone approaching Mansfield's personal writing within the pantheon of French literature today will still find themselves negotiating this quagmire of myths and falsehoods.

I believe that successful translations of Mansfield's fiction which would accurately reveal both her artistry and her personal philosophy have also yet to be written, and indeed can only be written by someone completely familiar with her work in English. This is not, however, to deny the difficulties of producing translations from writing that many would consider 'untranslatable'. As Lefevere concludes:

> We should make it easy on ourselves – we translators – and calmly tell the world that total equivalence [...] does not exist, and that the best we – and our readers – can hope for is some kind of optimal approximation. That is always possible.[41]

It is precisely this 'optimal approximation' in language, coupled with an adherence to form and meaning, as exemplified by Charles Mauron in his translation of *In a German Pension*, which will ultimately reveal the originality of Mansfield's personal artistic and philosophical aesthetic to the French reader.

---

41   André Lefevere, 'The Pragmatics of Translating a National Monument', in *Dutch Crossing*, ed. by José Lambert and André Lefevere (Bern/Leuven: Peter Lang/ Leuven University Press, 1993) 27–34 (p. 30).

Chapter Five
The Critical Trend: The Development of the Legend

'Le Prieuré. Voici le pin. Voici le hêtre,
Le parterre, le toit, l'eau triste des bassins…
O Mansfield, pour mourir, c'est donc là que tu
vins?
C'est là que tu fermas pour toujours ta paupière?
Que de regrets, hélas, hantent les seuils de
pierre!'

Dominique Renouard, 'La Tombe de Katherine
Mansfield: En revenant de la tombe de Katherine
Mansfield et du Prieuré', *La Nouvelle revue*, 161
(1938), 58.

In this final chapter, I shall demonstrate how a reputation can be created
a d a personality falsified with very little effort by a few well placed lit-
e rary critics, which is exactly what happened to Katherine Mansfield in
France. This will take the form of a chronological exposé of articles and
books on Mansfield in France, since this is the most logical way of demonstrating how the legend evolves. The chapter will concentrate primarily on the development and entrenchment of the legend up to the 1940s,
followed by a briefer overview of the situation since the 1950s.

Though in England Mansfield is not perceived as a literary giant,
nevertheless she commands respect; her short stories have never once
been out of print since her death. The contrast to how she is viewed in
France could not be more marked. There, her saint-like persona has been
set in stone since it was invented in a few short years after her death and
the critics who have attempted to oust this popular perception have seen
their viewpoints submerged by the huge tidal wave of French critical
opinion, determined to uphold this falsely created persona at whatever
cost to historical accuracy.

I shall also argue that this critical opinion was almost exclusively a
Catholic and reactionary one. The beginning of the twentieth century
saw a huge Catholic literary revival in France, with religious thought be-

coming associated with literary works, as a reaction against the Positivism, Naturalism and materialism of the nineteenth century. Richard Griffiths explains how, as the twentieth century progressed, a few of the writers associated with the movement, 'entrenched themselves more and more firmly in the most extreme positions';[1] this revolution, for Griffiths, 'showed itself to be in this sense a reaction of the Right' (p. 4). I shall demonstrate in this chapter how this Catholic revival played its part in the hagiography of Mansfield's life.

In 1898, Charles Maurras founded a specific movement whose influence would extend up to the Second World War and beyond – the *Action Française*. 'Maurras stood for order, anti-individualism, tradition, patriotism; he saw in the Catholic Church one of the main means of achieving these ends' (Griffiths, p. 16). For the followers of the *Action Française*, there was only one sure way of achieving their goals – the restoration of the French monarchy. Their views appeared daily in the movement's mouthpiece – the newspaper *Action Française*, which also has its own part to play in the legend surrounding Katherine Mansfield's personality in France.

This reactionary, right-wing, Catholic revival would go on to have a lasting influence on a certain section of French literary critics, many of whom would go on to become devotees of Mansfield – see Appendix H for brief bio-sketches of the most prominent French Mansfield critics discussed in this chapter. The irony for Mansfield scholars is that she is now generally regarded as one of the forerunners of twentieth-century Modernism, and yet the perpetrators of the Catholic revival were, for the most part, reacting *against* the Modernists. Although, because of its right-wing tendencies, support from the Vatican for the *Action Française* tailed off in the 1920s, nevertheless, as Griffiths notes:

> A large portion of the Church still favoured essentially right-wing views [...] Indeed, tradition, order and patriotism [...] were in many cases the causes for certain Catholics' support of Pétain in 1940 [...] In the order of dictatorship many saw a refuge from their new bogey, the *Front Populaire*, and ultimately communism (p. 356).

1   Richard Griffiths, *The Reactionary Revolution: The Catholic Revival in French Literature 1870–1914* (New York: Frederick Ungar, 1965), p. 4.

One journal which most frequently links Mansfield critics is the *Nouvelle revue française* (*NRF*); many of them were either regular contributors, or indeed in one or two cases, editors. In Chapter One I discussed the importance of Paris as the worldwide literary melting pot in the late-nineteenth and early-twentieth-centuries; Justin O'Brien, analysing the importance of the *NRF* comments that: 'no periodical so uniformly symbolized the twentieth century in Europe as it did'.[2] Founded by André Gide in 1909:

> It was from the beginning both a center [sic] of literary creation and a critical review. Beside its essays and shorter reviews in which the keenest and most disciplined minds in France commented on the artistic manifestations of the age, appeared novels, poems, plays, stories, and manifestoes by the new writers whom the periodical was constantly discovering (O'Brien, p. xii).

Another journal which has an important role to play in the Mansfield legend is the more conservative *Revue des deux mondes*, known as the 'antechamber' of the Académie Française; the appendix to this chapter demonstrates just how many of the Mansfield hagiographers were members of that august institution.

Mansfield's Living Reputation

The first brief critical appraisal of Katherine Mansfield to be found in France, appears, during her lifetime, in the book *Le Roman anglais de notre temps* by Abel Chevalley. Her name is mentioned under two separate chapter headings; in Chapter Ten, entitled 'Les Jeunes', her name is listed amongst the promising young writers, and in Chapter Eleven, 'Le Roman anglais depuis la guerre', she merits another brief mention:

> Les œuvres de Rebecca West (notamment *The Return of the Soldier*) et celles de Katherine Mansfield (et notamment une nouvelle: *Prelude*) sont d'autres exemples non moins intéressants de cette floraison contemporaine qui, tout en reproduisant

---

2   Justin O'Brien, ed., From the NRF: *An Image of the Twentieth Century from the Pages of the Nouvelle Revue Française* (New York: Farrar, Strauss and Cudahy, 1958), p. xi.

la forme du roman traditionnel, en sacrifie volontairement le parfum moral et social si ardent pendant les générations précédentes.[3]

Within the above quotation is embodied one of the postulations which have dogged the French critical approach to Mansfield's work since its inception – namely that it lacks any social or moral dimension. This is an important misrepresentation of her art in France, and as a result of it we shall see how Mansfield's work was instead placed on an ethereal plain from which successive generations of critics have attempted to either topple it or to maintain its precarious distance from all things earthly.

In the previous autumn of 1921, Mansfield's stories had come to the attention of the French literary establishment (even though there would be no translations of her work until after her death), when *Bliss and Other Stories* was entered for the 'Prix Femina Vie Heureuse' of 1921. I have discovered an unpublished letter held in the McFarlin Library, University of Tulsa, from Michael Sadleir, her publisher at Constable's, who had entered her for the prestigious French award for 'a book written in English', where he discusses her chances of winning:

A line of congratulation on the success of BLISS in being recommended to the Femina Vie Heureuse French Committee for consideration for the 1920/21 Prize. I hope it gets it. From the literary point of view I think its only serious competitor is THE BLACK DIAMOND but I notice with some concern that DANGEROUS AGES in this country had a larger number of votes than either of the other two. It was necessary to send immediately five copies of BLISS to Paris for the French Committee and one to the Chairwoman (the French Ambassadress) at the French Embassy.[4]

Mansfield wrote back: 'Thank you very much for sending the books to Paris on my behalf. But I shall not get the prize. Prizes *always* pass me by. Which is sad. For they are nice things' (CL4, p. 314, 7 November 1921). She was right; the prize went to Rose Macaulay for *Dangerous Ages*.[5] The other runner-up alongside Mansfield, was Brett Young's *The*

3   Abel Chevalley, *Le Roman anglais de notre temps* (London: Humphrey Milford, 1921), p. 238.
4   Unpublished typescript letter, from Michael Sadleir to Mansfield, 4 November 1921. (University of Tulsa, McFarlin Library, Department of Special Collections, series 1, Katherine Mansfield Correspondence).
5   Rose Macaulay, *Dangerous Ages* (London: Collins, 1921).

Black Diamond.[6] Being a contender, however, inevitably raised her profile within French literary circles.

Mansfield's Death Viewed in England

The weekly journal *The Nation and the Athenaeum*, which had been edited by Mansfield's husband Murry until February 1921, placed an anonymous obituary in the 'Wayfarer' column on 13 January 1923, four days after her death on 9 January:

> I deeply mourn the untimely death of Katherine Mansfield (Mrs. Middleton Murry) [...] Katherine Mansfield's spiritual excellence lay in the reflective power of a mind that caught up a thousand rays of revealed or half-revealed consciousness, and gave them out again in a serene order and a most delicate pattern [...] These gifts were joined to a great physical beauty, and, by reason of the sustaining power of a rare spirit, seemed to be little clouded by physical suffering, up to the hour when its bright light was extinguished.[7]

This obituary, undoubtedly written by a friend of Murry's, is critical in terms of instigating and disseminating a legend which in France has continued to the present day. The sycophantic tone, the stress on Mansfield's spirituality, her beauty, her suffering and other-worldliness will be found in countless articles, biographies and memoirs of Mansfield in France, as this chapter will reveal. This is where the hagiography begins – four days after her death, in an English journal, recently edited by her husband. A week later, in the same journal, another of Murry's friends, H. M. Tomlinson, continues the eulogising tone in a page-long memoir dedicated to Mansfield:

> And she suggested the power – an illusion, possibly, created by her luminous pallor and her look of penetrating intelligence – of that divination which is supposed to belong to those not quite of this world [...] She would listen without comment, and then tell the truth from her place above good and evil [...] She stood between this world and the next, and saw our disillusionments and disappointments at the

6   Brett Young, *The Black Diamond* (London: Collins, 1921).
7   Anon., 'A Wayfarer', *Nation & Athenaeum*, 32, 13 January 1923, p. 575.

end of a long, clear, perspective [...] Katherine Mansfield never once came down to flatter us. She remained aloof. She had no choice; she had been set apart by destiny, and was waiting.[8]

This same sycophantic tone is also to be found in many pages of the *Adelphi*, one of London's foremost literary journals, edited by Murry from 1923–1930. In the immediate aftermath of her death, Murry started printing several pieces of Mansfield's work in every issue, and this editorial policy continued for two years. As the months went by, the sycophantic line became ever more pronounced, the amount of space given over to the Katherine Mansfield publicity machine became ever greater, until even her closest friends and admirers turned away in disgust. As Frank Lea remarks, Mansfield, 'became the presiding genius of the paper – till even the friendly Bennett was forced to remonstrate, whilst with the unfriendly it became an article of faith that Murry was "exploiting his wife's reputation"'.[9]

During her lifetime Mansfield had three collections of short stories published. At the time of her death she had almost become a celebrity, receiving fan mail and good reviews for her work. She was about to hit the 'big time'. Then she died. Without Murry her star would not have shone so brightly, for three small volumes of short stories would not have been enough to maintain an iconic status over the next hundred or so years. But, following her death, Murry collected together all her papers, diaries, letters, and unpublished stories and gradually, over a number of years, created many volumes from these loose papers and notebooks, the detritus of a writer's life.

As early as six months after the fawning English obituaries discussed above, Conrad Aiken wrote a review of one of these posthumous volumes – *The Dove's Nest* – in *The Nation & The Athenaeum* (the same periodical as that in which Tomlinson's obituary appeared):

> The stories in 'The Dove's Nest' are not her best [...] They merely deepen one's impression of the smallness and repetitiveness of Miss Mansfield's art [...] She had discovered that she lacked the power and simplicity of the first-rate artist.[10]

8   H. M. Tomlinson, 'Katherine Mansfield', *Nation & Athenaeum*, 32, 20 January 1923, p. 609.

9   Frank Lea, *The Life of John Middleton Murry* (London: Methuen, 1959), p. 113.

10   Conrad Aiken, 'The Short Story as Confession', *Nation & Athenaeum*, 33, 14 July 1923, p. 490.

Raymond Mortimer, writing in *The New Statesman* the week before, was of an equally dismissive opinion, stating:

> Upon the thirty stories contained in *Bliss* and *The Garden Party* her rank as a writer of fiction must now always depend, and I cannot believe that her artistic reputation will ever stand higher than it does at present [...] [T]he peculiar characteristics of her art were her use of Tchekhov and her gift for seeing others as they see themselves [...] [T]here are moments [...] when his influence on English writers appears positively disastrous.[11]

These generally unfavourable reviews started the evolution, in England, of a dismissal of her work in general, and this negative opinion dominated, for the most part, English literary appreciation of her writing until the late 1950s. Thus, in England, the seeds of an 'other-worldly' personality were never allowed to germinate, since her reputation was always tainted by the fact that she was Murry's deceased wife. Over time he became progressively more disliked in literary circles, scathingly caricatured in Aldous Huxley's novel *Point Counter Point* as Denis Burlap.[12] As early as May 1925, writing in *The Nation & The Athenaeum*, Huxley's aversion to Murry's hagiography of his dead wife was already plainly evident:

> Each of Miss Mansfield's stories is a window into a lighted room. The glimpse of the inhabitants sipping their tea and punch is enormously exciting. But one knows nothing, when one has passed, of what they are really like. That is why, however thrilling at a first reading, her stories do not wear.[13]

The main reason for Murry's literary ostracisation was precisely this over-exposure of his dead wife's work and his aim to publish as

---

1*   Raymond Mortimer, 'The Dove's Nest and Other Stories', *New Statesman*, 21, 7 July 1923, p. 394.

12   Aldous Huxley, *Point Counter Point* (London: Chatto & Windus, 1928). Like many of Huxley's novels, Point Counter Point has little actual plot. Much of the novel consists of penetrating personality sketches and long intellectual conversations. Denis Burlap, is a facetious and hypocritical individual who idolizes (and thinks himself like) Saint Francis. In his biography of Murry, Frank Lea states: '[Murry] had been more outraged by Burlap than he cared to admit. His first impulse had been to challenge Huxley to a duel' (Lea, p. 159).

13   Aldous Huxley, 'The Traveller's Eye-View', *Nation & Athenaeum*, 37, 16 May 1925, p. 204.

much of her literary remains as the public could stomach, whilst at the same time editing out any material which he felt did not correlate with the image of her he was trying to put across, as discussed in my chapter on the translations. Murry's editorial stance remained more or less the same until his death in 1957. He made a good deal of money out of Mansfield's books; one does not have to be too great a cynic in order to view this production-line of his dead first wife's literary remains as an easy money making venture. It certainly paid for the upkeep on his next three wives.

There is no space here to discuss the development of the critical response to Mansfield's writing in England. Suffice to say that it was a measured response, with, as we have seen, the odd eulogy from close friends soon after her death, followed by more muted praise for her work, together with the ever-present snub to Murry for his role in her reputation. This attitude was summed up by Katherine Anne Porter in 1937:

> The misplaced emphasis [...] [is perhaps owed] [...] to her literary executor [Murry], who has edited and published her letters and journals with a kind of merciless insistence, a professional anxiety for her fame on what seems to be the wrong grounds, and from which in any case his personal relation to her might have excused him for a time. Katherine Mansfield's work is the important fact about her, and she is in danger of the worst fate that an artist can suffer – to be overwhelmed by her own legend, to have her work neglected for an interest in her 'personality' (Porter, p. 435).

Mansfield's Death Viewed in France

Murry, with his wide knowledge of French literature, had numerous contacts in French literary circles. As Frank Lea points out in his biography:

> [In 1922] Murry made the acquaintance of most of the leading French men of letters, to whom he was already well known as the 'presenter' of Proust and Gide to the English public – Valéry and Charles Du Bos for example, who became his friends and life-long admirers (Lea, p 89).

It was, however, to be two years after her death before French reviewers became generally aware of the name of Katherine Mansfield.

The critic Louis Gillet, a Catholic, an anglophile, and a reader of *The Adelphi* was the first person to draw attention to the dead artist in France. Although the two men had not met, Gillet was aware of Murry's literary reputation in France, and the fact that Mansfield was his wife made her an eminently suitable subject for literary discussion. As an antidote to the notoriety of such home grown writers as Rachilde and Colette, the attraction of a saintly young literary role-model for the literary and critical establishment in France was obvious. In her book *Masks of Tradition: Women and the Politics of Writing in Twentieth Century France*, Martha Noel Evans discusses the narrator of Colette's *La Vagabonde*, who, 'characterizes herself in contradictory but equally negative versions of the writer: the bluestocking and the whore'.[14] She goes on to discuss a concept which she terms 'negative inclusion'; in other words:

> The woman writer must come to terms with herself in relation to literary tradition not as an absence – which might in fact bestow on her a certain freedom of self-definition – but rather as a trivialized and distorted presence (p. 13).

Of course this theory also applies to dead as well as living female writers at a point in time where the literary establishment was overwhelmingly male and reactionary. This chapter will demonstrate how Mansfield was taken up by the male, Catholic literary right, transmuted into a trivialised and distorted presence, and thereby 'absorbed into a hierarchical system of political organisation, defined in essentialist, oppositional terms' (Evans, p. 17).

Gillet's article, which appears in *La Revue des deux mondes* in 1924, is of paramount importance to the initial development of the Katherine Mansfield legend in France. It is an exploratory, subjective, highly personalised review, which immediately takes the stance of idolising the artist, in a romantically poetic way. Gillet seems not so much impressed by her art as by her life, which he views in an almost saintly light. He cites Murry as his biographical source. We do not know to what extent, if any, he distorted or misrepresented the facts put before him, but it is important to note that Murry was on hand to offer biographical material:

14   Martha Noel Evans, *Masks of Tradition: Women and the Politics of Writing in Twentieth Century France* (Ithica: Cornell University Press, 1987), p. 20.

'Elle acquit', m'écrit son mari, M. John Middleton Murry, à qui je dois tous les renseignements qu'on vient de lire'.[15] Here then we find the origins of a cult in France, the first signs of Mansfield as literary icon:

> C'était [une] *femme* [...] de délicatesse, d'adorable pureté féminine, sans que jamais une seule fois l'auteur se mêlât d'aborder ces problèmes moraux [...] Elle n'avait rien de la suffragette. Elle paraissait née dans un astre étranger à la question sociale, sur une planète innocente, avant l'état de péché et le monstrueux âge de fer de l'industrie moderne. Elle semblait venir d'une étoile plus belle, et elle en conservait une atmosphère radieuse flottante autour de sa personne et dans la pou dre d'or de ses cheveux (p. 932).

Its similarity in tone to the obituary by Tomlinson discussed above is remarkable.

Within the article are to be found at least ten statements which we now know to be false. Some are relatively unimportant, such as his stating that her hair was the colour of 'poudre d'or' when it was black; that she barely managed to exist on a small allowance when in fact her annual income at the beginning of her literary career was £100 – more than most working class families saw in a year; she was not married to Murry in 1915, as stated, but in 1918; her final days, although the statement that they were spent 'dans une vieille maison à Fontainebleau' is literally correct, omits the fact that they were spent in the esoteric company of Gurdjieff and his followers at his Institute for the Harmonious Development of Man.

The emphasis in Gillet's article is on Mansfield as a charming 'jeune fille' with a quasi-angelic persona, coupled with the gift of genius. Saint-like and child-like images and vocabulary are everywhere: 'C'était *femme* des pieds à la tête'; 'une sorte de charme lointain'; 'la moitié de son être flottait dans l'invisible'; 'brisée, sans avenir'; 'elle ne tenait plus à ce monde que pour donner le souffle aux enfants de son cœur'. Her essential innocence as an artist is also stressed: 'Elle paraissait née dans un astre étranger à la question sociale, sur une planète innocente, avant l'état de péché et le monstrueux âge de fer de l'industrie moderne'. He has, however, not yet discovered her 'spirituality', which forms the basis for his next review in 1929. This first article, however, although full of

15   Louis Gillet, 'Katherine Mansfield', *Revue des deux mondes*, 24 (15 December 1924), 929–42 (p. 932).

praise for the young, dead writer, does not immediately bring Mansfield any general critical acclaim in France.

The second article on Mansfield in France, published four years after the first, written by Gabriel Marcel, appears in the pages of the *NRF*. Marcel, a hitherto professed agnostic, is baptised into the Catholic Church a month after the above article appears, at the age of forty. As Seymour Cain notes, in his biography of Marcel:

> This event was the culmination of a long, circuitous journey, starting from a non-religious family background and a secular philosophical training, proceeding though the intense and patient enquiries recorded in the metaphysical journals, and ending in complete acceptance of traditional Christian faith.[16]

His article is based on the recent publication in England of the *Journal* and *Letters*, and its more objective approach is in contrast to the earlier article by Gillet. Marcel lays emphasis on the spirituality of her situation – notably her illness and the death of her brother – and combined with it her attitude to life:

> Les indications, si précieuses soient-elles, que nous fournissent *Le Journal* et *La Correspondance*, sur l'atmosphère spirituelle dans laquelle s'épanouit le génie de Katherine Mansfield, ne sont pourtant pas ici l'essentiel [...] Ce qui fait à mes yeux la valeur sans prix de ces livres, c'est l'approfondissement constant d'une certaine situation spirituelle.[17]

In highlighting this spiritual element, Marcel was echoing Murry's editorial approach in England towards his wife's literary remains. Frank Lea states that the late 1920s were a difficult time personally and spiritually for Murry:

---

16 Seymour Cain, *Gabriel Marcel* (London: Bowes and Bowes, 1963), p. 50. Cain describes how Marcel's conversion came about after a 'seemingly slight incident revealed to him his unconscious intention [...] that he "had to choose Catholicism": Marcel's review of a work by the Catholic writer François Mauriac (*Dieu et Mammon*) elicited a friendly letter from Mauriac, ending with the query: "But, then, why aren't you one of us?" These words set going a spiritual experience which is recorded in the most touching passages in Marcel's journals' (Cain, pp. 50–51).

17 Gabriel Marcel, 'Lectures', *NRF*, 32 (February 1929), 268–73 (p. 270).

The coincidence of the economic Depression with [his second wife's physical] decline, following that of the War with Katherine's, had so enhanced his sense of the precariousness of existence that the notion of some occult 'correlation between my personal condition and that of the world' was to shape, or distort, his thinking for the rest of his life (Lea, p. 163).

In the light of his own personal reawakening to religion, he sought to show the spiritual, if not religious, side of his dead wife's writings too. Griffiths notes how: 'we, who have become so accustomed to spiritual themes in the novel and in the theatre, both in England and France, can hardly realise what a revolution in literary taste this new trend illustrated' (Griffiths, p. 357).

Marcel, however, does not see Mansfield's spirituality as having a Christian foundation at all: 'religion infiniment éloignée du Christianisme qui ne l'attirait point, qui peut-être même en quelque manière lui répugnait' (p. 271). Finally, he states what Gillet omitted to say, concerning Mansfield's exact whereabouts at the time of her death, namely that she was residing – 'dans une colonie théosophique'. He continues: 'Il n'y faut point voir, comme on est infiniment trop tenté de le faire, le geste désespéré d'une malade, mais un effort ultime pour réaliser enfin l'accord de sa pensée et de sa vie, de soi-même avec soi' (p. 273).

Both the above articles highlight the initial development of the critical approach in France. Already, we can see a division of opinion, an all-encompassing idolisation versus a more down-to-earth approval, eventually giving way, as we shall see, to astonished disbelief in some quarters at the path the reputation takes.

Gillet, of course, as the presenter of Mansfield to the French speaking world has to give his interpretation of the *Letters* and *Journal*, which he does, again in *La Revue des deux mondes* on 1 May 1929, three months after the appearance of Marcel's review. The article commences thus, after a silence of four and a half years:

C'est elle-même, c'est elle, la créature de paradis qui nous apparaissait là-bas, radieuse, au bord d'un golfe du Pacifique; c'est Kezia, c'est Beryl, l'Eve, que nous voyions sortir toute neuve de son bain matinal, fraîche comme la lumière des premiers jours du monde. Voici les lettres, les reliques de Katherine Mansfield.[18]

18   Louis Gillet, 'Les Lettres de Katherine Mansfield', *Revue des deux mondes*, 51 (1 May 1929), 213–27 (p. 213).

The religious implications of the word 'reliques' sets the tone of the article as Gillet attempts to define Mansfield's spiritual personality, giving it a Christian, and for him, Catholic foundation. He may well have been attempting to counterbalance the effect of Marcel's less overtly Christian approach. He speaks of her spiritual metamorphosis and says: 'Ce progrès est le grand intérêt des *Lettres* et du *Journal*. Ces textes permettent de suivre presque jour par jour le travail de la "grâce", ils révèlent un aspect de cette âme que nous ne soupçonnions guère, l'importance qu'a eue dans sa vie la crise religieuse' (p. 217). His emphasis centres on the fact that although she never actually embraced Christianity, nevertheless, her spiritual journey was on a more refined, ethereal level than most professed Christians could ever hope to attain, and that this same journey is to be upheld as an example worthy of our attention – and our adoration. Even her connection with Gurdjieff at Fontainebleau is now viewed as the final step in her peculiarly successful spiritual journey. Thus, the hagiography of Mansfield's life is now firmly established. Gillet's voice, the voice of eulogy, stands out loud and clear.

Reception of French Translations

However, Gillet and Marcel were still reading her works in English. Between 1928 and 1932, four of Mansfield's books are translated into French – two collections of short stories, *Bliss*, and *The Garden Party*, plus the *Letters* and *Journal*. (See Appendix F for a complete list of publications dates for Mansfield primary texts in England and France.) A much wider circle of critics are now able to help develop her burgeoning reputation in France, though its origins remain in Louis Gillet's original concept of Mansfield, both as a personality and as a literary artist. As the only real French 'specialist' on Mansfield at the time of the French translations, he is asked to write one of the prefaces, namely for *Bliss* (*Félicité*). It is his original article of 1924 – now six years old – slightly abridged, that he uses, and which necessarily biases the majority of French readers towards the stance expounded within it. No one has any reason not to believe the facts Gillet presents. So far as the *Journal* and

Letters were concerned, the critics had decided that Mansfield was an essentially spiritual writer, seeking hidden truths to explain the meaning of life. It is Gabriel Marcel who writes the preface to the *Lettres*.

Thus, in 1931, there are at least eleven articles devoted to Mansfield in French periodicals and newspapers, all with critical convergences. A collective examination of four of the most prominent reveals an interesting pattern of postulations, factual distortions, cognitive revelations and similarities of subject matter.[19] Although, as stated earlier, four volumes of her writing had now been translated into French, the two volumes of stories are not reviewed at all. All four articles are reviews of the *Lettres* with only one mentioning the *Journal* as well.

Of the *Lettres*, Benjamin Crémieux states:

> C'est plus qu'un livre, c'est une prise de contact direct avec un être adorable de fraîcheur, de spontanéité, de noblesse, et, en dépit de son mal, de vitalité. Son œuvre est celle d'un écrivain richement doué, mais c'est une œuvre entre les autres, malgré son timbre particulier. On peut l'aimer plus, l'aimer moins. Mais ces Lettres... (Crémieux, p. 243).

Although the other reviewers are not so dismissive of Mansfield's fiction, nevertheless their general lack of interest in the stories would seem to indicate a certain symbiosis of thought. All four articles bear witness to the influence of Gillet and Marcel, with Gillet's stance predominating (his voice is, of course, present in the preface to *Félicité*), evidence for which is to be found in the vocabulary of the Crémieux extract above.

Lack of space, perhaps, dictates the absence of any real biographical detail in the Crémieux article, but the other three seem to positively relish the chance to recount the 'tragic' life story in their own words. Bertrand's offering is particularly interesting, for the wealth of highly exaggerated, colourful and sometimes false detail splashed across its pages:

> A dix-huit ans, première crise morale; sa famille la rappelle en Nouvelle-Zélande. Le pays natal, vu de Londres, n'est plus pour elle qu'une prison, ou pire, 'un désert

19 Benjamin Crémieux, 'Le Carnet de Benjamin Crémieux – Katherine Mansfield', *Annales politiques et littéraires*, 2 (15 September 1931), 243–44. Pierre Deffrennes, 'La Correspondance de Katherine Mansfield', *Études des pères de la compagnie de Jésus*, 209 (Oct–Dec 1931), 314–24. G.-Jean Aubry, 'Katherine Mansfield', *Revue de Paris*, 6 (Nov–Dec 1931), 57–71. G. P. Bertrand, 'L'Attitude spirituelle de Katherine Mansfield', *Cahiers du sud*, 18 (1931), 646–65.

intellectuel'. Elle retourne, mais se révolte, mène pendant deux ans une existence nomade, parcourt à cheval l'intérieur de l'île, obtient enfin de ses parents la liberté et une maigre pension (Bertrand, p. 651).

This notion of 'une existence nomade' is laughable when one recalls that the months Mansfield spent in New Zealand prior to her return to England consisted of a busy social round of garden parties, concerts and soirées, as befitted one of the daughters of the chairman of the Bank of New Zealand. Gillet's coining of the term 'maigre pension', which, as we know, was simply not true, appears in two more of the articles – 'ces subsides étaient maigres' (Aubry, p. 59), 'une maigre pension' (Deffrennes, p. 315).

Gillet's earlier reference to Mansfield's French ascendancy in the family name of Beauchamp also seems worthy of note to the reviewers – 'd'une famille d'origine probablement française' (Aubry, p. 58), 'la famille de Beauchamp où d'aucuns se plaisent à voir une ascendance française' (Bertrand, p. 651), 'elle dort son dernier sommeil dans cette terre française d'où venaient probablement ses lointains aïeux' (Aubry, p. 71).[20]

Crémieux extends the notion of her attachment to France:

> Et ce qui, du premier coup, retient et charme un Français dans ces *Lettres*, c'est une vision fraîche et neuve de la France. Personne mieux que Katherine Mansfield n'a senti et évoqué le charme de Paris, celui de Provence et n'a compris le petit peuple citadin ou rural de notre pays (Crémieux, p. 243).

This point will be expounded by later reviewers and become a source of contention in the pro- and anti- Mansfield debate.

One further biographical note highlighted by all four critics, concerns the final months of Mansfield's life spent with Gurdjieff at his 'Institute for the Harmonious Development of Man' at Fontainebleau. Bertrand appears either not to have read either Marcel's or Gillet's 1929 articles, or else to be deliberately misleading, when he states, 'elle entra enfin dans une petite maison de retraite dans la forêt de Fontainebleau' (Bertrand, p. 659). The other articles reveal the true state of affairs but are hesitant about its meaning: 'Elle a cru trouver une atmosphère propre

---

20 The notion of her burial in France was not missed by Gillet either: 'Elle repose, relique charmante de l'Angleterre, confiée à la terre française qui déjà garde dans son sein la cendre fraternelle' (Gillet: 1924, p. 942).

à son dessein dans un étrange phalanstère russe' (Aubry, p. 71); 'K. Mansfield se retira dans une société de théosophes russes, près de Fontainebleau' (Deffrennes, p. 323).

All the reviews are an attempt to explain Mansfield spiritually – the spiritual journey she undertook as a result of her illness, her essential sincerity and goodness, in short, all the qualities which they claimed could be found in the *Lettres* and *Journal*. The fact that they should dwell on such things is, in large part, due to Murry's editing of the originals, and his attempt to bring out the spiritual quality of his wife's writings, as mentioned earlier. Pierre Deffrennes, a Jesuit priest, writing for the Catholic reader in a religious journal, follows the path already taken by Gillet – explaining Mansfield in terms of her religious development. He feels that Mansfield's soul and mind are constantly at war – her soul embracing wholeheartedly the essential tenets of the Christian faith, while her mind constantly refuses to acknowledge any orthodox religious convictions. Of her sincerity he says:

> Celle de K. Mansfield est une sincérité parfaitement intègre à la face d'une présence transcendante – quoi qu'elle en pense, – qui est pure, qui donne la vie, qui est joie, qui est Dieu en un mot, soit qu'on prononce ce mot ou non, à laquelle elle aspire de s'unir (Deffrennes, p. 319).

None of the other articles develops the religious theme to this extent, but nevertheless they all stress the essential purity of her art and her mind. Georges-Jean Aubry uses the adjective 'virginal' three times. He briefly mentions the stories, as does Bertrand – who, however, evades any discussion of her technique: 'il reste encore dans ses nouvelles un charme indéfinissable qu'aucune critique ne saurait révéler. [...] Son véritable secret est mort avec elle' (Bertrand, p. 665). For Bertrand and the others, her *Lettres* offer a great moral example, portraying the highest form of spirituality; he concludes by saying that had she lived, she might have become the greatest prose writer of her generation.

First Signs of Disillusionment

It is perhaps fitting that the year 1931 ends on an elegiac note, since all the reviews up to and including 1931 tend that way. However, not every critic in France could have admired Mansfield's work and the excess of praise is bound, sooner or later, to motivate someone to dispute the growing hagiography. This is precisely what happens.

In 1932, Robert Brasillach reviews the French translation of the *Journal*. His tone is measured, slightly critical, though not without praise:

> Il y a près de dix ans que cette jeune femme, après une longue maladie, mourut, encore inconnue en France [...] On traduisit en français deux recueils de nouvelles [...] qui acquirent aussitôt à la jeune morte un public peu étendu mais fidèle. Soudain la publication de ses *Lettres*, l'an dernier, fit naître autour de son souvenir mille affections et mille témoignages. Voici qu'aujourd'hui paraît son *Journal* (Stock), et Katherine Mansfield est entrée désormais dans une région spirituelle [...] De tous côtés, sa vie, ses souffrances, ses rêves, ses désirs, sont repris et traduits en échos fidèles par d'autres vies, d'autres désirs.[21]

He feels able to dismiss her art as not having anything like the quality of Rosamond Lehmann or Emily Brontë, though he places the *Lettres* and *Journal* amongst the best of their genre.

The effect is generative. André Thérive, in another review of the French translation of the *Journal*, takes the denigrating stance one step further: 'Il me sera permis, non pas d'avouer une déception, mais de tracer les limites de l'intérêt que ces textes éveillent. Et elles sont fort étroites'.[22] He is shocked by Mansfield's criticisms of France and the French in the *Journal*: 'On n'a pas eu le scrupule d'expurger le texte des remarques désagréables pour notre pays', and calls a comparison she makes between France and England, 'le comble de la puérilité' (p. 3).

The voice of dissent has finally appeared, and one would expect it to start the demythologisation process, forcing her circle of admirers to reappraise her. Initially, this was not to be the case, as future articles reveal.

21   Robert Brasillach, 'Katherine Mansfield', *Candide*, 22 September 1932, p. 4
22   André Thérive, 'Les Livres', *Le Temps*, 7 July 1932, p. 3.

Myth Continues Unabated

1933 is an important year for the development of the legend, due in part to the publication by Francis Carco in *Les Annales politiques et littéraires* of his 'Souvenirs sur Katherine Mansfield', published in two parts on 27 January and 3 February.[23] Their relationship is described in detail in Chapter Two, where I demonstrate how Carco based the predatory and exploitative character of Winnie on Mansfield in his 1916 novel *Les Innocents*, whilst she was still alive. Carco could not alter his novel, but he certainly could and does change his attitude towards Mansfield once she is dead and in particular his written portrayal of her. With the passage of time, Mansfield's reputation in its ascendancy, and not wishing to rock any critical boats, his biographical portrait of Mansfield is considerably softened and romanticised in order to accommodate the new sentimental French legend surrounding her: 'Quand je la menais, avec John Middleton-Murry, dans les bals de la rue Lappe (qui n'étaient point alors bien fréquentés), sa présence suffisait à tout rendre plus émouvant, plus pur' (I, p. 103). Today, we see Carco's falsification of actual events as an attempt to continue and enhance the reputation that Mansfield had so far achieved in France and thereby bask himself in some of the reflected glory. He states in this article that, but for the fact that his address was found amongst her papers, he would have remained silent about his connection with her: 'Je n'aurais jamais rien écrit sur Katherine Mansfield si mon ancienne adresse du quai aux Fleurs ne s'était trouvée reproduite dans sa *Correspondance*' (I, p. 98). His 'touching' presentation of his friendship with Mansfield and his continual insistence upon its platonic quality must have made the French literary world wonder at his modesty in concealing his relationship with such a literary star for so long. Once revealed, however, he is swift in attaching

---

23   Francis Carco, 'Mes Souvenirs sur Katherine Mansfield', *Annales politiques et littéraires*, 100 (27 January 1933), 98–104, and continuing with the second part in the following week's issue (3 February 1933), 137–40, hereafter referred to as 'Carco I and II'.

himself to the momentum of the growing legend by publishing the above two articles on three separate occasions.[24]

Carco describes their friendship as, 'folle d'ailleurs, mais absolument pure' (II, p. 137) ; of her trip to the battlefront at Gray he states categorically, 'Ce n'est point en pareils lieux [...] que j'aurais proposé à la jeune Anglaise de venir me rejoindre si mes intentions n'avaient été parfaitement correctes et désintéressées' (II, p. 137). Of course, this statement was a direct falsehood, since a sexual liaison was very much on the agenda – for both of them – but having thus absolved himself from any difficulties, he moves on, commending Gillet's hagiographical preface to the translation of *Bliss* (*Félicité*), by saying: 'Rien de plus pénétrant, de plus subtil n'a été dit de Katherine Mansfield. Elle vivait dans cette fantasmagorie' (II, p. 139), and he himself is able to confirm how, 'elle souffrait de vivre parmi tant de laideur et de corruption' (II, p. 140). He revels in descriptions of the tears she shed for him: 'Mystères d'une âme d'enfant! Si pure! Si franche! Que de larmes Katherine Mansfield n'a pas versées!' (II, p. 139). Thus, from someone French, who actually knew Mansfield, comes 'proof' of her essential innocence and purity and the legend now has a firmer basis than ever before.

Several more articles appear in 1933. One in particular, by Denis Saurat in the *NRF* merits discussion, since it describes in detail life at the Prieuré at Avon with Gurdjieff, and briefly mentions Mansfield's stay there: '[Orage] allait me montrer l'endroit où Katherine Mansfield avait passé ses derniers jours. Endroit extraordinaire'.[25] The tone is almost that of a mini-pilgrimage. Elisabeth Tasset-Nissolle writing in *Le Correspondant* is equally in awe of Mansfield's now semi-legendary literary status:

Si le succès du *Journal* et des *Lettres* indiquait en France un renouveau du goût littéraire dans le sens de la pureté, Katherine Mansfield n'aurait pas livré sa

---

24 These articles were reprinted in various forms for many years after their original appearance. They were collected and reprinted separately in 1934 by *Le Divan*. They also form the tenth chapter of his autobiography *Montmartre à vingt ans* (Paris: Albin Michel, 1938), pp. 176–205, and were extended for another chapter in his second book of memoirs, *Bohème d'artiste* (Paris: Albin Michel, 1940), pp. 245–61.

25 Denis Saurat, 'Visite à Gourdjieff', *NRF*, 41 (1 November 1933), 686–98.

bataille en vain. Elle aurait semé son 'grain de vérité'. Et qui sait quel grand arbre une petite semence peut devenir?[26]

The eulogising of Mansfield's life is swept along by this tide of critical opinion. Jacques Bompard's article in *La Grande revue*, marking the tenth anniversary of her death in sixteen pages of elegiac and sycophantic prose, is critically unimportant except for the fact that he notes a slight topic of dissention beginning to arise: 'On a reproché à Katherine Mansfield des mots assez désagréables pour la France, inscrits dans son journal ou dans ses lettres' (perhaps referring to Thérive's article of 1932).[27] His reply: 'Mais comment en vouloir à cette jeune femme malade, que sa maladie précisément rendait sensible au moindre heurt, à la moindre dissonance?' (Bompard, p. 555) One of the main bones of contention is beginning to surface, namely that both the *Lettres* and *Journal* contain numerous derogatory remarks towards the French. In another article, Edmond Jaloux (who wrote the preface to the 1929 translation of *The Garden Party*), comments on a new translation incorporating a selection of stories from the posthumously published volumes, *The Dove's Nest* and *Something Childish*, entitled *La Mouche*.[28] He commences thus: 'Quand on parle de Katherine Mansfield, il faut donc parler de son âme',[29] and after a long elegiac discussion, concludes: 'A tous [les personnages de son imagination], elle accorde un peu de sa mélancolie à elle, de son féerique secret, de sa solitude' (Jaloux, p. 4). Although he is discussing a new translation of her stories, he still manages to focus this article on Mansfield's personality rather than her fiction. The year concludes with the apogée of hagiography, in an article by Jean-Louis Vaudoyer in *Les Nouvelles littéraires*, entitled 'La tombe d'une fée':

26   Elisabeth Tasset-Nissolle, 'Katherine Mansfield (1888–1923)', *Le Correspondant*, 25 September 1933, 900–08 (p. 908). In 1936, Tasset-Nissolle brought out a book entitled *Conquérantes* (Paris: Je Sers, 1936), discussing the lives of Elisabeth Fry, Florence Barclay, Joséphine Butler, Catherine Booth, Emmeline Pankhurst, Katherine Mansfield and Renée de Benoit.

27   Jacques Bompard, 'Sur une jeune femme morte: Katherine Mansfield', *Grande revue*, 140 (February 1933), 540–56 (p. 555).

28   Katherine Mansfield, *La Mouche*, trans. by Madeleine T. Guéritte et Marguerite Faguer, pref. by M. Guéritte (Paris: Stock, 1933).

29   Edmond Jaloux, 'L'Esprit des livres', *Nouvelles littéraires*, 14 October 1933, p. 4.

Une âme de poésie règne sur le monde imaginaire que Katherine Mansfield a créé; elle le transfigure, l'épure jusqu'à la désincarnation ; métamorphosant les personnages les plus humbles de la vie quotidienne, et les baignant dans la lumière dont Fra Angelico baigne ses élus, aux seuils du paradis.[30]

It becomes harder and harder for a dispassionate observer to understand how serious critics were writing articles such as the ones discussed above. But the legend in France surrounding the life and work of Mansfield allowed such extreme expression to seem natural and, indeed, correct.

Irreverence Returns

After Carco's 'revelations', the most important article of 1933 is Marcel Thiébaut's review of the recently published *The Life of Katherine Mansfield* by Ruth Mantz and John Middleton Murry.[31] This is the first biography of Mansfield, translated into French in 1935 and titled much more appropriately, *La Jeunesse de Katherine Mansfield*, since the book only covers the years up to 1912 and the beginning of her relationship with Murry.[32] For all biographical material after 1912, the authors refer the reader to the *Letters* and *Journal*, severely edited by – Murry. Of her troubled life from 1908–1911, much is left unsaid or else speculation on the part of Mantz replaces hard facts. And after 1912, the reader still has to rely on the *Letters* and *Journal*, in their expurgated form, in order to follow the last eleven years of her life. This is not a book to destroy myths, nor was it ever intended as such. I contend that it is this book, more than any other, which raises the stakes in the hagiography of Mansfield's life in France, and for which Murry is directly responsible.

30   Jean-Louis Vaudoyer, 'La tombe d'une fée', in *Nouvelles littéraires*, 4 November 1933, p. 2.
31   Ruth Elvish Mantz and John Middleton Murry, *The Life of Katherine Mansfield* (London: Constable, 1933).
32   Ruth Mantz and John Middleton Murry, *La Jeunesse de Katherine Mansfield*, trans. by M. T. Guéritte, pref. by Jean-Louis Vaudoyer (Paris: Stock, 1935).

The book is a sycophantic portrayal of an almost fictional character, so little does Mansfield as portrayed in the book resemble the Mansfield whose personality is suggested by her own writings. In the introduction, Murry plays down his role: 'I do not really deserve the position of collaborator [...] but since my contribution has been rather more than a mere revision [...] it has been thought best that we should share the responsibility for the work' (p. 1). The religious element is brought in almost immediately:

> Such candour and transparence [sic] are the product of a long travail of soul – of an incessant process of self-purgation, of self-refinement into that condition of crystal clarity for which Katherine Mansfield unconsciously struggled and towards the end of her life consciously prayed (p. 2).

Of her early misdemeanours and constant risk-taking he writes: 'This is the voice of the Life within urging Man to yet more Life. This is the voice to which Jesus of Nazareth was himself obedient unto death' (p. 10). Continuing the annexation of Mansfield to Christ, he argues:

> What has Jesus to do with Blake, with Keats, with Katherine Mansfield? He has everything to do with them. They belong to his pattern. They are the life-adventurers, who turn from the wisdom of prudence and seek the wisdom of experience (p. 11).

In mentioning Mansfield's name alongside such literary luminaries as Blake and Keats, and bringing Jesus into his argument for good measure, Murry entwines her life with theirs, so that by the end of the introduction it is hard not to see Mansfield as a wholly religious writer, whose journal was a consciously written spiritual undertaking. He goes further:

> Katherine's little boat, Lawrence's small ship – fraught with the essential soul in its act of desperate choice – these, this (for it is one single thing, one single power, frail as a thread, yet of force to bind the universe and move the world) – this is God (pp. 12–13).

So, Mansfield's name is not just linked with that of Jesus, but also now with God. It is here in this short introduction that I believe 'Saint Katherine' undergoes her ultimate step to canonisation. Finally, adding weight and authority to his article, Murry plays his master card; it is he whom

Mansfield married, he to whom she entrusted her life. The final sentence of the introduction ends thus:

> 'In spite of all,' she wrote to her husband in a letter found among her belongings, to be opened only after her death; 'no truer lovers ever walked the earth than we were – in spite of all, in spite of all' (p. 15).

Incorporating his own name into this saintly mix adds a certain patina and air of authority; she is telling him in that final letter how special their relationship was, and now he, in his turn, is telling the world.

After Mansfield's death, Murry underwent a spiritual conversion of sorts; as Frank Lea notes: 'Murry made at least four reputations – as an artistic and literary critic in his twenties, a religious in his thirties, a socialist in his forties, and a pacifist in his fifties'.[33] He goes on to explain how by the 1930s an opinion poll taken at Cambridge revealed Murry as 'the most despised literary figure of the time' (Lea, p. 52). By the 1950s he was 'either unmentionable or else forgotten' (p. 52). His crises of faith, coupled with his interest in the spiritual are marked by the publication of several religious volumes around this time, including *The Life of Jesus*, *Things to Come*, and *God: An Introduction to the Science of Metabiology*.[34] In 1938, he wrote *Heaven and Earth*, 'A collection of essays, assembled and amplified to substantiate the book that 'ours is a Christian civilisation. The Christianity it implies is explicitly Pauline''.[35]

The early 1930s as mentioned above, marks the nadir of Murry's reputation in England, as a result of the merciless promotion of his dead first wife and also because of his sycophantic writing on D. H. Lawrence.[36] As Lea acknowledges, 'Both in England and France, the rise of

33   F. A. Lea, *Lawrence and Murry: A Twofold Vision* (London: Bentham Press, 1975), p. 51.

34   John Middleton Murry, *The Life of Jesus* (London: Cape 1926), *Things to Come* (London: Cape, 1928), *God: An Introduction to the Science of Metabiology* (London: Cape, 1929).

35   Philip Mairet, *John Middleton Murry* (London: Longmans Green & Co., 1958), p. 38. John Middleton Murry, *Heaven and Earth* (London: Cape, 1938).

36   As well as numerous articles on D. H. Lawrence, Murry also wrote *Son of Woman: The Story of D. H. Lawrence* (London: Cape, 1931), *Reminiscences of D. H. Lawrence* (London: Cape 1933) and *Love, Freedom and Society: An Analytical Comparison of D. H. Lawrence and Albert Schweitzer* (London: Cape, 1957). Of the *Reminiscences*, Mairet states: 'The personal reminiscences occupy less than half

Lawrence's and Katherine's reputations undoubtedly contributed to the decline of Murry's' (Lea, p. 53). William Godwin also points out that, 'Murry has not only been underestimated for his own contribution to literature, but has been adversely, even bitterly, criticised for not being the friend or the husband he should have been'.[37] Murry wrote extensively on his relationship with Lawrence, though at the time of Lawrence's death the pair had had little contact for many years.

I have discovered a document purporting to be a 'biography' of Murry, written in 1930 by Lawrence, under the pseudonym 'J. C.' (Jesus Christ). This 'biography', entitled *The Life of J. Middleton Murry*, privately printed, consists of one A4 sheet folded in half, with the title on the outside. Opening the page one finds the following printed on the right hand side:

> John Middleton was born in the year
> of the Lord 1891? It happened also
> to be the most lying year of the most
> lying century since time began, but what
> is that to an innocent babe!

This would no doubt have generated a good deal of mirth amongst the London literary scene at the time of its printing. Murry's new found 'spirituality', together with the incessant promotion of his dead wife, was more than Lawrence and most of his literary friends and acquaintances could stomach.

The rest of the Mantz/Murry biography which ends, as stated earlier, in 1911, is novelistic in tone and subjective in content, taking its themes from Murry's introduction:

> What had come to pass in those later days was her emergence out of the valley of the shadow of Experience into the Light of Innocence regained, and just as William Blake turned to the child world to find terms to express his wisdom, so Katherine Mansfield turned back to Karori (p. 17).

With its language so reminiscent of Psalm 23, Ruth Mantz begins her biography of Mansfield. Throughout the biography, the language is the

the book. The rest comprises Murry's answer to the attacks upon him which followed the publication of *Son of Woman*' (Mairet, p. 38).

37   Ernest G. Griffin, *John Middleton Murry* (New York: Twayne, 1969), p. 21.

same: 'The mysticism which burned in her, later, with so fine a flame was then crudely flaring. She was drawn by the mystery of Christianity; a crucifix hung between the two Watts prints over her bed' (p. 185). The fact that this is a description of a young girl's room in a boarding school, the décor of which was none of her doing, is not a point to be highlighted in a biography such as this.

With a life described thus, sanctioned by no less a person than the subject's husband, with whom, by all accounts, she was deeply in love; it is no wonder that the reactionary, Catholic French press seize upon Mansfield with such gusto. This sanitised Katherine Mansfield is perfect for them. There are a few critics however, not so easily duped.

Marcel Thiébaut's article, in the *Revue de Paris* on 15 November 1933, is a review of the Mantz/Murry biography, offering more in the way of critical balance and objectivity, and thereby rekindling the voice of dissention.[38] The whole article is a subtle condemnation of the polemic that Mansfield was both genius and ethereal being and is more of an attempt to reflect on her true worth, discarding any previous prejudices. It may be viewed as the forerunner of an important article published in 1940 by Pierre Citron, where the condemnation is taken much further. Thiébaut's article is very much a tongue-in-cheek condemnation; an attempt at mocking the idolatry of the French critics, at delving behind the biographical facts thus far presented and searching for hidden truths. It is an irreverent examination of a legend.

He starts with a chronological exposé of the growth of Mansfield's reputation in France. Critics liked the stories, but couldn't say why. Their enthusiasm for her, however, was boundless: 'Que Katherine Mansfield avait dû être heureuse! Et dans quelle merveilleuse pureté elle semblait baigner!' (p. 462). The arrival of the *Journal* and *Lettres* with their obvious editorial lacunae, nevertheless serves to underline the pain and suffering of her life. Lack of the right kind of information, together with the overabundance of trivia is ridiculed, in an acidly amusing little affront: 'Sur les ascendants de Katherine Beauchamp on ne pourrait même, sans faire preuve de singularité, souhaiter plus amples informations' (p. 463). He sneers at her bourgeois Wellington upbringing: 'Karori, un faubourg de Wellington, si le mot faubourg peut convenir à un groupe de maisons nichées dans la verdure' (p. 463). He cites her mar-

38   Marcel Thiébaut, 'Parmi les livres', *Revue de Paris* (15 November 1933), 462–75.

riage to Bowden and her pregnancy – 'elle était enceinte et pas de son mari' (466). He does not believe Carco to be telling the truth in his 'Souvenirs'. There is even a moment of comedy in the article; when referring to Carco's article of 27 January 1933 (discussed above), he states:

> La couverture des *Annales* du 27 janvier nous montre M. Carco devant la porte [de son appartement Quai aux Fleurs]. Il vient glaner des souvenirs. Un doigt sur la sonnette, il lève la tête, comme s'il craignait la chute de quelque objet, tombé d'un étage (p. 469).

He hints at a rift between Carco and Murry and at a growing liaison between Carco and Mansfield during the English couple's stay in Paris. He also hints at the truth behind the 'platonic' events in Gray in 1915 and compares the episode to a fictional account in *Les Innocents*, where Winnie meets Milord at Besançon and where ethereal love is replaced by more base instincts. More importantly, and echoing Carco's description, he says of Winnie: 'Ce qu'il y a de pur et d'intact dans le personnage on ne le trouvera pas très aisément […] C'est une personne perverse et raffinée' (p. 469). His exposé finally leads him to comment: 'Un regard sur sa vie nous a éloignés de l'idéal visage de keepsake, tendre, charmant et fade que les premiers contes parus en France nous avaient fait imaginer' (p. 472). Towards the end of the article he finally loses patience with those critics who have created and upheld the legend surrounding Katherine Mansfield:

> L'enthousiasme de quelques lecteurs français incite à une mise au point. Katherine Mansfield! Katherine Mansfield! On dirait d'une nouvelle étoile de *première grandeur* dans le ciel littéraire. Quelles louanges réservera-t-on alors à notre Colette (justement admirée par Mansfield d'ailleurs), qui compte, elle, à son actif non pas quelques contes réussis, délicieux, mais dix livres admirables? (474)

Once more the gauntlet is thrown to Gillet and his followers. Thiébaut also discusses her vacillating opinions concerning France and the French culminating in the following sentence: 'C'était évidemment une personne instable' (p. 474). This postulation is a way for Thiébaut to finally hit his nail home, and as we have shown, Mansfield's attachment to France is one of the key features of the early warmth felt by the French towards the writer, with this warmth incubating, and subsequently germinating, the myth and cult-like tendencies which we have already exposed.

Whatever the reasons behind Thiébaut's exposé of the Mansfield cult, it is hard not to feel a sense of relief that someone has finally seen through the myth-making and arrived at a more accurate picture of Katherine Mansfield, the woman and the writer. Importantly, Thiébaut also acknowledges the editing and expurgations, alluded to at the end of the Mantz biography, which do not allow for a fuller appraisal of Mansfield in France at this time: '[…] en attendant que l'on publie les innomb- ables passages supprimés dans les *Lettres* et le *Journal*' (p. 474).[39]

The above article now generates several responses as the Mansfield devotees launch a counter-attack.

Mythologising Continues

For those who would continue the delusion, 1934 proves a fruitful year, with several pro-Mansfield articles and apparently no more dissenting voices. After five years silence, Gillet's voice is once more the loudest of the year. He sees his old postulations are still valid and his new article, again in *La Revue des deux mondes*, notwithstanding the new biographical material furnished by the Mantz/Murry biography, is indistinguishable from anything he has previously written:

> Sa tombe du cimetière d'Avon est l'objet de plus d'un pèlerinage et le gage d'une alliance avec la poésie anglaise […] Sous les ombrages de Fontainebleau dort ainsi cette douce morte, la perle de l'Océanie. C'est en ces jours glacés d'hiver, en ces heures d'anniversaire, au temps de l'Épiphanie, quand l'arbre dépouillé prépare sa résurrection, qu'il faut aller nous recueillir et évoquer cette jeune ombre.[40]

---

39   'Many of her letters have been published only in part, and some not published at all. And probably it will be many years yet before these can be published. But the publication, when it comes, will add little that is essential to the picture of herself that is contained in the *Journal* and the *Letters*. What she was, what she became, is told in them with far greater truth than any biographer could hope to achieve' (Mantz, p. 349).

40   Louis Gillet, '"Kass" ou la jeunesse de Katherine Mansfield', *Revue des deux mondes* (15 January 1934), 456–68 (p. 456).

The entire article is composed in this overtly adulatory vein, almost as if counterbalancing the perceived calumnies of Thiébaut's article. Gillet claims that the *Journal*, and more especially, the *Lettres*, has become essential bedside reading – 'un livre de chevet, une lecture spirituelle pour les âmes délicates' (p. 456). Of the promiscuous biographical events of 1908–9, now in the public domain following the Mantz/Murry biography (though still heavily expurgated), he says:

> Elle 'marche au canon', elle enjambe, si je puis dire, le corps de ses parents, pour conquérir sa liberté, épisode comme il y en a dans certaines vies de saints [...] Ce qui suit est tellement cruel qu'on voudrait s'épargner la douleur d'en rien dire (p. 463).

His excuse for her actions? Her age: she was only twenty (p. 464). He constantly refers to her as 'la petite' – an epithet which dates from the earliest of his articles. He has also not forgotten his earlier religious postulation: 'C'est dommage que les biographes de Kathleen Mansfield nous aient donné si peu de lueurs sur [...] son éducation religieuse' (p. 466). For those people who had actually known Mansfield, statements such as the one above must have seemed laughable. In 'Prelude', which, contains numerous implicit sexual innuendos, he finds only 'des impressions charmantes de piété enfantine, de prières gazouillées le soir, et ce sentiment du miracle de la fleur mystérieuse' (p. 467). For Gillet, the *Journal*, 'nous fait comprendre que l'art aussi peut être religion' (p. 468). He finally explains away her early promiscuity and removes any stain which may have sullied the image of the legend:

> Qu'avions-nous besoin de tout savoir? Pourquoi, pourquoi tout dire, cruel? [...] Comme une lune qui croît et décroît et reparaît toujours intacte et virginale après les nuées et les éclipses, nous continuerons d'admirer dans cette âme de cristal le courage invincible et – malgré tout – la pureté (p. 468).

In this article, Gillet is determined – at whatever cost to historical accuracy – to cling on to the vision of Mansfield which he himself was instrumental in creating, upholding her character as pure and saint-like.

Henry Bordeaux rallies to the cause a few days after Gillet's piece, also dismissive of Thérive's postulations, in an article deemed worthy of the front page of the *Figaro*, entitled, 'Katherine Mansfield nous aimait-elle?'[41] (See Chapter Two for an in-depth discussion of this issue). He comments on the way certain critics have viewed the *Journal* and *Lettres*: 'L'un ou l'autre imagine de citer, d'un air entendu, ses jugements sévères sur notre pays et nos compatriotes'. His response :

> Elle n'aimait pas la France? Allons donc! Elle ne trouve que là le charme de vivre. Ne lui en voulons donc pas de quelques coups de patte et baisons au contraire cette main fine qui dessine si bien les images de la vie (p. 1).

Of the other articles written in 1934, that of Marguerite d'Escola in *La Revue bleue politique et littéraire* is noteworthy for the fact that she discusses the stories at some length and not just the predictable choices of 'Prelude' and 'At the Bay'.[42] Her tone, however, is lifted straight from the pen of Gillet and is continually inaccurate in its nomenclature:

> Un enfant du soleil! Miroir et foyer, absorbant la lumière et l'irradiant:
> 'Mon Dieu, supplie Catherine, [sic] rends-moi transparente comme le cristal pour que la lumière brille à travers moi!' (p. 649).

This tone of sycophancy reaches new heights in September 1934, in an article by Rose Worms Barretta in *La Revue hebdomadaire*;[43] I quote the following breathless passage, in order to demonstrate how far the legend surrounding Mansfield's life has come in the ten or so years since her death in France:

> Pâle, jeune femme qui vous traîniez affaiblie sur les routes ensoleillées et enviiez l'activité joyeuse des paysannes, saviez-vous, lorsqu'en rentrant vous crayonniez des notes ou des lettres sur votre chaise longue, que votre effort ne serait pas perdu, que l'essence de votre joie demeurerait si lumineuse qu'elle irait après vous en éclairer d'autres, et que c'est un destin suffisant ici-bas que d'avoir un instant étincelé au soleil, comme un pur diamant qui reflète la beauté divine de la création? (p. 362)

41   Henry Bordeaux, 'Katherine Mansfield nous aimait-elle?', *Le Figaro*, 24 January 1934, p. 1.
42   Marguerite D'Escola, 'Katherine Mansfield', *Revue bleue politique et littéraire*, 17 (1 September 1934), 643–49.
43   Rose Worms Barretta, 'Les Petites servantes méridionales vues par Katherine Mansfield', *Revue hebdomadaire* (15 September 1934), 358–62.

Hagiography Heightened Further

The next four years, 1935–38, bring little movement towards a more balanced critical voice. In 1935, the French translation of the Mantz/Murry biography, *La Jeunesse de Katherine Mansfield*, is published, eliciting two reviews, both of which are legend-reinforcing. Émile Henriot, in *Le Temps*, describes Gillet and his band of like-minded critics as, 'de très fervents commentateurs et propagandistes de sa jeune gloire'.[44] He himself is in complete accord with their views: 'Elle était si loin de notre monde, déjà si détachée, si pure et montée si haut, qu'il ne peut s'agir que de vénération et de respect' (p.461).

An anonymous article in *Le Figaro* of March 1935,[45] contains a plethora of photos of Mansfield – reproductions from *La Jeunesse de Katherine Mansfield*, with invented captions such as 'Cette créature féerique', 'C'est alors qu'elle lui dit: 'Murry je vous aime'. It goes on to review the Mantz/Murry translated biography in a manner which we have now come to expect:

> Nous aimons Katherine Mansfield comme on aime les personnages de miracles et de contes de fées. Cette jeune femme, dont la sensibilité se tient délicieusement entre l'enfantin et l'éternel, demeure au-delà des portes de la mort le sourire de notre siècle (p. 5).

André Maurois' initial contribution to Mansfield criticism takes the form of a chapter in his book *Magiciens et Logiciens*, published in 1935, panegyrizing the writer and her art.[46] This article was used in abridged form for the collected edition of her stories translated into French, first published by Stock in 1955, and is still the preface one reads today, nearly fifty years after it was first written:

> Tout est bien, dirions-nous volontiers à notre tour, chaque fois que nous achevons un des plus beaux récits de Katherine Mansfield. Tout est bien, ou plus exactement tout est ainsi. Devant l'art le plus grand, le silence seul exprime le ravissement (OR, p. xviii).

44 Émile Henriot, 'Le Souvenir de Katherine Mansfield', *Le Temps* (12 March 1935), 456–61 (p. 456).
45 Anon., 'La Vitrine du Figaro littéraire', *Le Figaro*, 23 March 1935, p. 5.
46 André Maurois, *Magiciens et Logiciens* (Paris: Grasset, 1935).

A dearth of articles on Mansfield in France in 1936 is followed in 1937 by the reappearance of Émile Henriot's 1935 offering, discussed above, in book form, as one of his series of portraits in *De Marie de France à Katherine Mansfield.*[47] The book is dedicated to Henry Bordeaux, another Mansfield hagiographer. In the same year, the first French academic book on Mansfield is published – *Katherine Mansfield, sa vie, son œuvre, sa personnalité* by May Lillian Muffang. A brief extract from the introduction indicates the critical viewpoint of the work:

> Nous nous sommes attachés à retracer brièvement la vie, et à commenter sur l'œuvre de K. Mansfield, mais en nous orientant nettement vers l'étude d'une personnalité. N'est-ce pas, après tout, cette personnalité, si riche et si exquise, qui est l'essence même de K. Mansfield auteur? Et l'écrivain n'est-il pas, chez elle, étrangement subordonné à l'être psychologique et moral qu'elle était? (Muffang, p. 9)

The chapter on Mansfield's narrative art traces a new path for French critical appreciation of the stories, but this art is still not seen as being divorced from her personality, and Mansfield the cult figure is stamped on every page. Muffang discusses the radio broadcasts which, 'la T.S.F. ne craint pas de radiodiffuser, à l'"Heure des Enfants", telle ou telle de ses histoires' (p. 9). Tellingly, these broadcasts are for children, underlining how sanitised Mansfield's life and work in France has become. The introduction concludes:

> En France, il semble que sa gloire se soit établie grâce aux articles, [...] grâce aussi à l'efficace croisade qu'entreprirent [plusieurs critiques]. K. Mansfield a, aujourd'hui, chez nous, son cénacle, ses critiques attitrés, ses spécialistes, ses traductrices. N'était-ce pas une douce dette à payer à celle qui a tant aimé la France? (p. 9)

Muffang is here describing and acknowledging a veritable industry surrounding Mansfield in France.

In a quiet year for articles on Mansfield, August 1937 sees the publication in *Le Temps*, of 'Le Souvenir de Katherine Mansfield', by Edmond Jaloux, where he describes his pilgrimage to Mansfield's tomb in Fontainebleau, 'à quelques minutes du couvent des Carmes', as if this

---

47   Émile Henriot, De *Marie de France à Katherine Mansfield: Portraits de femmes* (Paris: Plon, 1937).

fact was of significance.[48] His reading of her work leads him to conclude: 'Elle se tenait auprès de son mari comme un élève auprès de son maître, avec une sorte de déférence d'enfant qui voudrait trouver un guide' (3). Revered as a quasi-saint, Mansfield would naturally have taken the role of the 'dutiful woman', which would, in its turn, have appealed to the reactionary Catholic writers extolling her virtues.

Fiftieth Anniversary of Birth

In 1938, a mass of articles and reviews are published to celebrate the fiftieth anniversary of Mansfield's birth. All the articles conform to the same opinions, reaffirming and heightening the postulations offered by the French hagiographers since 1924. Commemorative ceremonies take place all over France, notably in the south at Menton, where Mansfield had sought relief from her tuberculosis. The homogeneity of the tone and content of the articles serves to produce a reaffirmation of faith in the saint-like image which the French have created for themselves; the distinct lack of any consistent evidence to the contrary enables the legend to become firmly entrenched in the French mind. The emotional nature of the facts surrounding her life serves as a catalyst for the further development of the false persona, so that in the end fact and fiction are inextricably bound. Critical appraisal has become a matter of convention, with the same points highlighted, the same details glossed over, year in, year out. The poem entitled 'La Tombe de Katherine Mansfield' which begins this chapter, is a romantically charged evocation of a visit to Mansfield's grave and the Prieuré by moonlight in this fiftieth anniversary year. The front page of *Le Figaro littéraire* for 15 October 1938 (the day after Mansfield's birth date), features a lengthy article entitled 'Katherine Mansfield aurait cinquante ans'. Its contents are all too familiar:

---

48   Edmond Jaloux, 'Le Souvenir de Katherine Mansfield', *Le Temps,* 28 August, 1937, p. 3.

> Elle demeure, à travers le temps qui passe, l'héroïne d'une vie qui ne meurt pas; cette vie dont ses livres gardent l'écho ravissant, cette vie ou l'idée du bonheur fait un bruit de cristal qui vibre au point de se briser.[49]

The commemorations continue into 1939, when there are various articles written to acknowledge the time Mansfield spent in France. Gabriel Boissy gives a speech at a ceremony in Menton for the unveiling of a plaque at the Villa Isola Bella on 21 March 1939: 'Nous voici bien là, devant une âme franciscaine. Il n'est pas d'autre nom à cette divine douceur, à ce suave épanchement dans l'absolu et l'éternelle unité de l'être'.[50] Mansfield as Franciscan nun? Reporting of this kind would have done nothing to aid Murry's reputation back in England.

Henry Bordeaux' article, 'Pèlerinage au cimetière d'Avon', in *Les Nouvelles littéraires*, reproduces a speech he made 'pour l'inauguration du carrefour Katherine Mansfield, dans la forêt de Fontainebleau, le 10 juin 1939'.[51] In an all too familiar vein, he claims, 'Ce qu'il faut encore reconnaître à Katherine Mansfield, c'est une sorte de pudeur qui lui fait répudier tout ce qui est grossièreté ou trivialité […] Il ne lui en est demeuré aucune souillure' (p. 1). *La Revue hebdomadaire* of 1 July publishes the speech made at the same commemoration ceremony by Hugh Sellon, director of the British Institute in Paris at the time. He naturally concentrates on her attachment to France, stating:

> Cette clarté de vision, qui n'effraie pas la vérité, justement parce qu'elle sait que la vérité a en soi un élément qui ne peut être corrompu, est essentiellement française. Française dans sa logique et son absence de sentimentalisme. Française dans son sens des valeurs spirituelles.[52]

It would appear that the 'official' English response to the legend is to condone it and even encourage it.

---

49 Jean-Pierre Auguis, 'Katherine Mansfield aurait cinquante ans', *Le Figaro littéraire*, 15 October 1938, p.1.

50 Gabriel Boissy, 'Katherine Mansfield à Menton', *Nouvelles littéraires*, 8 April, 1939, p. 2.

51 Henry Bordeaux, 'Pèlerinage au cimetière d'Avon: Katherine Mansfield toujours vivante', *Nouvelles littéraires*, 27 May 1939, p. 1.

52 Hugh Sellon, 'Le Souvenir de Katherine Mansfield', *Revue hebdomadaire*, 26 (1 July 1939), 96–100 (p. 99).

Further Attack on the Legend

In 1940 Pierre Citron publishes an article entitled 'Katherine Mansfield et la France' in *La Revue de littérature comparée*, which is the longest and most developed against the legend to date.[53] Yet it would appear that if the pro-Mansfield critics bind themselves with similar arguments and postulations, so too, it seems, do the opposers of the legend. In this twenty page article, almost half is devoted to Mansfield's relationship with France, the French and their literary tradition. Citron nails his own colours to the mast from the outset when he claims on the first page: 'Bref, on ne peut discerner aucune influence décisive de la littérature ou de la culture françaises sur son art et sa personnalité' (p. 173). The second half of the article is an appraisal of the critical trend to date. It proves to what extent the superficial elements of her biography were taken up and incorporated to form the foundations of the legend. As the evidence mounts, it begins to seem probable that had she not lived at Bandol and Menton for long periods, or died at Fontainebleau, the French might not have been quite so interested in her personality, or indeed, her art.

Her artistic achievement forms part of the legend only in so far as her supposedly 'best' stories – 'Prelude', 'At the Bay', 'The Doll's House', are all perceived to be expressions of the child-like innocence, beauty and spirituality which her admirers consider to be her finest assets. And, of course, the best place to discover this saint-like spirituality is in the pages of the *Lettres* and *Journal*, which results in the stories becoming redundant in any critical appraisal.

Citron's article begins thus:

> Les rapports de K. Mansfield et de la France ont été en quelque sorte accidentels. On sait qu'elle a fait de longs séjours à Bandol, à Menton, mais les Français ne sont pas responsables de la beauté, ni du climat de la Côte d'Azur (p. 173).

In taking this stance and developing it at length, Citron ensnares himself in one of the many traps of Mansfield criticism in France. Even with the many examples he provides of her general abuse towards the French, by

---

53   Pierre Citron, 'Katherine Mansfield et la France', *Revue de littérature comparée* (April–June 1940), 173–93.

mentioning as he does, even one or two examples of her love of France, his argument becomes inconclusive. For, having admitted that, 'il arrive à K. Mansfield de porter des jugements favorables sur les Français. […] Elle aime la gaîté, la simplicité et le goût des Français du peuple' (p. 181), he weakens his case. He also states:

> Les jugements littéraires de K. Mansfield sont, comme toujours chez elle, l'expression de ses affinités ou de ses antipathies personnelles, beaucoup plus que le résultat d'un examen raisonné et motivé (p. 174).

This only succeeds in proving how any argument concerning her likes and dislikes is a futile pastime, since even the early expurgated editions of the *Lettres* and *Journal* demonstrate both her quixotic nature and the constant vacillation of her opinions. And nowhere does Citron mention her humour, which I have discussed at length in almost every chapter, and which would have added so much substance to his argument.

The most informative section of Citron's article is the appraisal he makes of the critical approach to her life since her death. He traces a path similar to the one taken in this chapter and arrives at some of the same conclusions:

> Tous les articles ressemblent plus ou moins à des extraits, des résumés ou des paraphrases des premiers articles de MM. Gillet, Jaloux et Marcel; il paraît admis généralement et sans discussion que les Lettres sont une des œuvres les plus 'essentielles' de toute la littérature (p. 185).

He notes that none of the myth-making critics, apart from Carco, had ever met Mansfield whilst she was alive, and, reserving a special mention for Carco himself, comments on the fact that his 'Souvenirs' were, in fact, only published *ten years* after her death. Summing up their response, he states:

> Peut-être n'ont-ils pas attaché à K. Mansfield une importance aussi grande qu'ils ont bien voulu le dire ensuite, lorsque le succès du *Journal* et des *Lettres* se fut manifesté sans qu'ils y aient eu part? (p. 182)

He claims that it is only thanks to Gillet's intervention that the publishing house Stock decided to 'launch' this unknown English authoress on the French reading public, with translations of four volumes in quick succession. However, in a manner similar to those critics he would condemn, he dismisses her stories as not being worthy of discussion. He does however bring to light what the opposition camp had been feeling whilst the myth had been taking shape. Though remaining silent, they considered her, so he says, 'comme une femme insupportable, égoïste, sentimentale, prétentieuse' (p. 186), and states what the excesses of her admirers have forced them to do:

> On se détourne plutôt de son œuvre, on considère sa vogue comme un snobisme collectif, spontané ou habilement lancé par l'éditeur; tant de louanges ont été répandues sur K. Mansfield, que ceux qui abordent son œuvre s'attendent à une révélation, et sont souvent déçus (p. 186).

This is the first article that discusses the possibility of the deliberate creation of a Mansfield legend by certain critics and publishers in France. Citron's argument however, is indecisive in allowing a condemnation of the myth to be upheld; his rejection is couched in vague terminology. He makes use of Thérive's earlier condemnation but is wrong in stating that he was the only person to dismiss the legend, since he does not appear to have read Thiébaut's article of 1933 with its tongue-in-cheek condemnatory stance. Thérive's was the first but not the only public voice of dissent.

In conclusion Citron says:

> Lors de l'apparition de ses œuvres en France, K. Mansfield a connu un succès si considérable, elle a reçu de tous les critiques des éloges si unanimes sous tous les rapports, qu'on ne peut se défendre d'une légère inquiétude. On a l'impression d'une renommée toute faite qui nous arrive d'Angleterre, et que chacun, par paresse, admet sans la contrôler (p. 192).

In fact, as I have argued, apart from the early months following her death, Mansfield never really had the same sort of posthumous reputation in England that she had in France, except the negative one of being Murry's wife. It was Murry who provided the details, in his edited books of Mansfield's posthumous works, in his introductions to innumerable volumes, together with his own autobiography, which fed the information eagerly absorbed by so many French critics. The actual foundations are made up of words – words with a particular emotional bias for the French, essentially masculine 'esprit' of the day – tragique / femme / enfant / tuberculose / jolie / amour / mort, together with Murry's exaggerated version of a life story which most people would only expect to come across in fiction.

Entrenchment and Solidification of Hagiography

By 1940, the opposition camp has openly declared its position, and, predictably, the admirers of Mansfield pay little, if any, attention. The only modification to the critical stance is that the stories, the bulk of which seem never to have been read by most French critics, gradually assume an importance in their own right, though still no one seems capable of disassociating her art from her life.

As I have already indicated, the gradual emergence of new biographical material to challenge the unblemished reputation is, depending on its quality, either absorbed into the reputation itself, or else rejected out of hand. This is certainly the case with the translation in 1941, of Murry's 1935 autobiography *Between Two Worlds*, with the catchy French title *Katherine Mansfield et moi*.[54] In the introduction, René Lalou makes an oblique reference to those who have accused Murry of helping to promulgate the legend of his dead wife in France, with a sympathetic stance: 'Serait-il juste d'accabler Murry parce que Katherine Mansfield attire irrésistiblement nos sympathies, qu'elle est ici l'héroïne alors qu'il n'est que le survivant?' (p. 10). Murry no doubt had an eye on the potential reading public in France when penning this book – the frontispiece to the translation calls it 'une adaptation'. Lalou states:

> La France agissait sur Katherine Mansfield comme un stimulant à sa puissance créatrice. 'La France avait beau lui paraître insupportable, elle y retrouvait, disait-elle, son pouvoir de minutieuse vision' : cette phrase de Murry ne laissera nul Français insensible (p. 15).

Here again we find that determined search for a connection between Katherine Mansfield and France being brought out sympathetically by a French critic.

54 John Middleton Murry, *Katherine Mansfield et moi*, trans. by Nicole Bordeaux and Maurice Lacoste, intro. by René Lalou (Paris: Fernand Sorlot, 1941).

217

Mansfield is now generating less critical interest than in the early years after her death, but the hagiographical stance is still much in evidence. The war inevitably puts paid to much critical activity, but 1946 is a fruitful and busy year for Mansfield criticism in France, perhaps partly explained by post-war pressure on French writers in general to write with patriotic sentiment; this is not a time to be rocking any critical boats. H. Daniel-Rops publishes a book entitled *Trois tombes, trois visages*.[55] Its three essays have as their subjects Rupert Brooke, Charles Du Bos and Katherine Mansfield. The essay on Mansfield, entitled 'Katherine Mansfield sous les feuilles mortes', gives an account of her time at the Prieuré prior to her death and – in a pudding distinctly over-egged – is hagiographical, highly religious, sexist and reactionary. On the beliefs of the Prieuré's inhabitants he states:

> Il est bien vrai que cette pauvre hérésie ne pouvait rien apporter de valable à cette âme d'exception [...] Le choix d'une femme s'exprime rarement par la logique. Mais chez des êtres que Dieu a marqués d'un signe, la portée des actes dépasse toujours l'intention qui les fait accomplir (pp. 12–13).

The entire essay is composed in this vein. Conversely, at around the same time in England, commenting on the new publication of her *Collected Stories*, V. S Pritchett writes the following:

> When we take Katherine Mansfield's stories as they are, we see what original and sometimes superlative use she made of herself. Rootless, isolated, puritan, catty, repentantly over-fond? She made stories clear as glass. Isolated, she seeks to describe how people feel and think when they are alone.[56]

The difference between the two pieces could not be more marked and exemplifies the way Mansfield was regarded on either side of the Channel. Daniel-Rops concentrates on Mansfield's life, Pritchett concentrates on her narrative art. The former is subjective and adulatory, the latter matter-of-fact and objective in its praise.

Two further books on Mansfield in 1946, in France and Belgium, only add to the legend surrounding her life and contribute little to the literary debate on her narrative skills. *A la rencontre de Katherine Mans-*

---

55   H. Daniel-Rops, *Trois tombes, trois visages* (Paris: La Colombe, 1946).
56   V. S. Pritchett, 'Books in General', *New Statesman and Nation*, 31, 2 February 1946, p. 87.

field by Bernard Marion, concentrates primarily on biographical and spiritual issues.[57] *La Vocation de Katherine Mansfield* by Odette Lenoël,[58] with a foreword by Daniel-Rops, is an emotionally charged and biased Catholic reading of Mansfield's spiritual evolution, concentrating on the ways in which her life was shaped by ill-health and suffering; Lenoël died shortly before the book was published, in similar circumstances to Mansfield's.

The amount of Mansfield critical activity in this year may explain why the American composer David Diamond writes a song entitled 'Souvent j'ai dit à mon mari', with words taken from the French *Journal* of Katherine Mansfield.[59] As far as I am aware, this piece of music is unknown to Mansfield scholars and has never been mentioned elsewhere. David Diamond (1915–present) is an American composer who has spent considerable periods in Paris; on his second visit in 1937, he stayed in Fontainebleau, whilst following the classes of the French composer, conductor and teacher Nadia Boulanger (1887–1979), at the Fontainebleau Conservatory of Music. She taught many of the most famous conductors and composers of the twentieth century. The piece is dedicated 'To Darius, Madeleine and Daniel Milhaud';[60] the words (for voice and piano), are as follows:

Souvent j'ai dit à mon mari: Nous en prenons un? Et il me dit: ah non non ma pauvre femme. Notre petit moment pour jouer est passé. Je ne peux rien faire que de rester dans une chaise en faisant des grimaces. Et ça fait trembler plus que ça ne fait rire un petit enfant.

57   Bernard Marion, *A la rencontre de Katherine Mansfield* (Brussels: La Sixaine, 1946).
58   Odette Lenoël, *La Vocation de Katherine Mansfield* (Paris: Albin Michel, 1946).
59   David Diamond, 'Souvent j'ai dit à mon mari', [text] from the *Journal* of Katherine Mansfield, in *Songs* (Philadelphia: Elkan-Vogel, 1946). A second song in the same book, entitled, 'My Little Mother' is also taken from Mansfield's *Journal*, though this time in English, and is dedicated to the American composer Theodore Chanier (1902–1961):
     My little Mother, my star, my courage, my own. I seem to dwell in her now. We live in the same world. Not quite this world, not quite another. Not a soul knows where she is. She goes slowly, thinking it all over, wondering how she can express it as she wants to, asking for time and for peace.
60   Darius Milhaud (1892–1974), was one of the most prolific French composers of the twentieth century. Two of his greatest friends were the writer Paul Claudel and the poet Francis Jammes, both Catholics.

Although these compositions do not directly aid the creation of the Mansfield legend per se, nevertheless they go some way to demonstrate how her life and writing had entered the French public's consciousness, to the extent that an American composer could use words taken from the French translation of the *Journal*, for a song dedicated to a French composer and his family, knowing that the provenance would be appreciated and understood. Mansfield's own connection with Fontainebleau may also have played a part in the evolution of these compositions.

In 1949, Simone de Beauvoir attempts the refreshingly different stance of concentrating on Mansfield as a fiction writer. In *Le Deuxième sexe*, she quotes extensively from several of Mansfield's stories in order to substantiate her own radically new and feminist viewpoint:

> A plus forte raison peut-on compter sur les doigts d'une main les femmes qui ont traversé le donné, à la recherche de sa dimension secrète: Emily Brontë a interrogé la mort, V. Woolf, la vie, et K. Mansfield parfois [...] la contingence quotidienne et la souffrance.[61]

This sort of response in France, however, even after the War, is rare and ultimately submerged by more hagiographical offerings. The years leading up to 1954 and Alpers' biography, produce nothing in France to counter the legend and much to heighten it; the position is now more or less entrenched. At around this time in England, Sean O'Faolin, in a mostly dismissive article on her stories, condemns Mansfield for writing, 'too easily, too lengthily, too self-indulgently' (O'Faolin, p. 55). Meanwhile, in France, with the critics still concentrating on her personal writing, the publication of the fuller edition of Mansfield's letters in England in 1952, prompts J. B. Fort to comment on her entry into the Prieuré, in *Les Études anglaises*:

> Katherine semble en train de se faire une âme monastique; c'est d'une sorte d'abdication, dans la mort du moi ancien qu'elle trouvera sa 're-birth'. La mort arrêtera brutalement le travail de cette seconde naissance. Mais était-il pour elle une autre façon de renaitre?[62]

---

61   Simone de Beauvoir, *Le Deuxième sexe*, vol. 2 (Paris: Gallimard, 1949), p. 626.
62   J. B. Fort, 'Katherine Mansfield et lui', part 1, *Études anglaises*, 5 (1952), 59–65 (pp. 64–65).

Le Drame secret de Katherine Mansfield by Roland Merlin, published in 1950, considers the last ten years of Mansfield's life in an all too familiar pattern of biased descriptions and suppositions.[63] Nothing hinders those who would continue the idolisation of Saint Katherine.

The thirtieth anniversary of Mansfield's death in 1953 is marked in France by a ceremony in Fontainebleau, and an official visit to her tomb. Reproducing word for word sections of his article from June 1939, Henry Bordeaux comments on the occasion, proclaiming yet again: 'Ce qu'il faut encore reconnaître à Katherine Mansfield, c'est une sorte de pudeur qui lui fait répudier tout ce qui est grossièreté ou trivialité [...] Il ne lui en est demeuré aucune souillure'.[64] The legend continues its solidification.

In 1954, there appears an article to mark the translation into French of the new edition of the *Lettres*. Its title tells the reader exactly what to expect of its contents: 'Un long cri d'amour, haletant, déchirant: La Correspondance de Katherine Mansfield révélée 30 ans après'.[65] The sensationalist title is followed by a breathless article recounting, yet again, the well-worn details of Mansfield's life.

There is also a new book, *Monsieur Gurdjieff*, by Louis Pauwels, which devotes many of its pages to a description of the last months of Mansfield's life, both in Paris and at the Prieuré, together with the events surrounding her death:

> C'est une femme, avec son corps, avec son cœur, avec son désir de jouir totalement de cette vie terrestre, qui referme la porte de sa chambre d'hôtel et s'en va vers la dernière aventure de sa vie.[66]

The author relies on Roland Merlin, a firm upholder of the legend, for much of his biographical detail. The book contains a chapter entitled 'Toutes les lettres qu'écrivit chez Gurdjieff Katherine Mansfield à son mari' (p. 243). A quiet period for Mansfield criticism, is followed in

63 Roland Merlin, *Le Drame secret de Katherine Mansfield* (Paris: Éditions du Seuil, 1950).
64 Henry Bordeaux, 'Le Souvenir de Katherine Mansfield', *Nouvelles littéraires*, 8 January 1953, p. 5.
65 Anne Manson, 'Un long cri d'amour, haletant, déchirant: La correspondance de Katherine Mansfield révélée trente ans après', *Paris-presse-l'intransigeant*, 16 April 1954, p. 2.
66 Louis Pauwels, *Monsieur Gurdjieff* (Paris: Éditions du Seuil, 1954), pp. 241–42.

1956 by a compilation of Mansfield stories from various collections, brought out under the title *La Garden Party et autres nouvelles*, number five in the deluxe series 'Grand prix des meilleurs romans étrangers'[67] (not to be confused with *La Garden Party et autres histoires*); this edition comprises three stories from *Félicité*, five from *La Garden Party*, and 'La Maison de poupées' from *La Mouche*, itself a compilation collection of various Mansfield stories, originally published in France in 1933. In that edition, 'La Maison de poupées' had been translated by Marguerite Faguer; it is especially translated for this edition by André Bay.

The first wholly independent biography which appears in 1954 in England,[68] containing much new material, is poorly received by the French press and sells less than a thousand copies in France when translated five years later in 1959;[69] the rest are remaindered. The author, Antony Alpers, wrote in 1985:

> France simply wouldn't *have* it. [They] were appalled at the desecration of St. Katherine and this book was remaindered very soon... F. Mauriac reviewed it in *Le Figaro*, but I don't think I saw any other French reviews.[70]

There are in fact further reviews of his translation. René Daumière for example, commences his article thus:

> Dans un récent numéro du 'Figaro Littéraire', François Mauriac se penche avec une sorte de tristesse attentive sur le cas de Katherine Mansfield, à propos d'un copieux ouvrage que vient de lui consacrer Anthony Alpers aux Éditions Pierre Seghers. Le titre de son article dit parfaitement ce qu'il veut dire: 'De Katherine Mansfield aux Tricheurs ou la petite fille qui retrouva son âme'.[71]

He wholeheartedly agrees with Mauriac's premise, that Mansfield's life is too precious a commodity to deserve a 'warts-and-all' biography. Commenting on Alpers, he states, 'Ses analyses [...] sont violentes et

---

67   Katherine Mansfield, *La Garden Party et autres nouvelles*, trans. by Marthe Duproix, J.-G. Delamain and André Bay, pref. by Francis Carco (Paris: Sauret, 1956).

68   Antony Alpers, *Katherine Mansfield: A Biography* (London: Jonathan Cape, 1954).

69   Antony Alpers, *Katherine Mansfield: L'Œuvre et la vie* (Paris: Seghers, 1959).

70   Autograph letter from Antony Alpers to Gerri Kimber, 13 April 1985.

71   René Daumière, 'La petite fille qui retrouva son âme: Katherine Mansfield', *Paris-Normandie*, 10 July 1959, p. 11.

dépourvues de la poésie [...] Il leur manque [...] les silences qui, pour un biographe, sont parfois la preuve indispensable de la véritable tendresse' (p. 77). After such a reaction, it is not hard to understand why the translation of Alpers' biography sells so few copies. This is followed in September by Gabrielle Gras' article where she states: 'Le livre d'Antony Alpers est une étude objective qui ne laisse rien filtrer de l'*aura* qui est pour la plupart des lecteurs le miracle de l'œuvre'.[72] Whilst acknowledging his prodigious research and honesty she, like Daumière, regrets the need for such openness, and reveals why the legend may have come about in the first place:

> Alpers, par sa sobre exactitude, échappe à ce besoin un peu louche du public de transformer les êtres de chair, de sang, de pensée, en héros de roman. Le lecteur romanesque qui aime les amantes torturées et les morts précoces met peu à peu dans la même lignée la Catherine pathétique de *Huthering Heights* [sic] et cette amante que fut Katherine Mansfield (p. 139).

This, for Gras, is the essence of the Mansfield legend – the need by the general public to create heroes and heroines, the fascination we all have with tortured souls and the romantic connotation of the tubercular who die an early death, their promise unfulfilled. And finally, Mauriac, in his review, regretting the need for so much painful detail in Alpers' biography, ends by commenting: 'La petite fille perdue s'est trompée de route. Mais elle a cherché, elle a aspiré. C'est tout ce qui nous est demandé. Le reste relève de la Grâce'.[73]

Also in 1959, appears a romantic novel based on the life of Mansfield by Elisabeth Morel, for the imprint, 'Club de la femme', with a short introduction by Louis Pauwels (author of the book on Gurdjieff discussed above). It is an unremittingly 'Mills and Boon' offering, generating no critical comment:

> Elle le regarda. C'était comme si elle le voyait pour la première fois dans un matin resplendissant:

72   Gabrielle Gras, 'Katherine Mansfield', *Europe* (September 1959), 135–39, (p. 136).
73   François Mauriac, 'De Katherine Mansfield aux tricheurs ou la petite fille qui retrouva son âme', *Le Figaro littéraire*, 15 April 1959, p. 1.

—Tu ne peux savoir comment j'ai attendu ce moment, comment j'ai désiré que tu viennes. Maintenant, et maintenant seulement, nous pouvons regarder ensemble l'avenir...[74].

It is at this point that the legend 'ossifies' and then loses momentum. A virtual critical silence in the ensuing seven years is followed by a plethora of articles in 1966, covering the re-publication of the *Œuvre romanesque*, with the same preface by André Maurois, originally published in 1955.[75] Writing in *Les Lettres françaises*, one anonymous reviewer writes: 'Pourquoi lire Katherine Mansfield? Son œuvre participe à la fois à l'art de la nouvelle et à l'art de vivre'.[76] In August, Jacques Cabau writes in *L'Express*: 'Elle termina sa partie de cache-cache avec les anges qu'elle seule savait apercevoir dans la vie quotidienne'.[77] In October, Philippe Boyer writes in *L'Esprit*: 'L'œuvre de Katherine Mansfield est tissée comme une dentelle fragile qui serait l'unique trace d'un monde heureux et disparu, d'un paradis perdu'.[78] All three examples demonstrate the 'fixed' attitude now being taken by Mansfield critics, the homogeneity of thought processes and judgments.

The emergence of new biographical material to challenge the unblemished reputation is, depending on its quality, either absorbed into the reputation itself, or else rejected out of hand. The dissenting voice seems more or less to have disappeared and turned its back on the whole affair. In 1970 Christiane Mortelier discusses the Mansfield legend in *Les Études anglaises*: 'La personnalité et les écrits de Katherine Mansfield n'ont guère cessé d'exercer une étrange fascination sur le public français depuis 1924'.[79] Her article follows a path very similar to Pierre Citron's of thirty years before, though her stance is more measured than

---

74   Elisabeth Morel, *Katherine Mansfield*, pref. by Louis Pauwels (Paris: Club de la femme, 1959), p. 217.
75   The editor (from 1942), at the publishing house Stock at this time was the poet and novelist, André Bay (1919–present).
76   Anon., 'Passionnément éprise du spectacle du monde', *Lettres françaises*, 7 July 1966, p. 6.
77   Jacques Cabau, 'Tempêtes dans une tasse de thé', *L'Express*, 15 August 1966, p. 36.
78   Philippe Boyer, 'Librarie du mois', *Esprit* (October 1966), 558–61 (p. 560).
79   Christiane Mortelier, 'Origine et développement d'une légende: Katherine Mansfield en France', *Études anglaises*, 4 (October–December 1970), 357–68 (p. 357). (A translation of her earlier article in English).

Citron's tone of disbelief at how his compatriots could be so taken in. In 1972, Stock reissues the *Œuvre romanesque* yet again. On this occasion the dust-jacket claims:

> C'est l'œuvre d'un écrivain qui éprouve tout à la fois 'la grâce de vivre' et la 'grâce d'écrire' [...] Il s'agit de l'une des toutes premières œuvres où une femme ose enfin être vraiment féminine. Ce classique représente donc aussi une œuvre de pionnier (OR, 1966 edition).

The legend has remained static up to the present day. In 1979, a new biography in French by Marion Pierson-Piérard appears, entitled *La Vie passionnée de Katherine Mansfield*, with the sub-title, 'mieux qu'un roman, une vie vécue',[80] followed in 1987 by the *Brève vie de Katherine Mansfield* by Pietro Citati.[81] Both are hagiographical in tone and content, following the earlier style of the biographies by Mantz, Lenoël and Merlin. Claire Tomalin's 1987 biography of Mansfield, *A Secret Life*, is translated into French in 1990. The book cover states:

> L'image d'une Katherine Mansfield iconisée, assainie, sans défaut, voulue par John Middleton Murry, son mari – dont on peut dire avec quelque raison qu'il fit 'bouillir les os de sa femme pour en faire de la soupe' – ne pouvait qu'accroître l'effroi qui s'emparait d'elle à l'idée que soient révélés les secrets de sa jeunesse.[82]

The French publishers have recognised that this book contains important new biographical material, especially concerning Mansfield's early years, yet it generates no new critical discussion.

In March 2006, Stock brings out a new expanded edition of Mansfield's stories.[83] In the preface, Marie Desplechin states: 'Quelquefois, je pense que Katherine Mansfield est morte trop jeune pour mourir vraiment. Elle est restée suspendue, entre le ciel et nous' (12). A full page article in the newspaper *Sud-ouest*, reviewing this new edition, together with a large, digitally enhanced photo of Mansfield from 1913, is re-

80   Marian Pierson-Piérard, *La Vie passionnée de Katherine Mansfield* (Brussels: Éditions Labor, 1979).
81   Pietro Citati, *Brève vie de Katherine Mansfield*, trans. by Brigitte Pérol (Paris: Quai Voltaire, 1987).
82   Claire Tomalin, *Katherine Mansfield: Une vie secrète*, trans. by Anne Damour (Paris: Bernard Coutaz, 1990).
83   Katherine Mansfield, *Les Nouvelles*, pref. by Marie Desplechin (Paris: Stock, 2006).

markable for the way it seems to take us right back to the early days of Mansfield criticism, back almost eighty years to the hagiography and bias. André Maurois is cited, Louis Pauwels is mentioned, 'John Middleton' [sic] is cited as if he had just given an interview to the writer:

> John Middleton raconte qu'après la publication du recueil 'Félicité' où la nouvelle 'Prélude' apparaît en tête de volume, elle commence à recevoir des lettres des gens simples, qui aiment son œuvre et surtout la petite Kézia qu'on y rencontre. 'Elle se sentit responsable envers ces lecteurs-là. A eux, elle devait la vérité, rien que la vérité. Cette préoccupation du vrai, du vrai dans ce qu'elle écrivait, du vrai en son âme afin qu'elle fût digne de s'exprimer, devient la passion dévorante des dernières années de sa vie.'[84]

Le Figaro also publishes a review of the same book, in a similar vein: 'Katherine Mansfield avait ce don de magicienne de transformer l'instant en cristal d'éternité [...] Ses personnages, pourtant si vulnérables devant l'insoutenable vanité des choses et si inquiets de la fuite du temps, ont passé le siècle sans ciller'.[85] It is hard not to contain a sense of disbelief, when one considers that as recently as 2006, critics in France are still peddling the same old distorted views which Murry and the band of French hagiographers were promulgating in the 1920s. We have come full circle, and appear to be back where we started.

André Bay, the literary editor at Mansfield's French publishers, Stock, from 1942–1961, and co-translator of the 'definitive' version of the *Journal*, wrote the following in answer to some of my queries. I quote from it extensively, since it summarises many of the findings of this chapter:

> Les amis de Katherine Mansfield, ou du moins ceux qui s'intéressent à elle, sont depuis longtemps mes amis [...] Lorsque je suis entré chez Stock à la fin de la guerre, K. M. était déjà un auteur de la maison où elle avait été publiée avant la guerre avec beaucoup d'autres auteurs de qualité. Je l'avais lue, je l'admirais, je l'aimais au point d'entreprendre moi-même la traduction intégrale du *Journal* dont Stock n'avait publié que des extraits. Avec l'aide de J. M. Murry, j'ai rassemblé toutes les nouvelles en un seul volume, publié les trois volumes de correspondances. Mais elle était déjà célèbre avant '39. Toutes sortes de raisons jouaient en sa faveur : son frère mort sur le front et enterré en France, Beauchamp, sa vie en France, à Paris (la chambre qu'elle avait occupée place de la Sorbonne avait dû

---

84   Lionel Niedzwiecki, 'Une musique de l'âme', *Sud-ouest*, 26 March 2006, p. 10.
85   Astrid Éliard, 'Katherine Mansfield', *Le Figaro*, 23 March 2006, p. 19.

changer plusieurs fois de papier, les admirateurs arrachent le papier peint en souvenir d'elle…), sa mort à Fontainebleau, sa tombe à côté de celle de Gurdjieff,
etc…etc…

Il n'existe aucune archive chez Stock, si ce n'est les contrats, encore sont-ils
maintenant tombés en désuétude puisque son œuvre est dans le domaine public. Je
doute fort qu'on puisse vous donner une réponse quelconque sur les ventes dans
les années trente. Elles étaient très faibles en tout cas, de l'ordre de 2 à 3000 ex.
D'ailleurs, K. M. ne s'est jamais beaucoup vendue, et ce n'est que depuis
l'existence des livres de poche que *La Garden Party*, son plus gros succès, a pu
dépasser les 20.000. En France, la vente est souvent inversement proportionnelle à
l'importance donnée à un auteur. Il en fut ainsi pour Virginia Woolf. Dans ces
deux cas cependant le nombre des fidèles n'a cessé d'augmenter.[86]

For Bay, Mansfield's attraction for the French reading public can be at-
tributed to just a few factors: the death and burial of her brother in
France, the time she spent living in France, together with her own death
and burial in France. Her French book sales have never been massive but
as Bay informs us, this has no bearing on her status in the literary world,
which remains high. Although the letter was written some twenty years
ago, the reception of the new 2006 edition of the stories in France as
outlined above, demonstrates how little has changed in the intervening
years.

The French critics' insistence on concentrating on just a few small aspects of Mansfield's life and work has fabricated a peculiarly French
persona. My research into Mansfield's reputation in France has demonstrated how, after her death, those first French critics who took up this
cause, encouraged by Murry's own output, instigated a myth which has
continued to the present day.

The literary establishment in France grasped any salient biographical trifle relating to Mansfield, in order to substantiate their growing
hagiography – her beauty, her ill health, her supposed love of France and
the French, her romantic yet doomed love affair with Murry, her search
for the spiritual. But the fact remains that the persona they were slavishly
promoting, with very little critical dissent, bore only a passing resemblance to the figure known to her family and friends. The ethereal spirituality and general 'otherworldliness' perceived by the French critics in

86   Autograph letter from André Bay to Gerri Kimber, 8 October 1984.

Mansfield's writing, ignores the constant echoes of darkness, bitterness and also humour, which inform all her work. Their vision of a Mansfieldian prelapsarian world of fairies, parties, songs and dolls' houses, is far removed from the world Mansfield actually wrote about, which included the gassing of soldiers at the Front, the orgasm experienced by a school girl in a French class, together with compelling depictions of women's struggles for various kinds of liberty. For Mansfield's band of obsessive fans in France, however, she was encapsulated as a soul whose apparently fey and melancholic personal writing expressed a super-sensitivity, incompatible with the real world. Her reputation in France is therefore not based on sober academic judgement but on the more fluctuating and less controllable tide of personal and intuitive argument. The 1920s was a period ripe in France for a Mansfield figure to be launched, and the tide of this new critical process carried her reputation to the limits of subjective, interpretative criticism, with the French critics frequently finding themselves hoist by their own infatuation.

Those first French critical reviews instigated a myth which has continued to the present day. Most subsequent discussion has been based on the work of these initial critics; there is one root – a base of 'knowledge' from which information tends to be retrieved. A point is then reached where this information becomes solidified, leading to opposition to any alternative viewpoints, almost as if Mansfield's reputation had been talked up in some mysterious collective way, at whatever cost to objective critical judgment. It thus becomes irrelevant whether the initial research was based on deliberate misrepresentation or accidental misunderstanding – these so-called 'facts' have been in the public domain for so long that they *must* be true. The appendix to this chapter (Appendix H), collects together the bio-sketches of the most important critics discussed here, and reveals how those critics who helped perpetrate the legend were mostly Catholic, and mostly right-wing; many were members of the Académie Française. They all saw Mansfield as exemplifying their 'ideal woman', and promoted her as such to the general French reading public. Homogeneity, in the case of Katherine Mansfield in France, has led to a serious misrepresentation of a popular literary figure.

Conclusion

In this book, I have offered an innovative approach to an understanding of the development of Katherine Mansfield's reputation in France, as well as providing completely new research into specific French literary influences within the corpus of her writing.

Through a detailed examination of every reference to France and the French in Mansfield's personal writing never previously undertaken, I have been able to provide both a comprehensive picture of her time in France, together with an analysis of her perceptions on France and the French. As a result, we can perceive how Mansfield was aware of most of the French literary activity taking place during the years before and after the Great War. Her visits imbued her with a view of life, literature and art seen through a Gallic lens, which was to be of infinite and lasting value in her development as a writer. Life was seen from a different perspective when Mansfield was in France and her work was always informed by her own experience. She appears to have required constant journeying and a sense of instability in order to bring her creative temperament to the surface. Indeed, this was one of the ways she was to demonstrate Modernism – through her commitment to experimentation, which allowed her to move in directions not previously thought of.

Mansfield's fiction was influenced by French authors – Baudelaire and Colette in particular (with Murry being a constant source of new ideas in this regard during their relationship). Her brief liaison with Francis Carco fuelled her creative endeavours, leading directly to the composition of two stories, 'An Indiscreet Journey' and 'Je ne parle pas français'. Mansfield assimilated ideas and techniques through her reading of Colette, which she incorporated into her own fiction. Both women writers were searching for a new mode of expression, capturing the transitory nature of life, bringing ordinary moments and commonplace people into sharp relief; this notion lead them towards a theatrical quality in their work, via the use of monologue and dialogue. Out of her reading of Colette, Mansfield would come to reject the literary conventions associated with an intricately plotted narrative, and instead rely on direct and indirect narrative, producing constantly shifting focuses of perspective, and creating an intense interiority in some of her stories, developing into the 'stream-of-consciousness' technique.

Mansfield's contiguity with the French Symbolist and Decadent movements shows in her creative life where we see how some of her finest stories would not have come into being without her knowledge of Decadent and Symbolist texts. The practical aesthetics of Symbolism all became trademarks of Mansfield's mature Modernist, narrative technique, as did her satirical observances on the surfaces of the modern city landscape, redolent of Baudelaire's Parisian prose poems. Mansfield's use of symbols increased the emotional and intellectual capacity of her stories. Most of Mansfield's published fiction dates from 1914. She died in 1923 at the age of thirty-four, and towards the end of her life was too sick to write much of any consequence. Thus, the most productive phase of her short writing career coincided with the duration of the First World War and its immediate aftermath. This book has exposed how significant this historical conjunction was in terms of her literary output, since for Mansfield it resulted in a sense of cultural, historical and social fragmentation, brought about and reinforced by her war-time experiences, especially the death of her beloved younger brother, and effectuated her ensuing development of the Modernist short story.

Subjective editorial decision-making controls Mansfield's personal writing in translation. When the translation of the *Journal* and *Letters* are assessed together with the short stories, perhaps the most overriding feature which seems to be lost in translation is her humour. The more sober themes implicit in her fiction do seem to be able to cross over from English into French, whereas the humour almost *never* does. Mansfield took great delight in exposing the mundane snobberies of middle-class life, glorying in its inanities, sometimes placing a character with a single, deft comical phrase, and being consistently awake to the age-old comedy of misunderstanding. The sharp-witted, sarcastic comedienne perceived in her original writing however, becomes a dull, sober 'thinker' in translation. Thus, in this book, a close textual comparison of Mansfield's writing in the original and in translation, demonstrates how a careful reading of comparable texts from two national cultures, can offer a paradigm for interrogating the internal receptions of other canonical and non-canonical writers.

Murry's over-exposure of his dead wife's work and his aim to publish as much of her literary remains as the public could stomach, whilst at the same time editing out any material which he felt did not correlate with the image of her he was trying to convey, generated a wave of protest amongst those who had known her, which tainted her reputation in England, and hence any unbiased discussion of her work for many years.

The French critics, however, saw how Mansfield might exemplify – in contrast to more salacious home grown writers such as Rachilde and Colette – an ideal, sanitised version of a female writer. They seized on romantic, feminine details which could promote this vision: her beauty, her ill health, her supposed love of France and the French, her doomed 'tragic' relationship with Murry, her search for the spiritual. But the persona they were slavishly promoting, with very little critical dissent, bore almost no resemblance to the personality that is visible in Mansfield's original writings.

Balanced literary criticism can only really evolve from infusions of new ideas and approaches, over and above those which may already have been postulated. It would appear that no new arguments in the Mansfield debate have ever been allowed to take a secure foothold in France – the French critics seem determined to protect her from history itself. Yet all reputations need to be periodically reappraised in the light of changing intellectual trends. The final impression is of Mansfield as a Madame Tussaud-like waxwork figure in French literature, fixed, permanent and immutable. A demythologising process has been attempted by a few critics as a means of reassessing some parts of her reputation in the eighty years since her death, to no avail. Those critics who helped perpetrate the legend were mostly Catholic, and mostly right-wing; many were members of the Académie Française. They all saw Mansfield as exemplifying their 'ideal woman', and promoted her as such to the general French reading public. This homogeneity of critical judgement, in the case of Katherine Mansfield in France, has led to a serious misrepresentation of a popular literary figure.

The encapsulation of most of the themes of this book – Mansfield's time in France, the seeming inability of the French to understand her humour, the mis-translations of her words, the French perception of her as a serious, spiritual personality, all of the above are exposed in the following account.

Near the end of a letter to Murry written from Menton in the South of France, Mansfield wrote, 'You will find ISOLA BELLA in poker work on my heart' (CL4, p. 107, 12 November, 1920). Pokerwork is the art of decorating wood or leather by burning a design with a heated metal point. Outside the Katherine Mansfield memorial room, on the wall of the Villa Isola Bella where she lived for several months, the French mounted a plaque, with the following translation of the above quotation: 'Vous trouverez Isola Bella gravée sur mon cœur'. As mentioned in Chapter Five, Gabriel Boissy gave a speech at the unveiling ceremony of this plaque, on 21 March 1939, where he proclaimed: 'Nous voici bien là, devant une âme franciscaine. Il n'est pas d'autre nom à cette divine douceur, à ce suave épanchement dans l'absolu et l'éternelle unité de l'être' (Boissy, p. 2).

Not only does the plaque wrongly state that the words are taken from a letter to Murry of *10* November 1920, but, as C. K. Stead elaborates:

> There are two ways of reading this quotation. Pokerwork can be rather tatty and amateurish in its execution, so it's half-mocking the whole idea of things being engraved on the heart. And/or, pokerwork involves burning, and she may be hinting at the pain of the period in Menton and Ospedaletti. Whichever way you choose to read it, the solemn 'straight' French translation is really a misrepresentation of this beautifully ambiguous phrase.[1]

I am indebted to C. K. Stead for pointing out the above 'beautifully ambiguous' quotation to me, which encapsulates the general French approach to Mansfield, and exemplifies virtually every argument posited in this book. The use of the word 'gravée', as in 'engraved', implies a perceived serious, indelible manifestation of Mansfield's emotional and spiritual attachment to the Villa Isola Bella – and by extension, to France itself. The *actual* ambiguity of the implied meaning behind the phrase epitomises Mansfield's love/hate relationship with France and the French and her own vacillating response to the country which enriched both her life and her aesthetic response in so many ways.

---

1   Letter from C. K. Stead to Gerri Kimber, 6 September 2006.

Appendices

Appendix A
Time Spent in France – Brief Chronology

1906	Easter	Short visit to Paris and Brussels with her sisters, accompanied by her aunt, Belle Dyer.
1908	21–24 Oct	In Paris for a naval wedding, with her friend Margaret Wishart.
1912	May	Short 'honeymoon' in Paris with JMM. First introduction to Francis Carco.
	Dec	In Paris for Christmas with JMM and others
1913	Dec	KM and JMM relocate to Paris, residing at 31 rue de Tournon.
1914	26 Feb	Financial difficulties force them to return to London.
1915	15 Feb	KM returns alone to Paris (having obtained some money from her brother) and proceeds to Gray. Spends four days there with Francis Carco.
	25 Feb	KM back in England. Reconciliation with JMM.
	18 March	Travels alone to Paris in order to write, staying in Carco's flat on the Quai aux Fleurs.
	31 March	Returns to England.
	5 May	Once more at Quai aux Fleurs, in order to write.
	19 May	Back in England.
	[7 Oct]	[Leslie Beauchamp, KM's adored brother, 'blown to bits' in France]
	Mid Nov	KM and JMM leave for South of France, staying initially at Cassis and then moving on to Bandol.
	7 Dec	JMM returns to London, leaving KM at Hotel Beau Rivage, Bandol.
	31 Dec	JMM rejoins KM at Villa Pauline, Bandol
1916	7 April	With JMM, returns to England, to live with the Lawrences near Zennor in Cornwall.

1918	7 Jan	For health reasons, returns unaccompanied to Hotel Beau Rivage, Bandol. Exhausting war-time journey leaves her ill.
	21 March	KM and her companion, Ida Baker, leave Bandol for the return journey home to England, but only make it as far as Paris, due to war-time travel restrictions. They stay at the Select Hotel, Place de la Sorbonne.
	11 April	Finally arrive back in England.
1919	[11 Sep]	[KM and Ida travel to the Riviera, because of KM's ill-health, staying initially at San Remo, Italy.]
1920	21 Jan	Moves across the border to the French Riviera, staying at L'Hermitage, a private nursing home.
	15 Feb	Moves into the Villa Flora, Menton, staying with her cousin, Miss Beauchamp, and Miss Fullerton.
	27 April	Leaves Menton for London.
	11 Sep	Sets off for the Villa Isola Bella, Menton, accompanied by Ida, as a tenant of Miss Beauchamp and Miss Fullerton.
1921	[4 May]	[KM and Ida move to Baugy, Switzerland. With JMM, stay in Switzerland for several months]
1922	30 Jan	KM leaves Switzerland for Paris, staying at the Victoria Palace Hotel, in order to see Dr Manoukhin and undertake his revolutionary tuberculosis treatment.
	4 June	Leaves Paris to return to Switzerland.
	[16 Aug]	[Travels to London, sees A. R. Orage, attends lectures given by P. D. Ouspensky.]
	2 Oct	Goes to Paris with Ida, staying at The Select Hotel.
	16 Oct	She moves to Gurdjieff's Institute for the Harmonious Development of Man at Fontainebleau.
1923	9 Jan	KM dies at Fontainebleau.

Appendix B
Stories Written in France

December 1913   'Something Childish But Very Natural' – Paris
March–May 1915 'The Aloe' – Paris
May 1915   'An Indiscreet Journey' – Paris
May 1915   'Spring Pictures' – Paris
May 1915   'The Little Governess' – Paris
February 1916   'The Aloe' (amended) – Bandol
March 1916   'The Aloe' (completed) – Bandol, Villa Pauline
January 1918   'Je ne parle pas français' – Bandol, Hotel Beau Rivage
February 1918   'Sun and Moon' – Bandol, Hotel Beau Rivage
February 1918   'Bliss' – Bandol, Hotel Beau Rivage
October 1920   'The Singing Lesson' – Menton, Villa Isola Bella
October 1920   'The Young Girl' – Menton, Villa Isola Bella
November 1920   'The Stranger' – Menton, Villa Isola Bella
November 1920   'Miss Brill' – Menton, Villa Isola Bella
November 1920   'Poison' – Menton, Villa Isola Bella
November 1920   'The Lady's Maid' – Menton, Villa Isola Bella
December 1920   'The Daughters of the Late Colonel' (completed) – Menton, Villa Isola Bella
February 1921   'Life of Ma Parker' – Menton, Villa Isola Bella
February 1922   'The Fly' (completed) – Paris, Victoria Palace Hotel
February 1922   'Honeymoon' – Paris, Victoria Palace Hotel

Appendix C
Stories Set in France or Containing a French Influence

Aug 1911	'The Journey to Bruges', London
Spring 1913	'Épilogue I: Pension Seguin', London
Spring 1913	'Épilogue II: Violet', London
Spring 1913	'Épilogue III: Bains Turcs', London
Early 1915	'The Little Governess', Paris
May 1915	'Spring Pictures', Paris
May 1915	'An Indiscreet Journey', Paris
Jan 1917	'The Lost Battle', London
May 1917	'In Confidence', London
Sep 1917	'Feuille d'Album', London
Feb 1918	'Je ne parle pas français', Bandol
May 1918	'Carnation', Cornwall
Jan 1920	'The Man without a Temperament', Ospedaletti
July 1920	'The Escape', London
Oct 1920	'The Young Girl', Menton
Nov 1920	'Poison', Menton
Jan 1922	'The Dove's Nest', Switzerland
Feb 1922	'Honeymoon', Paris

Appendix D
French Authors Known to Have Been Read by Mansfield

Amiel, Henri-Frédéric (1821–81)
Aubanel, Théodore (1829–86)
Balzac, Honoré de (1799–1850)
Barbey-D'Aurevilly, Jules (1808–89)
Barbusse, Henri (1873–1935)
Bofa, Gus (1883–1968)
Boulestin, Marcel (1878–1943)
Carco, Francis (1886–1958)
Codet, Louis (1876–1914)
Colette (1873–1954)
Daudet, Alphonse (1840–97)
Dérème, Tristan (1889–1941)
Deroulède, Paul (1846–1914)
Duhamel, Georges, 1884–1966)
Flaubert, Gustave (1821–80)
Gide, André (1869–1951)
Laforgue, Jules (1860–87)
Mallarmé, Stéphane (1842–98)
Margueritte, Paul (1860–1918)
Maupassant, Guy de (1850–93)
Merimée, Prosper (1803–70)
Mistral, Frédéric (1830–1914)
Pellerin, Jean (1885–1921)
Rachilde (1860–1953)
Sainte-Beuve, Charles-Augustin (1804–69)
Sand, George (1804–76)
Stendhal (1783–1842)
Tharaud, Jérôme (1874–1953)
Valéry, Paul (1871–1945)
Villiers de L'Isle-Adam, Auguste (1838–89)

Appendix E
Selected English/French Cultural Chronology
During Mansfield's Life-Time

	ENGLAND	FRANCE
1890	James, *The Tragic Muse*	Claudel, *Tête d'Or* Villiers de l'Isle-Adam, *Axël* Zola, *La Bête Humaine*
1891	Wilde, *The Picture of Dorian Gray*	[Maupassant goes insane]
	Hardy, *Tess of the D'Urbevilles*	[Rimbaud dies] Huysmans, *Là-bas* Mallarmé, *Pages* Gide, *Les Cahiers d'André Walter*
1894	The quarterly journal, the *Yellow Book* launched	[The conviction of Dreyfus for treason] Debussy, 'L'Après-midi d'un Faune'
1895	Wilde, *The Importance of Being Earnest* [The trial of Oscar Wilde]	
1896	Chekhov, *The Seagull*	Alfred Jarry, *Ubu Roi*
1897		Rostand, *Cyrano de Bergerac*
1898		Zola's article, 'J'accuse'
1899	[Beginning of the Boer War] Symons, *The Symbolist Movement in Literature*	Zola, *Fecondité*
1900	Freud, *Interpretation of Dreams*	[Matisse begins 'Fauvist' movement]
1901	[Death of Queen Victoria]	[First Nobel Prize for Literature, awarded to Sully Prudhomme]
1902		Gide, *L'Immoraliste*
1903	[Emmeline Pankhurst founds the Women's Social and Political Union]	

1904		[Nobel Prize for Literature, Frédéric Mistral]
1907	Forster, *The Longest Journey*	Picasso, 'Les Demoiselles d'Avignon' [Cubist exhibition in Paris]
1909		Matisse, 'The Dance' [Diaghilev's Russian ballet in Paris]
1910	[Post-Impressionist exhibition in London] [Death of Edward VII, accession of George V]	
1911	Mansfield, *In a German Pension* Murry and Mansfield found *Rhythm*	Paul Claudel, *L'Otage* Colette, *La Vagabonde*
1912	[Sinking of the Titanic] Lawrence, *The Trespasser*	['Futurist' exhibition in Paris] Claudel, *L'Annonce faite à Marie*
1913	Lawrence, *Sons and Lovers* [Suffragette demonstrations in London]	Proust, *Du côté de chez Swann* Apollinaire, *Alcools*, *Les Peintres cubistes* Colette, *L'Envers du music-hall* Colette, *L'Entrave* Alain-Fournier, *Le Grand Meaulnes*
1914	[Outbreak of World War I] Joyce, *Dubliners* [Founding of *Blast* and *Egoist*] Pound (ed.), *Des Imagistes* [Wyndham Lewis founds 'Vorticist' movement]	Gide, *Les Caves du Vatican* Carco, *Jésus-la-Caille*
1915	Woolf, *The Voyage Out* Lawrence, *The Rainbow* Brooke, *1914 and other Poems* Madox Ford, *The Good Soldier*	[Nobel Prize to Romain Rolland]

1916	Joyce, *A Portrait of the Artist as a Young Man* Shaw, *Pygmalion*	Apollinaire, *Le Poète assassiné* Carco, *Les Innocents* Barbusse, *Le Feu*
1917	Eliot, *Prufrock and Other Observations* Jung, *The Unconscious* [Revolutions in Russia] [America enters the War]	Valéry, *Le Jeune Parque* Apollinaire, *Les Mamelles de Tirésias* Duhamel, *La Vie des martyrs*
1918	Votes for women age thirty and over in Britain] Joyce, *Exiles* [End of World War 1] [Rutherford splits the atom] Strachey, *Eminent Victorians*	Giraudoux, *Simon le pathéthique* Duhamel, *Civilisation 1914–1917* Proust, *A l'ombre des jeunes filles en fleurs* [Debussy dies]
1919	[Treaty of Versailles] Woolf, *Night and Day*	Picasso, 'Pierrot and Harlequin' Gide, *La Symphonie pastorale* [Breton founds periodical *Littérature*] [Renoir dies]
1920	Lawrence, *Women in Love* Mansfield, *Bliss* De la Mare, *Poems 1901–18* Eliot, *The Sacred Wood* Fry, *Vision and Design*	Apollinaire, *La Femme assise* Montherlant, *La Relève du matin* Proust, *Le Côté de Guermantes* Valéry, *Le Cimetière Marin, Odes, Album des vers anciens* [Dada Festival in Paris]
1921	Huxley, *Crome Yellow* Lawrence, *Women in Love*	Breton and Soupault, *Les Champs magnétiques* Giraudoux, *Suzanne et le Pacifique* Proust, *Sodome et Gommorrhe* [Nobel Prize to Anatole France] [Trial of Barrès]

1922	Eliot, *The Waste Land*	Bergson, *Durée et simultanéité*
	Joyce, *Ulysses*	Colette, *La Maison de Claudine*
	Mansfield, *The Garden Party*	Valéry, *Charmes*
	Woolf, *Jacob's Room*	[Proust dies]
	Galsworthy, *The Forsyte Saga*	
	Lawrence, *Aaron's Rod*	
1923	[Katherine Mansfield dies at Avon, Fontainebleau, 9 January]	

Appendix F
Publication Dates for Mansfield Primary Texts

TITLE	ENGLAND	FRANCE
In a German Pension	1911	1939
Bliss and Other Stories	1920	1928
The Garden Party and Other Stories	1922	1929
The Doves' Nest and Other Stories	1923	
Poems	1923	1946
Something Childish and Other Stories	1924	
Journal	1927	1932
The Letters	1928	1931
The Aloe	1930	1987
Novels and Novelists	1930	
La Mouche (Selection)		1933
The Scrapbook	1939	1944
Collected Stories	1945	1955
Sur La Baie (Selection)		1946
Le Voyage Indiscret (Selection)		1950
Letters to John Middleton Murry	1951	1954
Journal – Definitive Edition	1954	1956
Collected Letters Vol. 1	1984	
Collected Letters Vol. 2	1987	
Collected Letters Vol. 3	1993	
Collected Letters Vol. 4	1996	
The Katherine Mansfield Notebooks	2002	

Appendix G
Characteristics of Literary Texts by Jean DeLisle[1]

Literary texts are identified by the following six criteria:

1. In a literary work, the writer communicates *his vision of the world*, his personal perception of the reality that he has chosen to describe. Speaking always for himself, he describes *his* feelings, *his* reactions, and *his* emotions. [...] In a literary work, then, the expressive function of language is predominant.

2. An imaginative and creative work also has the *power to evoke*. Not all of the message is explicit. A large part of it remains unexpressed, hence the major role played by connotation in literature. The order of words, the rhythm of sentences, and the patterns of sound may all have an evocative power that is relevant to the message and must be conveyed by the translator [...]

3. In a literary work, *form is important in and of itself*. [...] Language is not merely a means of communication, as it is in pragmatic texts, it is also an end in itself. In no other type of writing are form and content so inextricable. Poetry and artistic prose seek not only to communicate, but also to elicit an emotional response [...]

4. Literary works are *not restricted to a single interpretation*. The richer a work of literature is, the more levels of meaning it contains and the more interpretations are possible [...]

5. Literature is also characterised by a certain *timelessness*. Although it is the product and mirror of a particular era, a great literary work transcends space and time. It may be re-translated periodically, but that is to preserve its content and give new life to its form [...]

---

1   Jean Delisle, *Translation: An Interpretive Approach* (Ottawa: Univ. of Ottawa Press, 1988), pp. 14–15.

6. Lastly, a work of art stands the test of time because it is informed by *universal values*. The old works are still read today, not simply because they are aesthetically pleasing, but also because their themes have not grown stale. Love, death, religion, the human condition, the agony of existence, and relationships with others are themes for all places and all times

In the IoL's [Institute of Linguists] *Notes for Candidates*, the criteria for assessing translations are given as follows:

1. Accuracy: the correct transfer of information and evidence of complete comprehension;
2. The appropriate choice of vocabulary, idiom, terminology and register;
3. Cohesion, coherence and organisation;
4. Accuracy in technical aspects of punctuation, etc.[2]

2   Jeremy Munday, *Introducing Translation Studies: Theories and Applications* (London: Routledge, 2001), p. 30.

Appendix H:
Prominent Mansfieldian French Literary Critics

* Indicates member of the Académie Française.

*Marcel **ARLAND** (1899–1986), French novelist, literary critic and journalist. Co-founded the dadaist periodical *Aventure*. He directed the Nouvelle Revue Française (NRF) from 1953–1977.
Elected to the Académie Française in 1968.
Preface to *Journal – Édition Definitive* (1956).

André **BAY** (1919–present), poet and novelist. Literary editor (from 1942) at Mansfield's French publishing house, Stock.
Translator of 'La Maison de poupées' (1956).
Co-translator of *Journal – Édition Définitive* (1956).
Introduction to *Lettres à John Middleton Murry* (1954).

*Henry **BORDEAUX** (1870–1963), lawyer, novelist and essayist. His books exemplify traditional, moral, religious and family values.
Elected to the Académie Française in 1919.

Robert **BRASILLACH** (1909–1945), extreme right-wing novelist, journalist and literary critic. Considered the Nazi Party's rallies in Nürnberg to be the highest artistic creations of our time. Prisoner of war in 1940–41, after which became a supporter of collaboration, he was eventually executed in 1945 after a highly-publicised trial.

Jacques **CABAU** (1931–1989), Anglophile and literary critic. Known especially for his studies of American writers, notably Edgar Allan Poe and Upton Sinclair.

Francis **CARCO** (1886–1958), poet of the Fantaisiste school, as well as a novelist, dramatist, and art critic. The only Frenchman to have had a relationship with Mansfield. His novels are frequently picturesque, if slightly seedy, portrayals of Montmartre and the Parisian underworld.

Pierre **CITRON** (1919–present), biographer and literary scholar, notably for work on Balzac, Giono and also Berlioz.

Benjamin **CRÉMIEUX** (1888–1945), Jewish, right-wing drama and literary critic at the *NRF*, specialising in Italian literature. He became a senior editor at the *NRF*'s publishing house, Gallimard, only to find himself 'removed' from his position during the Second World War. He died in Buchenwald concentration camp.

*H. **DANIEL-ROPS** (1901–1965), pseudonym of Henri Petiot. He combined the roles of essayist and novelist with his role as a history teacher until 1945, after which he concentrated solely on writing. Deeply religious, his Catholicism informed virtually his entire output. After 1939 he turned his back on fiction to become a Church historian. He became editor-in-chief of the publishing firm of Fayard.
Elected to the Académie Française in 1955.

*Louis **GILLET** (1876–1943), literary critic, art historian, and Anglophile. Devoted much of his time to studies of English-speaking authors, notably Shakespeare, Joyce and D. H. Lawrence. Long-standing contributor to the *NRF*.
Elected to the Académie Française in 1935.
Preface to Félicité et autres nouvelles (1928).

*Émile **HENRIOT** (1889–1961), poet, novelist, journalist and literary critic.
Elected to the Académie Française in 1945.

*Edmond **JALOUX** (1878–1949), prolific novelist, translator, and critic.
Preface to La Garden Party et autres histoires (1929).
Elected to the Académie Française in 1936.

Georges-Jean **AUBRY** (1882–1950), translator and critic. Contributor to the *NRF*, most widely known for his friendship with Joseph Conrad, whose books he translated into French.

René **LALOU** (1889–1957), literary critic and prolific translator. Translated, amongst others, works by Virginia Woolf, D. H. Lawrence and Shakespeare.

Gabriel **MARCEL** (1889–1973), Catholic, reactionary philosopher, drama and music critic. Influenced the development of existentialism. Contributor to the *NRF*.
Preface to the one volume edition of the *Lettres* (1931).
[Anne Marcel, wife – translator of *Lettres à John Middleton Murry* (1954)].

*François **MAURIAC** (1885–1970), most important French Catholic novelist of 20th century. Was awarded the Nobel Prize for Literature in 1952.
Elected to the Académie Française in 1933.

*André **MAUROIS** (1885–1967) – pseudonym of Émile Herzog. Biographer, novelist, essayist, and prominent personality in French letters for fifty years. A great Anglophile, he was a member of the British forces in World War 1 and spent most of his working life promoting English Literature and culture.
Elected to the Académie Française in 1938.
Preface to L'œuvre romanesque (1966).

Charles **MAURON** (1899–1966), philosopher, writer, critic. Best known as an Anglophile, Bloomsbury collaborator and prolific translator of amongst others, Virginia Woolf, T. E. Lawrence and E. M. Forster. He was the inventor of psychological criticism as a form of literary analysis, examining the links between a writer's work and his life.
Translator of *Pension allemande* (1939).

Louis **PAUWELS** (1920–1997), prolific French journalist and writer. In 1948 he became a follower of the teachings of Gurdjieff for fifteen months, which was the catalyst for a book discussing Mansfield and Gurdjieff, and which would also influence him in writing his famous book *Le Matin des magiciens* (1960). Towards the end of his life he turned his back on all things esoteric and reconverted to Catholicism.

Denis **SAURAT** (1890–1958), Anglo-French scholar, writing on a wide range of topics, with interests in the occult, and particularly the Kabala. Became associated with the Department of French at King's College, London from 1920, and for many years was the director of the French Institute in London.

André **THÉRIVE** (1891–1967), novelist and literary critic of *Le Temps*.

*Jean-Louis **VAUDOYER** (1883–1963), art critic, poet and novelist. Criticised in some circles for taking on the administration of the Comédie Française during the Occupation.
Elected to the Académie Française in 1950.

Bibliography

Katherine Mansfield:
Principal Works (in order of publication)

In a German Pension (London: Stephen Swift, 1911)
Prelude (Richmond: Hogarth Press, 1918)
Je ne parle pas français (Hampstead: Heron Press, 1919)
Bliss and Other Stories (London: Constable, 1920)
The Garden Party and Other Stories (London: Constable, 1922)
The Doves' Nest and Other Stories (London: Constable, 1923)
Poems (London: Constable, 1923)
Something Childish and Other Stories (London: Constable, 1924)
Journal, ed. by J. Middleton Murry (London: Constable, 1927)
The Letters, 2 vols, ed. by J. Middleton Murry (London: Constable, 1928)
The Aloe (London: Constable, 1929)
Novels and Novelists, ed. by J. Middleton Murry (London: Constable, 1930)
The Short Stories (New York: Alfred A. Knopf, 1937)
The Scrapbook, ed. by J. Middleton Murry (London: Constable, 1939)
Collected Stories (London: Constable, 1945)
Letters to John Middleton Murry 1913–1922, ed. by J. Middleton Murry (London: Constable, 1951)
Journal, Definitive Edition, ed. by J. Middleton Murry (London: Constable, 1954)
Letters and Journals, ed. by C. K. Stead (London: Penguin, 1977)
The Urewera Notebook, ed. by Ian A. Gordon (Oxford: Oxford University Press, 1978)
The Collected Stories (London: Penguin, 1981)
The Aloe with Prelude, ed. by V. O'Sullivan (Wellington: Port Nicholson Press, 1982)

The Collected Letters, Volume One, 1903–1917, ed. by V. O'Sullivan and M. Scott (Oxford: Clarendon Press, 1984)

The Stories of Katherine Mansfield – Definitive Edition, ed. by Antony Alpers (Auckland: Oxford University Press, 1984)

The Collected Letters, Volume Two, 1918–1919, ed. by V. O'Sullivan and M. Scott (Oxford: Clarendon Press, 1987)

Poems, ed. by V. O'Sullivan (Oxford: Oxford University Press, 1988)

Selected Letters, ed. by V. O'Sullivan (Oxford: Oxford University Press, 1989)

The Collected Letters, Volume Three, 1919–1920, ed. by V. O'Sullivan and M. Scott (Oxford: Clarendon Press, 1993)

The Collected Letters, Volume Four, 1920–1921, ed. by V. O'Sullivan and M. Scott (Oxford: Clarendon Press, 1996)

The Katherine Mansfield Notebooks, 2 vols, ed. by M. Scott (Canterbury: Lincoln University Press, 1997)

Notebooks, Complete Edition, ed. by M. Scott (Minnesota: University of Minnesota Press, 2002)

Principal Biographies in English

Alpers, Antony, *Katherine Mansfield: A Biography* (London: Jonathan Cape, 1954)

—— *The Life of Katherine Mansfield* (London: Jonathan Cape, 1980)

Baker, Ida, pseud. 'Lesley Moore', *Katherine Mansfield: The Memories of L.M.* (London: Michael Joseph, 1971)

Boddy, Gillian, *Katherine Mansfield: The Woman and the Writer* (Harmondsworth: Penguin, 1988)

Gordon, Ian, *Katherine Mansfield*, Writers and Their Work, No. 49 (London: Longmans, Green & Co., 1954)

Mantz, Ruth Elvish and J. M. Murry, *The Life of Katherine Mansfield* (London: Constable, 1933)

Meyers, Jeffrey, *Katherine Mansfield: A Biography* (London: Hamish Hamilton, 1978)

—— *Katherine Mansfield: A Darker View* (New York: Cooper Square
Press, 2002)
Nathan, Rhoda B., *Katherine Mansfield* (New York: Continuum, 1988)
Phillimore, Jane, *Katherine Mansfield: Life and Works* (Hove: Wayland,
1989)
Tomalin, Claire, *Katherine Mansfield: A Secret Life* (London: Viking, 1987)
Woods, Joanna, Katerina: *The Russian World of Katherine Mansfield*
(Auckland: Penguin, 2001)

Critical Works on Mansfield in English

Benet, Mary Kathleen, *Katherine Mansfield, George Eliot, Colette and
the Men They Lived With* (Boston: G. K. Hall & Co., 1984)
Berkman, Sylvia, *Katherine Mansfield: A Critical Study* (London: Ox-
ford University Press, 1951)
Burgan, Mary, *Illness, Gender and Writing: The Case of Katherine
Mansfield* (Baltimore: Johns Hopkins University Press, 1994)
Dada-Büchel, Marianne, *Katherine Mansfield's Dual Vision* (Basel:
Franke, 1995)
Daly, Saralyn, *Katherine Mansfield* (New York: Twayne, 1965)
Dunbar, Pamela, *Radical Mansfield: Double Discourse in Katherine
Mansfield's Short Stories* (London: Macmillan, 1997)
Gunsteren, Julia van, *Katherine Mansfield and Literary Impressionism*
(Amsterdam: Rodopi, 1990)
Hanson, Clare, ed., *The Critical Writings of Katherine Mansfield* (Lon-
don: Macmillan, 1987)
—— ed., *Re-reading the Short Story* (Basingstoke: Macmillan, 1989)
—— and Andrew Gurr, *Katherine Mansfield* (Basingstoke: Macmillan,
1981)
Hayman, Ronald, *Literature and Living: A Consideration of Katherine
Mansfield and Virginia Woolf* (London: Covent Garden Press, 1972)
Hughes, Peter, intro., *Katherine Mansfield Manuscripts in The Alexander Turnbull Library* (Wellington: National Library of New Zealand, 1988)

Kaplan, Sydney Janet, *Katherine Mansfield and the Origins of Modernist Fiction* (NY and London: Cornell University Press, 1991)

Kinoshita, Yukiko, *Art and Society: A Consideration of the Relations Between Aesthetic Theories and Social Commitment with Reference to Katherine Mansfield and Oscar Wilde* (Chiba: Seiji Shobo, 1999)

Kirkpatrick, B. J., *A Bibliography of Katherine Mansfield* (Oxford: Clarendon Press. 1989)

Kobler, J. F., *Katherine Mansfield: A Study of the Short Fiction* (Boston: Twayne, 1990)

Lawlor, P. A., *A Katherine Mansfield Enthusiast: The Work of Guy N. Morris* (Wellington: Beltane Book Bureau. 1951)

Michel, Paulette and Michel Dupuis, eds., *The Fine Instrument: Essays on Katherine Mansfield* (Sydney: Dangaroo Press, 1989)

Moore, James, *Gurdjieff and Mansfield* (London: Routledge & Kegan Paul, 1980)

Morrow, Patrick, *Katherine Mansfield's Fiction* (Ohio: Bowling Green State University Press, 1993)

Murray, Heather, *Double Lives: Women in the Stories of Katherine Mansfield* (Dunedin: University of Otago Press, 1990)

Murry, John Middleton, *Katherine Mansfield and Other Literary Portraits* (London: Peter Nevill, 1949)

Nathan, Rhoda B., ed., *Critical Essays on Katherine Mansfield* (New York: Hall and Co., 1993)

New, W. H., *Reading Mansfield and Metaphors of Form* (Quebec: McGill-Queen's University Press, 1999)

O'Sullivan, Vincent, *Katherine Mansfield's Selected Stories: Norton Critical Edition* (New York: Norton, 2006)

Pilditch, Jan, ed., *The Critical Response to Katherine Mansfield* (Connecticut: Greenwood Press, 1996)

Ricketts, Harry, ed., *Worlds of Katherine Mansfield* (Palmerston: Nagare Press, 1991)

Robinson, Roger, ed., *Katherine Mansfield: In From the Margin* (Louisiana: Louisiana State University Press, 1994)

Scott, Margaret, *Recollecting Mansfield* (Auckland: Random House, 2001)

Smith, Angela, *Katherine Mansfield: A Literary Life* (Basingstoke: Palgrave, 2000)

—— *Katherine Mansfield and Virginia Woolf: A Public of Two* (Oxford: Clarendon Press, 1999)

Other Works Consulted in English

Atkin, Jonathan, *A War of Individuals: Bloomsbury Attitudes to the Great War* (Manchester: Manchester University Press, 2002)

Baldick, Chris, *The Oxford English Literary History Volume 10, 1910–1940: The Modern Movement* (Oxford: Oxford University Press, 2004)

Barlow, Adrian, *The Great War in British Literature* (Cambridge: Cambridge University Press, 2000)

Bassnett, Susan, *Translation Studies* (London: Routledge, 1991)

—— and Harish Trivedi, eds., *Post-Colonial Translation: Theory and Practice* (London: Routledge, 1999)

Bates, H. E., *The Modern Short Story from 1809 to 1953* (London: Robert Hale, 1988)

Baudelaire, Charles, *The Complete Verse: Volume 1*, trans. and intro. by Francis Scarfe (London: Anvil Press Poetry, 1986)

—— *The Parisian Prowler – Le Spleen de Paris, Petits Poèmes en Prose*, trans. by Edward K. Kaplan (Georgia: University of Georgia Press, 1989)

Benstock, Shari, *Women of the Left Bank: Paris, 1900–1940* (Austin: University of Texas Press, 1986)

Bergonzi, Bernard, *The Turn of a Century: Essays on Victorian and Modern English Literature* (Basingstoke: Macmillan, 1973)

Bertocci, Angelo Philip, *Charles Du Bos and English Literature* (New York: Columbia University Press, 1949)

Best, Victoria, *An Introduction to Twentieth Century French Literature* (London: Duckworth, 2002)

Bevan, David, ed., *Literature and War* (Atlanta: Rodopi, 1990)

Birkett, Jennifer and James Kearns, *A Guide to French Literature: From Early Modern to Postmodern* (Basingstoke: Macmillan, 1997)

Bowen, Elizabeth, intro, *Faber Book of Modern Stories* (London: Faber and Faber, 1937)

Brook, G. L., *The Language of Dickens* (London: Deutsch, 1970)

Brower, Reuben A., ed., *On Translation* (New York: Oxford University Press, 1966)

Cain, Seymour, *Gabriel Marcel* (London: Bowes and Bowes, 1963)

Carswell, John, *Lives and Letters: 1906–1957* (London: Faber and Faber, 1978)

Caws, Mary Ann and Sarah Bird Wright, *Bloomsbury and France: Art and Friends* (New York: Oxford University Press, 2000)

Cooper, Barbara and Mary Donaldson-Evans, eds., *Modernity and Revolution in Late-Nineteenth-Century France* (Newark: University of Delaware Press, 1992)

Cornell, Kenneth, *The Symbolist Movement* (Yale: Yale University Press, 1951)

Daiches, David, *New Literary Values: Studies in Modern Literature* (London: Oliver and Boyd, 1969)

—— *The Novel and the Modern World* (Chicago: University of Chicago Press, 1939)

Daly, Nicholas, *Modernism, Romance and the Fin de Siècle: Popular Fiction and British Culture, 1880–1914* (Cambridge: Cambridge University Press, 1999)

Delabastita, Dirk, ed., *Wordplay and Translation* (Namur: St Jerome Publishing, 1996)

Delisle, Jean, *Translation: An Interpretive Approach*, trans. by Patricia Logan and Monica Creery (Ottawa: University of Ottawa Press, 1988)

Demoor, Marysa, *Their Fair Share: Women, Power and Criticism 1870–1920* (Aldershot: Ashgate Publishing Ltd., 2000)

Diamond, David, *Seven Songs* (Philadelphia: Elkan-Vogel, 1946)

Downing, Lisa, *Desiring the Dead: Necrophilia and Nineteenth-Century French Literature* (Oxford: Legenda, 2003)

Du Bos, Charles, *What is Literature?* (London: Sheed & Ward, 1940)

Duclaux, Mary, *Twentieth Century French Writers* (London: Collins, 1919)

Eliot, T. S., *Essays Ancient and Modern* (London: Faber and Faber, 1936)

—— *Prufrock and Other Observations* (London: The Egoist Press, 1917)

—— *The Sacred Wood: Essays on Poetry and Criticism* (London: Methuen, 1920)

Evans, Martha Noel, *Masks of Tradition – Women and the Politics of Writing in Twentieth Century France* (Ithica: Cornell University Press, 1987)

Fairlie, Alison, *Baudelaire: Les Fleurs du Mal* (London: Edward Arnold, 1960)

Faulk, Barry, J., *Music Hall and Modernity: The Late-Victorian Discovery of Popular Culture* (Athens: Ohio University Press, 2004)

Field, Frank, *Three French Writers and the Great War* (Cambridge: Cambridge University Press, 1975)

Flora, Joseph M., ed., *The English Short Story 1880–1945: A Critical History* (Boston: Twayne, 1985)

France, Peter, ed., *The New Oxford Companion to Literature in French* (Oxford: Clarendon Press, 1995)

Gane, Mike, *French Social Theory* (London: Sage, 2003)

Gildea, Robert, *The Third Republic from 1870 to 1914* (London: Longman, 1988)

Gillet, Louis, *Claybook for James Joyce*, trans. by Georges Markow-Totevy (London: Abelard-Schuman Ltd, 1958)

Glenavy, Beatrice, *Today We Will Only Gossip* (London: Constable, 1964)

Goldman, Dorothy, ed., *Women and World War 1: The Written Response* (Basingstoke: Macmillan, 1993)

Gordon, Lyndall, *Eliot's Early Years* (Oxford: Oxford University Press, 1977)

Greicus, M.S., *Prose Writers of World War 1* (London: Longman, 1973)

Griffin, Ernest G., *John Middleton Murry* (New York: Twayne, 1969)

Griffiths, Richard, *The Reactionary Revolution – The Catholic Revival in French Literature 1870–1914* (New York: Frederick Ungar, 1965)

Gurdjieff, George Ivanovitch, *The Herald of Coming Good* (Angers: Privately Printed, 1933)

Hanscombe, Gillian, *Writing for their Lives: The Modernist Women, 1910–1940* (London: Women's Press, 1987)

Hanson, Clare, *Short Stories and Short Fictions, 1880–1980* (London: Macmillan, 1985)

Harvey, Sir Paul, ed., *The Oxford Companion to English Literature*, 4th edition (Oxford: Clarendon Press, 1973)

Harwood, John, *Eliot to Derrida: The Poverty of Interpretation* (Basingstoke: Macmillan, 1995)

Hawthorne, Melanie C., *Rachilde and French Women's Authorship: From Decadence to Modernism* (Nebraska: University of Nebraska Press, 2001)

Head, Dominic, *The Modernist Short Story: A Study in Theory and Practice* (Cambridge: Cambridge University Press, 1992)

Hiddleston, J. A., *Baudelaire and 'Le Spleen de Paris'* (Oxford: Clarendon Press, 1987)

Holmes, Diana, *French Women's Writing: 1848–1994* (London: Athlone Press, 1996)

—— *Rachilde: Decadence, Gender and the Woman Writer* (Oxford: Berg, 2001)

—— *Women Writers: Colette* (Basingstoke: Macmillan, 1991)

Holmes, James, ed., *The Nature of Translation: Essays on the Theory and Practice of Literary Translation* (The Hague: Mouton and Co., 1970)

Houston, John Porter, *Joyce and Prose: An Exploration of the Language of Ulysses* (Lewisburg: Bucknell University Press, 1989)

Huffer, Lynne, *Another Colette: The Question of Gendered Writing* (Michigan: University of Michigan Press, 1992)

Hulme, T. E., *Speculations: Essays on Humanism and the Philosophy of Art*, ed. by Herbert Read. (London: Kegan Paul, Trench, Trubner, 1936)

Huneker, James, *Iconoclasts: A Book of Dramatists* (New York: Scribners, 1905)

Hutchins, Patricia, *James Joyce's World* (London: Methuen, 1957)

Kaplan, Edward K., *Baudelaire's Prose Poems: The Esthetic, The Ethical, and The Religious in The Parisian Prowler* (Athens: University of Georgia Press, 1990)

Lawrence, D. H., *The Life of J. M. Murry by J.C.* (Privately printed: 1930)

Lea, Frank, *Lawrence and Murry: A Twofold Vision* (London: Brentham Press, 1985)

—— *The Life of John Middleton Murry* (London: Methuen, 1959)

Lefevere, André, *Translation, Rewriting and the Manipulation of Literary Fame* (London: Routledge, 1992)

Levenson, Michael, ed., *The Cambridge Companion to Modernism* (Cambridge: Cambridge University Press, 1999)

—— ed., *A Genealogy of Modernism* (Cambridge: Cambridge University Press, 1984)

Lloyd, Rosemary, *Mallarmé: The Poet and His Circle* (Ithica: Cornell University Press, 2005)

Lohafer, Susan, *Reading for Storyness: Preclosure Theory, Empirical Poetics and Culture in the Short Story* (Baltimore: Johns Hopkins University Press, 2003)

Lottman, Herbert, *Colette: A Life* (London: Secker and Warburg, 1991)

Mairet, Philip, *John Middleton Murry*, Writers and Their Work No. 102 (London: Longmans, Green & Co., 1958)

Maurois, André, *From Proust to Camus – Profiles of Modern French Writers*, trans. by Carl Morse and Renaud Bruce (London: Weidenfeld and Nicolson, 1967)

Menand, Louis, *Discovering Modernism: T. S. Eliot and his Context* (Oxford: Oxford University Press, 1987)

Moore, George, *Confessions of a Young Man* (London: Swan Sonnenschein, 1888)

Moore, Harry T., *Twentieth Century French Literature* (Illinois: Southern Illinois University Press, 1966)

Mortimer, Raymond, *Duncan Grant* (Harmondsworth: Penguin, 1944)

Munday, Jeremy, *Introducing Translation Studies – Theories and Applications* (Abingdon: Routledge, 2001)

Murry, Colin Middleton, *One Hand Clapping* (London: Victor Gollancz, 1975)

Murry, John Middleton, *Between Two Worlds* (London: Jonathan Cape, 1935)

—— *Katherine Mansfield and Other Literary Portraits* (London: Peter Nevill, 1949)

—— *The Letters of John Middleton Murry to Katherine Mansfield*, ed. by C. A. Hankin (London: Constable, 1983)

—— *The Problem of Style* (London: Humphrey Milford, 1925)

—— *Poets, Critics, Mystics*, ed. by Richard Rees, pref. by Harry T. Moore (Illinois: Southern Illinois University Press, 1970)

—— *Still Life* (London: Constable, 1916)

Murry, Katherine Middleton, *Beloved Quixote, The Unknown Life of John Middleton Murry* (London: Souvenir Press, 1986)

O'Brien, Justin, ed., *From the NRF: An Image of the Twentieth Century from the Pages of the Nouvelle Revue Française* (New York: Farrar, Strauss and Cudahy, 1958)

O'Connor, Frank, *The Lonely Voice: A Study of the Short Story* (London: Macmillan, 1963)

Ouditt, Sharon, *Fighting Forces, Writing Women: Identity and Ideology in the First World War* (London: Routledge, 1994)

Ouspensky, P. D., *In Search of the Miraculous* (London: Routledge, 1950)

Paul, David, ed., *Poison and Vision: Poems and Prose of Baudelaire, Mallarmé and Rimbaud* (New York: Vintage, 1974)

Petrilli, Susan, ed., *Translation, Translation* (Amsterdam: Rodopi, 2003)

Pound, Ezra, ed., *Des Imagistes* (London: Poetry Bookshop, 1914)

—— *Ripostes of Ezra Pound* (London: Stephen Swift, 1912)

Prendergast, Christopher, *Paris and the Nineteenth Century* (Oxford: Blackwell, 1992)

Quennell, Peter, *Baudelaire and the Symbolists: Five Essays* (London: Chatto and Windus, 1929)

Raitt, A. W., *The Life of Villiers de l'Isle-Adam* (Oxford: Clarendon Press, 1981)

Raitt, Suzanne and Trudi Tate, eds., *Women's Fiction and the Great War* (Oxford: Clarendon Press, 1997)

Riccardi, Alessandra, ed., *Translation Studies: Perspectives on an Emerging Discipline* (Cambridge: Cambridge University Press, 2002)

Richardson, Joanna, *The Bohemians: La vie de Bohème in Paris* (London: Macmillan, 1969)

Ridge, George Ross, *The Hero in French Decadent Literature* (Atlanta: University of Georgia Press, 1961)

Robinson, Christopher, *French Literature in the Nineteenth Century* (Newton Abbot: David and Charles, 1978)

Rothenstein, William, *Twenty-Four Portraits* (London: Chatto and Windus, 1923)

Sartori, Eva M., and Dorothy W. Zimmerman, eds., *French Women Writers* (Westport: Greenwood Press, 1991)

Saurat, Denis, *Modern French Literature: 1870–1940* (London: Dent and Sons, 1946)

Savory, Theodore, *The Art of Translation* (London: Jonathan Cape, 1968)

Schom, Alan, *Émile Zola: A Bourgeois Rebel* (London: Queen Anne Press, 1987)

Scott, Bonnie Kime, ed., *The Gender of Modernism: A Critical Anthology* (Bloomington: Indiana University Press, 1990)

Scott, Clive, *Translating Baudelaire* (Exeter: University of Exeter Press, 2000)

Shattuck, Roger, *The Innocent Eye: On Modern Literature and the Arts* (New York: Farrar, Strauss & Giroux, 1984)

Showalter, Elaine, ed., *Daughters of Decadence: Women Writers of the Fin-de-Siècle* (New Jersey: Rutgers University Press, 1993)

Smith, Angela K., *The Second Battlefield: Women, Modernism and the First World War* (Manchester: Manchester University Press, 2000)

Starkie, Enid, *From Gautier to Eliot: The Influence of France on English Literature 1851–1939* (London: Hutchinson, 1960)

Stephens, Sonya, *Baudelaire's Prose Poems: The Practice and Politics of Irony* (Oxford: Oxford University Press, 1999)

Symons, Arthur, *Selected Writings* (Manchester: Carcanet Press, 1974)

—— *The Symbolist Movement in Literature* (London: Heinemann, 1899)

—— *The Symbolist Movement in Literature*, intro. by Richard Ellmann (New York: Dutton, 1958)

Taylor, Jane, ed., *Double Vision: Studies in Literary Translation* (Durham: University of Durham, 2002)

Temple, Ruth Z., *The Critic's Alchemy: A Study of the Introduction of French Symbolism into England* (New York: Twayne, 1953)

Thompson, William J., ed., *Understanding Les Fleurs du Mal: Critical Readings* (Nashville: Vanderbilt University Press, 1997)

Thurman, Judith, *Secrets of the Flesh – A Life of Colette* (London: Bloomsbury, 1999)

Trodd, Anthea, *A Reader's Guide to Edwardian Literature* (Hemel Hempstead: Harvester Wheatsheaf, 1991)

Turnell, Martin, *The Art of French Fiction* (London: Hamish Hamilton, 1959)

Tylee, Claire M., *The Great War and Women's Consciousness: Images of Militarism and Womanhood in Women's Writings, 1914–64* (Basingstoke: Macmillan, 1990)

University of Edinburgh, Women's Union, *Atalanta's Garland: being the book of the Edinburgh University Women's Union, 1926* (Edinburgh: Edinburgh University Press, 1926)

Van Leuven-Zwart, Kitty and Ton Naaijkens, eds., *Translation Studies: Proceedings of the First James S. Holmes Symposium on Translation Studies* (Amsterdam: Rodopi, 1991)

Venuti, Lawrence, ed., *The Translation Studies Reader* (London: Routledge, 2000)

Villiers de L'Isle-Adam, *Cruel Tales*, trans. by Robert Baldick, intro. by A. W. Raitt (Oxford: Oxford University Press, 1985)

—— *Sardonic Tales (Contes Cruels)*, trans. by Hamish Miles (New York: Alfred A. Knopf, 1927)

Waelti-Walters, Jennifer, *Damned Women: Lesbians in French Novels* (Montreal: McGill-Queen's University Press, 2000)

Walker, Warren, S., *Twentieth-Century Short Story Explication: Interpretations, 1900–1966 of Short Fiction Since 1800* (Hamden, Conn: Shoe String Press, 1967)

Wallace, Lewis A. R., pseud. 'M. B. Oxon', *Cosmic Anatomy or the Structure of the Ego* (London: Watkins, 1921)

Walton Litz, A., Louis Menand and Lawrence Rainey, eds., *Modernism and the New Criticism: The Cambridge History of Literary Criticism*, Vol. 7 (Cambridge: Cambridge University Press, 2000)

Ward, Patricia A., ed., *Baudelaire and the Poetics of Modernity* (Nashville: Vanderbilt University Press, 2001)

Wheeler, Kathleen M., *Modernist Women Writers and Narrative Art* (Basingstoke: Macmillan, 1994)

Wilde, Oscar, *The Picture of Dorian Gray* (Oxford: Oxford University Press, 1999)

Willy, Margaret, *Three Women Diarists*, Writers and Their Work No. 173 (London: Longmans, Green & Co., 1964)

Wilson, Edmund, *Axel's Castle: A Study in the Imaginative Literature of 1870–1930* (London: Charles Scribner's, 1931)

Woolf, Leonard, *The Autobiography of Leonard Woolf* (London: Hogarth Press, 1964)

Woolf, Virginia, *Collected Essays*, vol. 1 (London: Hogarth Press, 1966)

—— *The Diary of Virginia Woolf: vol 2 1920–1924*, ed. by Anne Olivier Bell (London: Hogarth Press, 1977)

Worthen, John, *D. H. Lawrence: The Life of an Outsider* (London: Allen Lane, 2005)

Yeats, W. B., ed., *The Oxford Book of Modern Verse: 1892–1935* (Oxford: Clarendon Press, 1936)

Yee, Cordell, D. K., *The World According to James Joyce: Reconstructing Representation* (Lewisburg: Bucknell University Press, 1997)

Articles on Mansfield in English

Aiken, Conrad, 'The Short Story as Confession', *Nation & Athenaeum*, 33, 14 July 1923, p. 490

Anon., 'A Wayfarer', *Nation & Athenaeum*, 32, 13 January 1923, p. 575

Anon., 'Katherine Mansfield's Stories', *Times Literary Supplement*, 46, 2 March 1946, p. 102

Anon., 'The Garden Party and Other Stories by Katherine Mansfield', *English Review*, 34 (1922), 602

Baldeshwiler, Eileen, 'Katherine Mansfield's Theory of Fiction', *Studies in Short Fiction* (Summer 1970), 421–32

Boulestin, Marcel, 'Recent French Novels', *Blue Review: Literature, Drama, Art, Music*, 1.2 (June 1913), 138–40

Boyle, Kay, 'Katherine Mansfield: A Reconsideration,' *New Republic*, 92, 20 October 1937, p. 309

Clarke, Brice, M.D., 'Katherine Mansfield's Illness', *Proceedings of the Royal Society of Medicine*, 48 (April 1955), 1029–32

Corin, Fernand, 'Creation of Atmosphere in Katherine Mansfield's Stories', *Revue des langues vivantes*, 22 (1956), 65–78

Garlington, Jack, 'Katherine Mansfield: The Critical Trend', *Twentieth Century Literature*, 2 (July 1956), 51–61

Gerard, Albert, 'The Triumph of Beauty: Katherine Mansfield's Progress', *Revue des langues vivantes*, 18 (1952), 325–34

Huxley, Aldous, 'The Traveller's Eye-View', *Nation & Athenaeum*, 37, 16 May 1925, p. 204

King, Russell, S., 'Francis Carco's *Les Innocents* and Katherine Mansfield's *Je ne parle pas français*', *Revue de la littérature comparée*, 47 (1973), 427–41

Laurie, Alison, J., 'Queering Katherine' (AWSA 2001 conference proceedings), http://www.socsi.flinders.edu.au/wmst/awsa2001/pdf/papers/Laurie.pdf

Meyers, Jeffrey, 'Katherine Mansfield: A Bibliography of International Criticism, 1921–1977', *Bulletin of Bibliography* (July 1977), 53–67

—— 'Murry's Cult of Mansfield', *Journal of Modern Literature* (February 1979), 15–38

Mortelier, Christiane, 'The Genesis and Development of the Katherine Mansfield Legend in France', *AUMLA* (November 1970), 252–63

Mortimer, Raymond, 'The Dove's Nest and Other Stories', *New Statesman*, 21, 7 July 1923, p. 394

Murry, John Middleton, 'A Friend in Need to Katherine Mansfield', *Adelphi* (July–September 1948), 218–20

—— 'The Influence of Baudelaire', *Rhythm*, 2.14 (March 1913), xxiii–xxvii

—— 'In Memory of Katherine Mansfield', *Adelphi*, 1 (January 1924), 663–65

O'Faolain, Sean, 'Katherine Mansfield', *New Statesman and Nation*, 35, 17 January 1948, pp. 54–55

Pritchett, V.S., 'Books in General', *New Statesman and Nation*, 31, 2 February 1946, p. 87

Scott, Margaret, 'The Extant manuscripts of Katherine Mansfield', *Études anglaises* (1973), 413–19

Sitwell, Edith, 'Three Women Writers', *Vogue*, October 1924, p. 83

Tomlinson, H. M., 'Katherine Mansfield', *Nation & Athenaeum*, 32, 20 January 1923, p. 609

Uglow, Jennifer, 'Self-revelation and the self revealed', *Times Literary Supplement*, 13 January 1984, p. 47

Waldron, Philip, 'Katherine Mansfield's Journal', *Twentieth-Century Literature*, 20, 1 (January 1974), 11–18

Zorn, Marilyn, 'Visionary Flowers: Another Study of Katherine Mansfield's "Bliss"', *Studies in Short Fiction* (Spring 1980), 141–47

Principal Works and Editions in French
(in order of publication)

Félicité, trans. by J.-G. Delamain, pref. by Louis Gillet (Paris: Stock, 1928)

La Garden Party et autres histoires, trans. by Marthe Duproix, pref. by Edmond Jaloux (Paris: Stock, 1929)

Lettres, trans. by Madeleine T. Guéritte, pref. by Gabriel Marcel (Paris: Stock, 1931)

Journal, trans. by Marthe Duproix, intro. by J. M. Murry (Paris: Stock, 1932)

La Mouche, trans. by Madeleine T. Guéritte and Marguerite Faguer, pref. by Madeleine T. Guéritte (Paris: Stock, 1933)

Pension allemande et nouvelles diverses, trans. by Charles Mauron and Marguerite Faguer (Paris: Stock, 1939)

Cahier de notes, trans. by Germaine Delamain, intro. by J. M. Murry (Paris: Stock, 1944)

Nouvelles, trans. by J.-G. Delamain, Madeleine T. Guéritte, Marguerite Faguer and Marthe Duproix, pref. by Edmond Jaloux (Lausanne: Guilde du Livre, 1944)

Poèmes, trans. by Jean Pierre Le Mée (Paris: Éditions de la Nouvelle Revue Critique, 1946)

Sur la baie, trans. by Germaine Delamain, Marthe Duproix, Madeleine T. Guéritte, and Marguerite Faguer (Paris: Stock, 1946)

La Garden Party et autres histoires, trans. by Marthe Duproix, pref. by Edmond Jaloux (Paris: Stock, 1948)

Journal, trans. by Marthe Duproix, intro. by J. M. Murry (Paris: Stock, 1950)

Le Voyage indiscret, trans. by Didier Merlin (Paris: Éditions du Seuil, 1950)

Lettres, Vol. 1: 1913–1918, Vol. 2: 1918–1919, Vol.3: 1920–1922, trans. by Anne Marcel, intro. by André Bay (Paris: Stock, 1954)

L'Œuvre romanesque, trans. by J.-G. Delamain, Marthe Duproix, André Bay, Marguerite Faguer, Didier Merlin and Charles Mauron, pref. by André Maurois (Paris: Stock, 1955)

Journal, édition définitive, trans. by Marthe Duproix, Anne Marcel and André Bay, pref by Marcel Arland, intro. by J.M. Murry (Paris: Stock/ Les Librairies Associés, 1956)

La Garden Party et autres histoires, trans. by Marthe Duproix, pref. by Edmond Jaloux (Paris: Stock, 1956)

La Garden Party et autres nouvelles, trans. by Marthe Duproix, J.-G. Delamain and André Bay, pref. by Francis Carco (Paris: Sauret, 1956)

Félicité, trans. by J.-G. Delamain, pref. by André Maurois (Paris: Stock, 1966)

L'Œuvre romanesque, trans. by J.-G. Delamain, Marthe Duproix, André Bay, Marguerite Faguer, Didier Merlin and Charles Mauron, pref. by André Maurois (Paris: Stock, 1966)

Journal, édition définitive, trans. by Marthe Duproix, Anne Marcel and André Bay, pref. by Marcel Arland, intro. by J. M. Murry (Paris: Stock, 1973)

Le Voyage indiscret, trans. by Didier Merlin (Paris: Éditions du Seuil, 1973)

L'Œuvre romanesque, trans. by J.-G. Delamain, Marthe Duproix, André Bay, Marguerite Faguer, Didier Merlin and Charles Mauron, pref. by André Maurois (Paris: Stock, 1973)

Félicité, trans. by J.-G. Delamain, pref. by Louis Gillet (Paris: Stock, 1982)

Journal, édition complète, trans by Marthe Duproix, Anne Marcel and André Bay, pref. by Marcel Arland, intro. by J. M. Murry (Paris: Stock, 1983)

Pension allemande et nouvelles diverses, trans. by Charles Mauron and Marguerite Faguer (Paris: Stock, 1984)

L'Aloès, trans. by Magali Merle (Paris: Presses Pocket, 1987)

La Garden-Party et autres nouvelles, trans. and pref. by Françoise Pellan (Paris: Gallimard, 2002)

Katherine Mansfield: Les Nouvelles, pref. by Marie Desplechin (Paris: Stock, 2006)

Principal Biographies in French

Alpers, Antony, *Katherine Mansfield: L'Œuvre et la vie* (Paris: Seghers, 1959)

Citati, Pietro, *La Brève vie de Katherine Mansfield* (Paris: Quai Voltaire, 1991)

Lenoël, Odette, *La Vocation de Katherine Mansfield* (Paris: Albin Michel, 1946)

Mantz, Ruth and J. M. Murry, *La Jeunesse de Katherine Mansfield*, trans. by M. T. Guéritte, pref. by Jean-Louis Vaudoyer (Paris: Stock, 1935)

Marion, Bernard, *A la rencontre de Katherine Mansfield* (Brussels: La Sixaine, 1946)

Morel, Elisabeth, *Katherine Mansfield*, pref. by Louis Pauwels (Paris: Club de la femme, 1959)

Murry, John Middleton, *Katherine Mansfield et moi*, trans. and intro. by René Lalou (Paris: Fernand Sorlot, 1941)

Pierson-Piérard, Marianne, *La Vie passionnée de Katherine Mansfield* (Brussels: Éditions Labor, 1979)

Tomalin, Claire, *Katherine Mansfield: une vie secrète*, trans. Anne Damour (Paris: Bernard Coutaz, 1990)

Critical Works on Mansfield in French

Béranger, Elisabeth, ed., *Katherine Mansfield: de l'œuvre à la scène* (Bordeaux: Presses Universitaires de Bordeaux, 1985)

Daniel-Rops, H., *Trois tombes – trois visages* (Paris: La Colombe, 1946)

Henriot, Émile, *De Marie de France à Katherine Mansfield* (Paris: Librairie Plon, 1937)

Joubert, Claire, *Lire le féminin: Dorothy Richardson, Katherine Mansfield, Jean Rhys* (Paris: Messène, 1997)

Merlin, Roland, *Le Drame secret de Katherine Mansfield* (Paris: Éditions du Seuil, 1950)

Muffang, May Lillian, 'Katherine Mansfield: Sa vie, son œuvre, sa personnalité' (unpublished thesis, University of Paris, 1937).

Other Works Consulted in French

Barbey d'Aurevilly, *Les Diaboliques* (Paris: Garnier-Flammarion, 1967)
Baudelaire, Charles, *Le Spleen de Paris: petits poèmes en prose* (Paris: Flammarion, 1997)
Beauvoir, Simone de, *Le Deuxième Sexe* (Paris: Gallimard, 1949)
Boylesve, René, *La Jeune fille bien élevée* (Paris: H. Floury, 1909)
Carco, Francis, *Bohème d'artiste* (Paris: Albin Michel, 1940)
—— *Les Innocents* (Paris: Albin Michel, 1916)
—— *Jésus-la-Caille* (Paris: Mercure de France, 1914)
—— *Mémoires d'une autre vie* (Paris: Albin Michel, 1934)
—— *Montmartre à vingt ans* (Paris: Albin Michel, 1938)
Colette, *L'Entrave* (Paris: Ollendorff, 1913)
—— *L'Envers du music-hall* (Flammarion: Paris, 1913)
—— *Mes Apprentissages* in *Œuvres de Colette*, vol. 3 (Paris: Flammarion, 1960)
—— *La Vagabonde* (Paris: Ollendorff, 1910).
Chevalley, Abel, *Le Roman anglais de notre temps* (London: Humphrey Milford, 1921)
Clouard, Henri, *Histoire de la littérature française du symbolisme à nos jours: de 1914–1940* (Paris: Albin Michel, 1949)
Du Bos, Charles, *Journal: 1924–1925* (Paris: Éditions Corréa, 1948)
Duhamel, Georges, *Civilisation 1914–1917* (Paris: Mercure de France, 1918)
—— *Vie des martyrs* (Paris: Mercure de France, 1917)
Gillet, Louis, *Stèle pour James Joyce* (Marseille: Sagittaire, 1941)
Gourévitch, Jean-Paul, *Villiers de l'Isle-Adam: événements littéraires, artistiques et historiques* (Paris: Éditions Seghers, 1971)
Goyet, Florence, *La Nouvelle 1870–1925: description d'un genre à son apogée* (Paris: Presses Universitaires de France, 1993)

Kahn,, Gustav, *Symbolistes et Décadents* (Paris: Librairie Léon Vanier, 1902)

Maurois, André, *Magiciens et Logiciens* (Paris: Grasset, 1935)

Mirbeau, Octave, *L'Abbé Jules* (Paris: Ollendorff, 1888)

—— *Le Jardin des supplices* (Paris: Charpentier, 1899)

Mounin, Georges, *Les Problèmes théoriques de la traduction* (Paris: Gallimard, 1963)

Pauwels, Louis, *Monsieur Gurdjieff* (Paris: Éditions du Seuil, 1954)

Poe, Edgar Allan, *Nouvelles histoires extraordinaires*, trans. and intro. by Charles Baudelaire (Paris: Folio, 1972)

Raitt, A. W., *Villiers de l'Isle-Adam et le mouvement symbolique* (Paris: Librairie José Corti, 1986)

Tatilon, Claude, *Traduire: Pour une pédagogie de la traduction* (Toronto: Éditions du Gref, 1986)

Villiers de l'Isle-Adam, *Contes cruels*, ed. by Pierre Citron (Paris: Garnier-Flammarion, 1980)

—— *Œuvres complètes*, vol. 1, ed. by Alan Raitt and Pierre-Georges Castex (Paris: Éditions Gallimard, 1986)

Articles on Mansfield in French

Anon., 'La Vitrine du Figaro Littéraire', *Le Figaro*, 23 March 1935, p. 5

Anon., 'La vie de Katherine Mansfield par Antony Alpers', *Le Figaro littéraire*, 15 April 1959, p. 5

Anon., 'Les Lettres de Katherine Mansfield', *Le Figaro*, 12 July 1931, p. 5

Anon., 'Lettres de Catherine Mansfield' [sic], *Action française*, 9 August 1931, p. 7

Anon., 'Malentendus', *Le Figaro*, 1 June 1932, p. 5

Anon., 'Passionnément éprise du spectacle du monde', *Lettres françaises*, 7–13 July 1966, p. 6

Arland, Marcel, 'Katherine Mansfield ou la grâce d'écrire', *Nouvelle nouvelle revue française* (1954), 577–593

Auguis, Jean-Pierre, 'Katherine Mansfield aurait cinquante ans...', *Le Figaro littéraire*, 15 October 1938, p. 1

Barretta, Rose Worms, 'Les petites servantes méridionales vues par Katherine Mansfield', *Revue hebdomadaire*, 15 September 1934, 358–62

Bay, André, 'Le Journal définitive de Katherine Mansfield', *Carrefour*, 8 February 1956, p. 9

Bertrand, G. P., 'L'Attitude spirituelle de Katherine Mansfield', *Cahiers du sud* (December 1931), 646–65

Blanche, Jacques-Émile, 'Lectures sous la pluie', *Le Figaro*, 2 September 1931, p. 3

Boissy, Gabriel, 'Katherine Mansfield à Menton', *Nouvelles littéraires*, 8 April 1939, p. 2

Bompard, J., 'Sur une jeune femme morte: Katherine Mansfield', *Grande revue* (February 1933), 540–56

Bordeaux, Henry, 'Katherine Mansfield nous aimait-elle?', *Le Figaro*, 24 January 1934, p.1

—— 'Pèlerinage au cimetière d'Avon', *Nouvelles littéraires*, 27 May 1939, p.1

—— 'Le Souvenir de Katherine Mansfield', *Revue hebdomadaire*, 6 (May–June 1939), 265–79

—— 'Le Souvenir de Katherine Mansfield', *Nouvelles littéraires*, 8 January 1953, pp. 4–5

Boyer, Philippe, 'Katherine Mansfield: L'Œuvre romanesque', *Esprit (Nouvelle Série)* (October 1966), 558–16

Brasillach, Robert, 'Portrait: Katherine Mansfield', *Candide*, 22 September 1932, p. 3

Cabau, Jacques, 'Tempêtes dans une tasse de thé', *L'Express*, 15 August 1966, p. 36

Carco, Francis, 'Lettre de France: Le Roman français, introduction', in *Rhythm*, 2.10 (November 1912), 269–76

—— 'Lettre de Paris', in *Rhythm*, 2.2 (July 1912), 65–69

—— 'Mes Souvenirs sur Katherine Mansfield', *Annales politiques et littéraires*, 27 January 1933, 98–104

—— 'Mes Souvenirs sur Katherine Mansfield', *Annales politiques et littéraires*, 3 February 1933, 137–40

Charles, Gilbert, 'Une Âme transparente', *Le Figaro*, 9 July 1931, p. 5

—— 'L'Attitude spirituelle de Catherine Mansfield' [sic], *Le Figaro*, 14 Jan 1932, p. 5

—— 'Le 'Journal' de Catherine Mansfield' [sic], *Le Figaro*, 1 Nov 1931, p. 5

—— 'Le 'Journal' de Catherine Mansfield' [sic], *Le Figaro*, 27 May 1932, p. 5

Citron, Pierre, 'Katherine Mansfield et La France', *Revue de littérature comparée* (April–June 1940), 173–93

Crémieux, B., 'Katherine Mansfield', *Annales politiques et littéraires*, 2 (1931), 243–44

Crépin, André, 'Comptes Rendus: Katherine Mansfield & Other Literary Studies', *Études anglaises*, 12.3 (1959), 267–68

Daumière, René, 'La Petite fille qui retrouva son âme: Katherine Mansfield', *Paris-Normandie*, 10 July 1959, p. 11

Deffrennes, Pierre, 'L'Homme et sa plume: la correspondance de Katherine Mansfield', *Études par des pères de la compagnie de Jésus* (October–December 1931), 314–24

Éliard, Astrid, 'Katherine Mansfield', *Le Figaro*, 23 March 2006, p. 19

d'Escola, Marguerite, 'Katherine Mansfield', *Revue bleue politique et littéraire* (1 September 1934), 643–49

Fort, J. B., 'Katherine Mansfield et lui', *Études anglaises* (1952), 59–65

—— 'Comptes Rendus: The Journal of Katherine Mansfield', *Études anglaises*, 12.1 (1959), 76

Gateau, Andrée-Marie, 'Katherine Mansfield impressioniste', *Caliban (Toulouse)*, 6 (1969), 33–48

—— 'Poétesse, musicienne, et peintre d'un moment éphémère, ou Katherine Mansfield impressioniste', *Caliban (Toulouse)*, 5 (1968), 93–102

Gennari, Geneviève, 'Aux sources de la vocation féminine', *Table ronde*, 99 (March 1956), 72–75

Gillet, Louis, '"Kass": Ou la Jeunesse de Katherine Mansfield', *Revue des deux mondes*, 19, 15 January 1934, 456–68

—— 'Katherine Mansfield', *Revue des deux mondes*, 24, 15 December 1924, 929–42

—— 'Les Lettres de Katherine Mansfield', *Revue des deux mondes*, 51, 1 May 1929, 213–27

Gras, Gabrielle, 'Katherine Mansfield', *Europe* (September 1959), 135–39

Guyot, Edouard, 'Katherine Mansfield, par May Lillian Muffang', *Nouvelle revue française*, 49 (1937), 859–60

Harmat, Andrée-Marie, 'Ribni', *Annales de l'Université de Toulouse-le Mirail*, 9 (1973), 55–66

Henriot, Émile, 'Le Souvenir de Katherine Mansfield', *Le Temps* (12 March 1935), 456–61

Jaloux, Edmond, 'La Mouche, par Katherine Mansfield', *Nouvelles littéraires*, 14 October 1933, p. 4

—— 'Le Souvenir de Katherine Mansfield', *Le Temps*, 26 August 1937, p. 3

Jean-Aubry, G., 'Katherine Mansfield', *Revue de Paris*, 6 (November–December 1931), 57–72

Lamarche, Gustave, 'L'Équipe Murry-Mansfield', *Carnets viatoriens* (1947), 277–91

Manson, Anne, 'La Correspondance de Katherine Mansfield revelée trente ans après', *Paris-Presse L'Intransigeant*, 16 April 1954, p. 2

Marcel, Gabriel, 'Lettres étrangères', *Nouvelle revue française*, 32 (February 1929), 268–73

Matisse, Henri, 'Notes d'un peintre', *Grande revue*, 25 December 1908, 731–45

Mauriac, François, 'De Katherine Mansfield aux tricheurs ou la petite fille qui retrouva son âme', *Le Figaro littéraire*, 15 April 1959, p. 1

Mortelier, Christiane, 'Origine et développement d'une légende: Katherine Mansfield en France', *Études anglaises* (October–December 1970), 357–68

Niedzwiecki, Lionel, 'Une musique de l'âme', *Sud-Ouest*, 26 March 2006, p. 10

Renouard, Dominic, 'La Tombe de Katherine Mansfield', *Nouvelle revue*, 161 (1938), 58

Saurat, Denis, 'Visite à Gourdjieff', *Nouvelle revue française*, 41 (1 November 1933), 686–98

Sellon, Hugh, 'Le Souvenir de Katherine Mansfield', *Revue hebdomadaire*, 7 (1 July 1939), 96–100

Tasset-Nissolle, Elisabeth, 'Katherine Mansfield (1888–1923)', *Le Correspondant*, 25 September 1933, 900–08

Thérive, André, 'Les livres', *Le Temps*, 7 July 1932, p. 3

Thiébaut, Marcel, 'Parmi les livres', *La Revue de Paris*, 15 November 1933, 462–75

Vaudoyer, J. L., 'La Tombe d'une fée', *Nouvelles littéraires*, 4 November 1933, p. 2

Verney, Alain, 'Histoire de Katherine Mansfield', *France libre*, 15 March 1946, 391–99

Index

286

288

European Connections

edited by Peter Collier

'European Connections' is a new series which aims to publish studies in Comparative Literature. Most scholars would agree that no literary work or genre can fruitfully be studied in isolation from its context (whether formal or cultural). Nearly all literary works and genres arise in response to or at least in awareness of previous and contemporary writing, and are often illumin-ated by confrontation with neighbouring or contrasting works. The literature of Europe, in particular, is extraordinarily rich in this kind of cross-cultural fertilisation (one thinks of medieval drama, Romantic poetry, or the Realist novel, for instance). On a wider stage, the major currents of European philosophy and art have affected the different national literatures in varying and fascinating ways.

The masters of this comparative approach in our century have been thematic critics like F.R. Leavis, George Steiner, and Jean-Pierre Richard, or formalist critics like I.A. Richards, Northrop Frye, Gérard Genette and Tzvetan Todorov, but much of the writing about literature which we know under specific theoretical labels such as 'feminist' (Julia Kristeva, Judith Butler), 'marxist' (Georg Lukacs, Raymond Williams) or 'psychoanalytical' criticism (Charles Mauron, Jacques Lacan), for instance, also depends by definition on taking literary works from allegedly different national, generic or stylistic traditions and subjecting them to a new, comparative grid. The connections of European with non-European writing are also at issue—one only has to think of the impact of Indian mythology on Salman Rushdie or the cross-fertilisation at work between a Spanish writer like Juan Goytisolo and the Latin American genre of 'Magical Realism'. Although the series is fundamentally a collection of works dealing with literature, it intends to be open to interdisciplinary aspects, wherever music, art, history, philosophy, politics, or cinema come to affect the interplay between literary works.

Many European and North American university courses in literature nowadays teach and research literature in faculties of Comparative and General Literature. The series intends to tap the rich vein of such research. Initial volumes will look at the ways in which writers like Thackeray draw on French writing and history, the structure and strategies of Faulkner's fiction in the light of Proust and Joyce, Goethe's relation to the Spanish picaresque tradition, Victorian reactions to Eugène Sue, and George Mackay Brown's interest in Hopkins and Mann. Offers of contribution are welcome, whether studies of specific writers and relationships, or wider theoretical investigations.

Proposals from established scholars, as well as more recent doctoral students, are welcome. In the major European languages, the series will publish works, as far as possible, in the original language of the author.

The series editor, Peter Collier, is a Fellow of Sidney Sussex College, and Senior Lecturer in French at the University of Cambridge. He has translated Pierre Bourdieu (*Homo Academicus*, Polity Press, 1988), Emile Zola (*Germinal*, Oxford World's Classics, 1993), and Marcel Proust (*The Fugitive*, Penguin, 2002), has edited several collections of essays on European literature and culture (including *Visions and Blueprints*, with Edward Timms, Manchester University Press, 1988, *Modernism and the European Unconscious*, with Judy Davies, Polity Press, 1990, *Critical Theory Today*, with Helga Geyer-Ryan, Polity Press, 1990, and *Artistic Relations*, with Robert Lethbridge, Yale University Press, 1994), and has written a study of Proust and art (*Mosaici proustiani*, Il Mulino, 1986). He is a member of the British branch of the International Comparative Literature Association.